715

THE NATIONALISED INDUSTRIES

THE NATIONALISED
INDUSTRIES

Policies and Performance since 1968

RICHARD PRYKE

Martin Robertson · Oxford

First published in 1981 by Martin Robertson, Oxford.

British Library Cataloguing in Publication Data

Pryke, Richard
　The nationalised industries.
　1. Government ownership – Great Britain –
　History
　I. Title
　338′ .0941　　　HD4145

ISBN 0-85520-241-6 (case)
ISBN 0-85520-242-4 (pb)

Typeset in 10/12 pt Baskerville by Bookmag, Inverness
Printed and bound in Great Britain
by Book Plan, Worcester

Contents

List of Tables

Preface

A book on the nationalised industries requires no prefatory justification. I must, however, make three points clear. First, the statistical series which form the backbone of my study are subject to a margin of error. They have involved enormous time and trouble and are, I believe, a first rate job. However this does not necessarily mean that they are accurate to the last decimal point, and the figures for the National Freight Corporation should be treated with some caution. Instead of continually drawing attention to the difficulties of measurement in the text I make the point here. Second, I now take a much less favourable view of the nationalised industries' performance, and indeed of public ownership itself, than before. I hope and believe that my views have changed because the facts have altered and because I know more about the subject. However the reader should know of my change of views in case, as Lord Kaldor has suggested, I have become over-critical. Third, I have relied heavily on information which I have obtained from conversations, interviews and, especially in the case of BSC, confidential documents. I have not, of course, been able to give my sources where I have relied on interview material and there seemed little point in the case of documents which are not publicly available.

I should like to acknowledge the help that I have had from many people in nationalised industries and departments who must remain anonymous and to thank the following for their assistance, though they are not, of course, responsible for the opinions I have expressed or the factual errors I may have made: John Barber; Professor Bhaskar, who kindly let me read his book *The Future of the UK Motor Industry* before publication; Russell Black; Charles L. Brown; Duncan Burn; Michael Corby, who kindly let me read his book *The Postal Business 1969-1979* in draft; John Dodgson; Peter Ennor; R.G. Garwood; Malcolm Hamer; Richard Hancock; E.T. Judge; Richard

viii PREFACE

Lecomber, who explained depletion costs for gas extraction; Peter McGrath; Peter Mackie; G. Millard; John Murray; Professor Ken Gwilliam; D.G. Rhys; John Roper M.P.; Michael Shanks; Peter White; Derek Whittaker; and Sir Reginald Wilson.

I should like to gratefully acknowledge the financial assistance that I received from the Houblon Norman Fund. I should also like to thank Naomi Canter for her super efficient typing. Finally I am most grateful to my wife for bearing with me through another protracted literary pregnancy.

RICHARD PRYKE

Department of Economics
University of Liverpool
August 1980

Note on Statistics

All financial figures, unless otherwise stated, have been converted into pounds of 1978 purchasing power with a price index for all final goods and services sold on the home market. Most text figures can be converted to their original price level by dividing them by the following factors. The first figure is for the calendar year; the second is for the twelve months April–March beginning during the year shown.

1963	3.76	3.73	1973	2.12	2.05
1968	3.07	3.03	1974	1.78	1.69
1969	2.91	2.87	1975	1.42	1.36
1970	2.72	2.67	1976	1.23	1.19
1971	2.50	2.45	1977	1.09	1.07
1972	2.32	2.28	1978	1.00	0.98

My financial figures can be converted into pounds of 1979 purchasing power by multiplying them by 1.13 and into pounds of October–December 1979 purchasing power by multiplying them by 1.19.

Wherever a change in prices, costs, or profits is mentioned this should be understood as referring to the real rise or fall after allowing for general inflation. The surplus after depreciation, but before interest or subsidy, is described as the net profit (or surplus) while the surplus before allowing for depreciation will be described as the gross profit (or surplus). References to operating costs, or simply to costs, relate to expenditure before depreciation or interest. Depreciation has throughout been put on a replacement cost basis unless otherwise stated. VAT has been excluded throughout.

The construction of the output and related indices is explained in the notes at the foot of each of the initial tables in the industry chapters. In order to calculate the output per unit of labour and capital, indices for the quantities of labour and capital employed were combined with weights proportional to the remuneration that labour received and which it was deemed that capital should have obtained. The latter amount was taken to be depreciation at current replacement cost, during the base year in question, together with a return of 5% on net fixed assets at replacement cost. The replacement cost figures used here were derived from CSO estimates.

CHAPTER 1

Introduction

This book examines the recent economic performance of those large trading bodies that are in public ownership and have been so for a considerable period. It covers not only coal, electricity, British Rail and those other nationalised industries with which virtually everyone is familiar but also the National Freight Corporation and the National and Scottish Bus Groups which are less well known. British Leyland has also been included because, although it has only been in public ownership since 1975, it is of considerable interest and importance and much has happened since it was taken over. The eleven industries and undertakings with which we shall be concerned are together responsible for nearly 10% of the total output of the nation. It can be seen from Table 1.1 that they range in size from telecommunications which, during 1977, produced almost 2% of the gross domestic product (GDP) to the Freight Corporation, which accounted for only 0.2%. Apart from telecommunications there are four other nationalised industries that contribute 1% or more of the GDP — electricity, gas, coal and BR — while postal services, BSC and BL each produce between 0.5 and 1%.

The part that the nationalised industries play in the economy is also shown by their employment and capital expenditure. In 1977 they had about 1,750,000 workers, which represented 7% of total employment, and they were responsible for over 16% of gross fixed capital formation, excluding housing. As this suggests the nationalised industries tend to be capital intensive. In 1977 electricity, telecommunictions, British Airways, gas and BSC invested between 2½ and 5 times as much per worker as industry and communications as a whole. On the other hand BL, NFC, the buses and the postal services invested less than average, although only in the latter was investment very low.

1

TABLE 1.1   *Public Enterprise in Perspective, 1977*

	Proportion of gross domestic product, before stock appreciation	Employment	Proportion of total working population in employment	Proportion of gross domestic fixed capital formation, excluding housing	Gross domestic fixed capital formation per employee as % of average for industry and communications[i]
	(%)	(000)	(%)	(%)	(%)
Telecommunications	1.9	237	1.0	4.2	400
British Electricity Boards	1.7	178	0.7	4.0	500
British Gas	1.1	100	0.4	1.2	260
NCB collieries	1.0	292	1.2	1.4	100
British Rail[a]	1.0[c]	220	0.9	1.3[g]	130
Postal services	0.8[d]	201[d]	0.8	0.1	15
BSC: iron and steel	0.6	182	0.7	2.4	290
BL: vehicles UK	0.6	161	0.6	0.6	85
British Airways airline activities	0.3[e]	54[f]	0.2	0.9[h]	370
National and Scottish Bus Groups	0.3[c]	80	0.3	0.2	60
National Freight Corporation	0.2	41	0.2	0.1[h]	80
Total	9.4	1,746	7.0	16.3	210
Subsidiary activities and other public enterprises[b]	3.3	605	2.4	6.3	230
All public corporations and enterprises	12.7	2,345	9.4	22.6	210

[a] Includes workshops.
[b] Includes Rolls Royce and Alfred Herbert; British Aerospace and Shipbuilders included on a full year basis. Figures in this row partly obtained as residuals.
[c] Includes subsidy.
[d] Includes sub-postmasters and their remuneration.
[e] Includes non-airline activities but excludes remuneration of overseas employees.
[f] Includes overseas employees, which are excluded from the final total.
[g] Includes expenditure of a capital nature on current account.
[h] Includes leased assets, which are not included for other public enterprises.
[i] SIC Orders 11–XX11 excluding petroleum and natural gas, but including a rough allowance for leased assets. Rounded figures are given.

The nationalised industries with which we are concerned fall into three broad groups: the fuel and power industries — gas, electricity and coal — which are examined in Part 1; those providing transport and communication services — BR, National and Scottish, NFC, British Airways and the Post Office — which are discussed in Part 2; and the two manufacturing undertakings — BSC and BL — which are covered in Part 3. The book concentrates on the industries' performance since 1968, partly because the previous period has been extensively written about and partly because the year constitutes a natural watershed. It was, for instance, the first full year of steel nationalisation, it saw the creation of British Leyland and it witnessed the passage of an important Transport Act which established the NFC, the National Bus Company and the Scottish Transport Group.

The year was also significant from an economic point of view because the Act instituted a new financial regime for BR under which it was supposed to pay its way with the benefit of a small and closely-controlled subsidy. Moreover 1968 should have been the beginning of a new era for the nationalised industries because of the publication during the previous year of an important White Paper on their *Economic and Financial Objectives*.[1] This was designed to raise their technical efficiency and improve the allocation of resources by the greater use of marginal cost pricing and the screening of investment projects, using the discounted cash flow method, to ensure that an adequate rate of return (8% and later 10%) would be earned. Although the period up to 1958 had been a disappointing one for the nationalised industries, even their critics conceded that their record had improved between 1958 and 1968, and I reached a generally favourable verdict in my book *Public Enterprise in Practice*.[2] How successful have the nationalised industries been during the past decade?

PART 1

Fuel and Power

CHAPTER 2

British Gas

The industry has been controlled by the British Gas Corporation (BGC) since the beginning of 1973, having previously been run by the Gas Council and twelve Area Boards.

BEFORE NATURAL GAS

During the 1950s and early 1960s the industry presented a very different aspect from today. Its output showed little tendency to increase because its prices were rising relatively fast due to its dependence on coal-based methods of production and the swift rise in the cost of the high grade coal that was required. British Gas, to perpetrate a convenient anachronism, was well aware of the need to find a cheaper source of gas. With considerable enterprise it arranged for the importation of liquified methane from Algeria. The scheme, which was the first of its type, started in 1964 and the same year saw the first plants for producing gas from light oil. This technique, which was the result of research by ICI and the industry, had a revolutionary effect because the plants had low capital and operating costs. They also produced gas at high pressure, which meant that it could be distributed through grid mains without the expense of pumping. The total cost of making gas by the new methods, including both capital charges and operating expenditure, was lower than the avoidable cost of continuing to make gas at old works and it was therefore worth scrapping carbonisation plant and constructing new works based on light oil.

This the industry proceeded to do with great vigour. Between 1963 and 1968 BGC eliminated about half its carbonisation plant and installed a large amount of new capacity to provide for the upsurge in demand. Over this period sales increased from 2.9 billion therms to 4.4 billion but the increase in the industry's weighted output was much less spectacular, at just under 40%, because of the swift decline in the production of coke and chemical by-products. Output per equivalent worker increased by 43% and there was a substantial reduction in staff costs per unit of output (23% over the period 1963–64 to 1968–69). The decline in fuel costs was even greater (38%) due to the substitution of light oil and natural gas for coal. The industry's prices fell by 16% and there was a marked improvement in the gross profit margin. In the domestic market the price of gas fell by 13% relative to electricity and by 8% relative to solid fuel. Gas sales were also stimulated by the introduction of improved gas fires and the spread of central heating.

Natural Gas

While British Gas was busy switching from coal to light oil natural gas was discovered in the southern part of the North Sea. The first discovery was made in the autumn of 1965 and gas began to be received during 1967. The following year saw the conclusion of the crucial negotiations in which it was agreed that the Corporation would be able to buy the gas, which the oil companies had found, at a very advantageous price. How did this happen and what issues were at stake?

One of the problems which governments face in licensing companies to prospect for gas (or oil) is that gas that is produced under favourable geographical or geological conditions will provide the licencee with an abnormally high profit. The two most obvious ways of transferring this rent to the community are to tax away the excessive profit or to hold an auction, in which case each licence will fetch a price equal to the (present) value of the rent that is expected. Because circumstances differ widely from one block of territory to another it is difficult to devise a suitable tax system and various objections have been made to the auction system. In particular it has been argued that there may be collusion among bidders; that if those who are bidding are over-cautious auction prices will be too low; and that if firms have to devote their funds to making advance payments to the government they will be unable to finance development work. None of these objections has any force. The oil industry is not a cartel and foreign and subsequently British experience has shown that when auctions are held the bids are competitive. As for the suggestion that bidders might be over- cautious, even Mr Michael Posner, who advances this argument, concedes that 'The risk aversion of oil companies does not seem great to outsiders — indeed quite the contrary'.[1] The suggestion that the oil companies do not command sufficient resources to both buy licences and drill wells is implausible in view of their financial strength and ability to borrow. Moreover, as Professor Dam pointed out at the time, it would have been possible to defer payment or conduct the auction in terms of a percentage of the profit: a procedure which was already in use in the United States.[2] The risk that licence holders would fail to exploit their concessions could have been guarded against by laying down a minimum level of drilling activity.

The Government did not give any serious conideration to either competitive bidding or taxation but adopted a system in which each production licence was to be paid for by a royalty of 12½% of the value of production. This, together with ordinary income tax, would, it was thought, extract about half of the profits that were earned. However, oil companies were not permitted to dispose of their gas for use as fuel to anyone except BGC unless the Minister decided that an unreasonably low price was being offered. This meant that the gas industry would, by using its monopsony power, be able to buy at a price which would do no more than meet the companies' costs of exploration and production. The advantage of this arrangement was obvious — the oil companies would be deprived of their excess profits — but it suffered from a weakness which was almost equally clear. If British Gas sold the natural gas at a price based on what it had cost, rather than for the maximum it would fetch, there would be insufficient to satisfy demand. This was argued forcefully at the time by Mr George Polanyi and was one of the principal grounds on which the oil companies urged that they should be paid a market price.[3]

They began by demanding around 6.2p per therm and the Gas Council's initial offer was 2.5p, but it was ultimately decided that the industry would pay 3.7p per therm and would be able to buy additional supplies during the non-winter months for 2.6p. This was far below the market price, i.e. what consumers would be prepared to pay at the margin for the supplies in question, less BGC's costs of distribution from the beach head. In order to dispose of the large quantity of gas that was available BGC would have to enter the market for crude heat and begin competing with heavy fuel oil for which medium-sized industrial consumers and the CEGB were paying 6.9p per therm in 1968. As the cost of pipelining gas from the beach to a central location was about 1.0p per therm, the market price for North Sea gas appeared to be at least 6p per therm.

Of course British Gas did not have to sell natural gas to industry at a price which only just covered its costs. It could just undercut the cost of heavy fuel oil and make a large profit. This would prove embarrassing and conflict with the industry's apparent obligation to provide its customers with gas at the lowest possible cost. British Gas would therefore be led into disposing of the surplus that it was earning on its industrial sales by reducing the price of gas in the domestic market until it was being sold at a loss. As cross-subsidisation of this type would involve misallocation, while the sale of gas to industry on a cost plus basis would lead to a shortage, the Government should have guarded against both dangers either by adjusting BGC's financial target so that it had to earn a high profit or by imposing a tax on North Sea gas to close the gap between the market and the monopsony price. This did not happen and it does not appear that the problem was ever clearly seen. It is perhaps significant that Mr Michael Posner, who was at the time Director of Economics in the Ministry of Power, does not discuss these issues in his book on *Fuel Policy*, although he recognises that the price which was set for North Sea gas was significantly below the market level.[4] In retrospect it is clear that the procedure that was adopted for allocating licences and setting the price of North Sea gas was ill-conceived. There should have been an auction.

The advent of natural gas posed the problem of whether consumers' appliances should be converted, so that it could be supplied direct, or whether it should be used as a feedstock for the industry's new gas-making plant, in which it could be reformed into town gas. This would avoid the cost of conversion but the industry would be put to the expense of operating gas works and installing new plant to meet the expansion of demand and replace capacity as it wore out. Conversion also had the important advantage that because natural gas has a higher calorific value it would more than double the effective capacity of mains and gas holders. As a result far less would have to be spent on reinforcing the distribution system. It was estimated that conversion would on balance lead to a large saving in costs, and the industry embarked on a ten year programme of conversion which was completed during 1977.[5] Conversion was handled with considerable success and an official Committee of Inquiry concluded that, 'The conversion operation has been carefully planned, well organised and competently executed. The labour force available has been adequate in numbers and quality . . . . The number of defects in conversion which have given rise to inconvenience and possible danger to consumers has not been excessive in relation to the size and complexity of the operation. In most cases they have been quickly rectified'.[6] Conversion has been undertaken remarkably quickly by foreign standards and has cost less than was originally estimated.[7]

OUTPUT, MARKET SHARE AND PRICING POLICY

Between 1968 and 1973 gas sales increased from 4.4 billion therms to 10.7 billion. During this period the original fields — West Sole and Leman Bank — built up to full production and the other main fields in the southern part of the North Sea — Hewett, Indefatigable and Viking — came into production. Since 1973 the Rough Field, which is comparatively small, is the only one to have come into operation in the southern sector, and the huge Frigg field in the north did not start producing until the autumn of 1977. As a result only a limited amount of gas was available. There could have been a very large increase in the supply and sale of gas during 1978, but it was decided to restrict the expansion of gas sales to premium uses. Nevertheless by 1978 consumption had risen to 15.3 billion therms, which was three and a half times more than in 1968.

As Table 2.1 shows the increase in the industry's (weighted) output was much less spectacular at around 80%. One reason why output increased less fast was that the growth in sales was most rapid in the industrial market where the revenue per therm is lowest. During 1968 industry accounted for 22% of the total quantity consumed: by 1978 the figure had risen to 41%. Meanwhile domestic sales, where the value per therm is greatest, fell from 64% to 47%, despite a large rise in the absolute quantity consumed (157%). However, the most important reason why the increase in output has been smaller than the growth in quantity is that the production and processing of gas, and the manufacture of by-products, have now ceased. This has been due partly to the switch to natural gas and

TABLE 2.1 British Gas: Output, Productivity and Finances

	Gas sold	Output	Employment	Average weekly hours worked by manual workers, October week	Output per equivalent worker	Real unit operating costs^a	Real unit staff costs^ab	Real staff costs per employee^a	Real staff costs per employee in manufacturing^a	Relative weekly earnings of manual men, October week	Real cost of fuel per unit^a	Real revenue per unit^ac	Revenue^ac	Gross surplus^ad	Gross of surplus as % of revenue^a	Net surplus^ae
	(therms m)	(1968=100)	(000)		(1968=100)	(1968-69=100)	(1968-69=100)	(1968=100)	(1968=100)	(1968=100)	(1968-69=100)	(1968-69=100)	(£m,1978 prices)	(£m,1978 prices)	(%)	(£m,1978 prices)
1963	2,894	71.7	124.6	46.7	69.9	130.3^f	130.4	90.4	87.2	98.3	162.3	119.4^f	1,737	256	14.7	..
1968	4,416	100.0	122.1	46.3	100.0	100.0	100.0	100.0	100.0	100.0	100.0	100.0	1,812	350	19.3	..
1969	4,973	106.3	120.0	47.0	107.3	94.6	96.9	105.0	103.0	101.3	76.8	93.3	1,781	326	18.3	..
1970	5,750	108.9	118.7	46.3	112.1	88.1	93.4	112.4	107.4	102.5	61.4	84.2	1,742	285	16.4	..
1971	7,490	121.4	114.9	45.2	130.5	74.8	82.5	121.0	110.3	105.8	48.1	75.2	1,804	367	20.3	..
1972	9,757	135.5	109.4	45.2	152.9	64.3	69.7	127.9	114.0	103.4	41.2	68.3	1,943	486	25.0	..
1973	10,700	143.5	104.8	46.2	167.4	58.8	65.1	136.6	118.1	100.9	42.4	61.0	1,903	447	23.5	..
1974	12,634	152.2	102.3	46.3	181.7	53.3	60.9	142.8	118.5	106.3	38.9	56.7	1,958	484	24.7	..
1975	13,081	154.9	102.7	43.8	188.4	50.3	63.5	148.5	123.7	114.0	33.4	57.5	2,051	614	29.9	..
1976	13,969	155.1	101.2	43.1	192.5	47.3	61.6	148.0	126.0	111.6	32.0	62.0	2,261	875	38.7	496
1977	14,549	167.2	99.8	43.4	209.7	49.3	58.9	157.2	123.3	111.2	42.3	65.2	2,607	1,013	38.9	584
1978	15,281	181.8	100.4	44.0	225.7	54.3	58.1	163.2	128.9	118.1	57.9	64.8	2,761	889	32.2	432

Note Output and employment figures were derived from financial year data. The output index consists of sub-indices (combined with 1963 and 1968 net output weights) for (i) gas distribution and appliance sales and (ii) activity at gas works as reflected by gas made and reformed, etc. The distribution sub-index comprises eight weighted indicators: gas sales by type of contract and consumer (using revenue weights) and number of appliances sold (net output weights for gas and appliances). Instead of treating gas works as a separate activity double deflation could have been used, in which case the cessation of production at works would have been reflected by increased purchases of natural gas. However, due to the very low price that was paid an enormous increase in net output would have been shown. The unit series were estimated using gross output at 1968-69 (and 1963-64) prices.

^a Financial year (April–March) beginning during year shown. ^b Excludes replacement expenditure now charged to revenue. Also excludes central heating installation and oil production as represented by their revenue. Includes expenditure on conversion to natural gas. Also includes depreciation and interest of North Sea exploration and production subsidiary in order that its gas should appear at cost. ^c Excludes central heating installation and oil. ^d Replacement expenditure now charged to revenue not deducted. Conversion expenditure and depreciation and interest of North Sea subsidiary deducted. ^e Before stock appreciation; but after interest of North Sea subsidiary. ^f Excludes sale and installation of appliances.

partly to conversion, which means that it can be supplied direct. If the production and reforming of gas had not been treated as a separate activity the rise in the industry's output would have appeared very much greater.

The large rise in the quantity of gas sold has led to a sharp increase in the industry's share of the energy market. Its proportion of expenditure on fuel by final users, for all purposes apart from transport, increased from 9% in 1968 to 23% in 1978 at 1973–74 prices (and from 10% to 33% on a thermal basis). This rise has been mainly due to the large decline in the price of gas which has fallen in both absolute terms and in relation to other fuels. For instance, in the domestic field the price of gas fell, over the period 1968–78, by 36% relative to electricity, by 40% in comparison with heating oil and by 42% in relation to solid fuel. Gas's share of the domestic market was already rising and would have continued to increase because of the spread of central heating and the fact that it was far more clean and convenient than solid fuel. Hence it seems doubtful whether any great reduction in price was required. In the industrial field the position was different because gas was, to begin with, far more expensive than oil and its market penetration was not increasing. Nevertheless, the price of gas was pitched excessively low. It appears from the increase in BGC's sales to, and revenue from, the industrial market between 1968–69 and 1971–72 that the Corporation was selling gas under its new bulk contracts at an average price of no more than 4.5p per therm; and it is known that in the case of the massive deal with ICI, that was negotiated in 1969, the price was 4.9p per therm.[8] This meant that gas was being sold at less than heavy fuel oil where, during the late 1960s and early 1970s, the price ranged from 6.0p (1970) to 8.3p (1971). Moreover a comparison with heavy fuel oil is only appropriate in the case of contracts for interruptible supplies which accounted for only about 40% of the additional industrial sales. Where contracts are for a firm supply the proper comparison is with gas oil which is substantially more expensive.

Why did BGC sell North Sea gas at such bargain prices? As we have seen the industry had been able to buy large supplies of natural gas at a very low price and the Gas Council and the Government decided that it was economically advantageous to absorb it at a rapid rate. Once it had committed itself to this policy BGC became worried that it would not be able to dispose of the large supply that was available. It was therefore led into selling it in a hurry at a knockdown price. After some initial hesitation there were plenty of takers which showed that the Corporation's anxiety was misplaced. By 1972 BGC had already arranged to sell all the gas which, granted its existing arrangements with the oil companies, was available for large users. As a result an embargo was placed on new bulk contracts and the Corporation started to turn away business. It also, at long last, increased its prices. By 1973 it was charging those customers whose contracts had expired a price which, for a firm supply, was slightly above the cost of gas oil and for an interruptible supply was equivalent to that of heavy fuel oil.[9]

However, when OPEC increased the price of oil, there was no corresponding rise in the price of gas. As late as 1978–79 the renewal price for a firm supply was 20% lower than the cost of gas oil, after allowing for the fact that gas does not involve storage and is easier and cleaner to use. By 1978–79 the renewal price of interruptible gas had been raised to that of heavy fuel oil, but it had been substantially lower between 1974 and the first part of 1977.[9] This was not due to an excess supply of gas, because the Corporation was short of gas until 1977. In this situation the appropriate response was obviously to charge a higher price. This would have encouraged consumers to economise and have led those customers who did not value gas very highly to switch to alternative fuels. However, the Gas Corporation had difficulty in adjusting the price of its industrial sales to market-related levels because of the Price Commission restrictions. Moreover, although it was possible to renegotiate contracts when they expired, the Corporation had entered into a number of long-term agreements that did not contain any satisfactory price escalation provisions. The contract with ICI was so badly framed that until recently BGC has been almost giving away gas. For instance in 1977 it supplied a huge quantity at a price which was only 15% of the market level. Although this was exceptional the Corporation's average charge during 1978–79 for firm and interruptible supplies was 30% lower than the (weighted) average cost of heavy fuel and gas oil.

BGC's average revenue per therm has been substantially lower than its marginal costs. During 1978–79 it paid 11.8p per therm for gas from the Frigg field and this represents the gas component in marginal cost since Frigg was the Corporation's most expensive source of supply.[10] After allowing for BGC's other expenditure, on an average cost basis, the total cost of supplying industrial and commercial consumers was about 18p per therm. However the average charge was more than 25% lower at 13p per therm. In the case of customers on interruptible contracts there is a considerable difference between average and marginal non-gas costs, but even if allowance is made for this the marginal cost, at nearly 14p per therm, was considerably higher than the average revenue of just over 11p. Only a small part of the discrepancy between costs and prices appears to be due to unfavourable contracts that were negotiated in the dim and distant past, and it seems clear that BGC entered into agreements which would not enable it to recover its prospective marginal costs. However, in its renewal contracts of 1978–79 the Corporation did charge the marginal cost price although, where a firm supply was being provided, this was so much below the cost of gas oil that BGC was once again courting the risk that it would run out of gas.[11]

Moreover, domestic consumers and other tariff users were being provided with gas at a price that, both on average and at the margin, was lower than BGC's cost of supply. For domestic credit consumers the figure was about 22.5p per therm after making a rough deduction in respect of meter reading and billing, as this is obviously a fixed cost. In 1978–79 the average revenue for domestic prepayment users was about 16.7p per therm ignoring the standing charge, and the price where more than a minimum amount was being used was only around 15p per therm.[11] This suggests that the Corporation was charging its larger domestic customers about a third less than the marginal cost.

Domestic prices would have been even lower if the Government had not compelled the industry to increase its tariffs during 1977. The Corporation was most reluctant to do this because it was already covering its interest payments. This suggests that its prices would have been only slightly higher if it had had a free hand during the period when price restraint was in operation and it made a small loss. The Corporation's charges have been so low because the average price at which it purchases gas has been well below the market level and it has therefore been able to satisfy its financial obligations without charging more. During 1978–79 it paid an average of only 4.3p per therm for natural gas because, although it was being charged a market price for Frigg gas, it was still only paying something like 2.4p for the gas that it received from the original fields in the southern part of the North Sea. Not only was the original price extremely favourable but the contracts with the oil companies do not enable them to adjust their charges in line with inflation, let alone with the cost of oil.

EMPLOYMENT AND PRODUCTIVITY

Between 1968 and 1978 the Corporation's labour force was reduced from 122,000 to 100,000, although, as can be seen from Table 2.1, most of the decline had already taken place by 1974. The fall in employment was entirely explained by conversion to natural gas and the virtual elimination of staff engaged on production. As there was a substantial increase in output, productivity rose sharply. Over the period 1968–78 output per equivalent worker (or OEW) increased by 125%. OEW allows for the change in the number of hours worked by manual, but not salaried, employees and is to be distinguished from output per man year (OMY) which does not allow for variations in average hours.

Because gas works have been treated as a separate activity in my output estimates the growth in OEW is not directly attributable to conversion to natural gas; although conversion has led to a reduction in employment this has been offset by the decline in production at gas works. However natural gas has indirectly been responsible for much of the rise in productivity because it has boosted sales and there is only a weak link between output and the number employed on distribution. About 30% of all workers are employed on customer servicing, which includes the installation and maintenance of appliances and meters. Figures are available from 1972–73 onwards for the number of jobs performed and they show that there has been a small decline. In addition 15% of the labour force are engaged on customer accounting and work at showrooms. Their workload largely depends on the number of customers, which increased by 10% over the period 1968–78, and on the number of appliances sold, which fell by 10%. The only other large block of workers, apart from administration and general services, is employed on transmission and distribution. There must have been an increase in activity here but it cannot have been anything like as large as the increase in sales. The mileage of mains in use increased by only 18%, and the length laid and relaid fell by 16%, although this work is largely undertaken by contractors.

Back in 1968 British Gas had ample scope for a more efficient use of labour. Only about 14% of all manual employees were on incentive payment schemes based on work study (WSIP) and little progress had been made in measuring and then improving the productivity of salaried staff. Those workers who were on WSIP had a performance of around 90, where 100 represents the standard which should be readily attainable. In contrast the performance of other manual workers only stood at around 50 and, after a thorough review of the situation, the Prices and Incomes Board concluded that there was 'considerable scope for improving labour productivity and securing cost reductions'. It also found that work measurement could be applied on an extensive scale to salaried staff and that where it had been used performance had increased, on average, by some 27%.[12] By 1978 about 75% of the industry's manual employees were on WSIP and productivity measurement had been applied to 25% of salaried jobs. According to British Gas, workers who are on WSIP now have a performance of over 90. However this gives a misleading impression of the gains which have been made because there is a tendency for incentive schemes to get slacker as time goes by. The performance of workers engaged on customer servicing ranged from less than 44 in the worst region to about 80 in the best, as measured under a scheme for monitoring productivity which is based on work study times.[13] It is clear that BGC still has considerable scope to improve the efficiency with which labour is used but that substantial, although not enormous, progress has already been made. Between 1972–73 and 1978–79 there was a rise of 10% in the number of jobs per manual employee on customer servicing and there has been some decline in the number of hours worked.

COSTS, PRICES AND PROFITS

During 1978–79 the Gas Corporation's unit costs were about 45% lower than they had been in 1968–69. They fell steadily until 1976–77 but then increased. This is largely explained by the movement of unit fuel costs. Between 1968–69 and 1976–77 there was a fall of two-thirds due to the decreasing use of coal and light oil and the increasing use of natural gas, which became progressively cheaper. However after 1976–77 unit fuel costs shot up because of the use of Frigg gas for which BGC was having to pay a market price. Nevertheless during 1978–79 the cost of fuel was still around 40% lower than it had been a decade earlier. Due to the huge rise in productivity there has also been a spectacular decline in unit staff costs. By 1978–79 they were about 40% lower than in 1968–69, and this despite an increase of 18% in the relative earnings of the industry's manual employees and of around 60% in staff costs per employee. This compares with a rise of only 30% in manufacturing.

In 1978–79 BGC's prices were 35% lower than they had been ten years earlier, although they were somewhat above the low point which had been reached in 1976–77. Because unit costs have declined more than unit revenue the Corporation's gross margin has improved from 19% in 1968–69 to 32% in 1978–79. During 1978–79 BGC had a net profit of £430 million which represented a return of 6.3% on capital employed at replacement cost. However the financial position would look very different if BGC had paid the full market price for North Sea gas. If it had had to pay a price equal to that of Frigg gas the Corporation would have incurred a net loss of approximately £830 million, which is another way of saying that its prices were too low.

RESERVES AND THEIR DEPLETION

During 1978 consumption of natural gas was equivalent to 65 million tonnes of coal (mtce). It is expected that by the early 1980s the supply will approach 80 mtce tonnes as a result of the build up of production from the Brent and Frigg fields. According to the Department of Energy's paper on *Energy Projections* the supply will build up to 85–90 mtce around 1990 'after which sales would begin to be curtailed' due to the exhaustion of reserves. It is stated that by the end of the century natural gas supplies could have fallen back to 65-70 mtce and 'may need to be supplemented by substitute natural gas (probably manufactured from coal)'.[14] The Department appears to be expecting that if the GDP grows by just under 3% per annum and the demand for energy increases relatively fast, BGC will use some 13 million tonnes of coal in 2000; but that if the economy grows by 2% p.a. and the demand for energy increases more slowly, none will be required. The Department now takes a far more cautious view of the need for substitute natural gas than at the time of the 1978 Green Paper on *Energy Policy* in which it was forecast that by 2000, BGC would require up to about 30 million tonnes of coal.[15] The fact that the energy planners have changed their minds so fast, and at a time when so little has changed, indicates that their forecasts should be regarded with scepticism and not with the polite respect that they are normally accorded.

It was assumed in the Green Paper that the remaining reserves of natural gas available to the UK amounted to 55 trillion cubic feet (tcf), including purchases from Norway. It was obvious at the time that this figure was unrealistically low and a figure of 60 tcf has now been adopted.[16] Of this, reserves of known gas in the southern sector of the North Sea would account for some 20 tcf. However, according to Professor Peter Odell's estimates the figure should be 33 tcf.[17] It is obviously possible that he is being over-optimistic but it does seem likely that the Department's figures are on the low side. The Gas Corporation's central estimate appears to be 70 tcf for all North Sea gas and it is known to believe that supplies will not begin to decline until some time between 2000 and 2010, even if no gas is discovered in those parts of the UK continental shelf that have not yet been explored.[18]

How long our reserves of natural gas last depends, of course, not only on their size but also on the rate at which they are exploited. The general principle which should govern the depletion of gas reserves, or of any other natural resource, is that extraction should be speeded up or slowed down until the current benefit obtained is just equal to the opportunity cost. The benefit will be indicated, other things equal, by the price which consumers pay for the gas, while the opportunity cost will consist of the current costs of production and distribution (including capital charges) and what is often termed the depletion cost. This is the present value of the future benefit which will be sacrificed if the gas is consumed now instead of being left in the ground to be used later. It is measured by the discounted difference between the price that would be paid during the year in which the gas would otherwise be consumed and the costs of production and distribution which would then be incurred. In other words the depletion cost is equal to the discounted future rent that is being forgone. (It is necessary to discount because present pounds are worth more than future pounds, if only because a pound in the hand can be invested in order to yield a future return. The factor by which a future pound must be divided in order to discover its present value is, therefore, the amount to which £1 will have increased at compound interest by the time it is received. If, for instance, the rate of interest is 10%, £1 invested in 1981 will be worth £1.21 in 1983 and £1 received in that year will have a present (i.e. 1981) value of 82.6p, viz. £1÷1.21.)

In order to discover whether extraction is proceeding too fast or too slowly it is therefore necessary to find out whether gas will on present plans be sold at a price which is less than its opportunity cost or, what amounts to the same thing, the long run marginal cost (LRMC). What is directly relevant here is gas from the UK continental shelf that is not produced in association with oil. The depletion cost element is irrelevant in the case of Norwegian or other imported gas because the rent will not be received by us. Gas which is associated with oil is not of direct relevance because, although its production can be deferred by reinjection, its use cannot be delayed indefinitely once extraction of the oil has commenced. However Norwegian and associated gas has an important indirect bearing on the LRMC because the greater the quantity that is used the longer the extraction of non-associated UK gas can be put off. However it will only be worth postponing its consumption so long as its LRMC exceeds the resource cost for UK associated gas and the financial cost in the case of Norwegian gas. If the opportunity cost of non-associated gas is lower its extraction should be speeded up, associated gas should be flared and new contracts for Norwegian gas should not be arranged. Hence the rate of extraction is optimal when the price of gas is equal to the LRMC and what may be regarded as the short run marginal cost, viz. the cost of imported and associated gas, plus distribution expenses. In practice the LRMC will reflect the cost of exploiting new reserves in the southern part of the North Sea, where the gas is not associated with oil, and the SRMC will depend on the cost of gas from the northern sector, whether imported or produced in association with oil. References to the price of gas obscure the fact that different prices prevail in different markets. This is right and proper because distribution costs differ, but the price net of these costs should be equal in each market to the SRMC and LRMC, also net of these costs.

The first step towards estimating the LRMC of gas is to discover what the net price of gas will be in 2005 which, as we have seen, is approximately when production of North Sea gas will start to decline if it is extracted at the planned rate. The net price in 2005 should not exceed what it will cost to produce substitute natural gas (SNG) from coal and could be lower if, for instance, natural gas could be imported in a liquid state at a favourable price. During 1978 it would have been possible, using the established Lurgi process, to produce SNG from British coal at a cost of about 32p per therm, including capital charges (as calculated with a 5% rate of discount). Technological progress will tend to reduce the cost of SNG, though the new processes which are at an advanced stage of development are unlikely to produce a saving of as much as 20%.[19] On the other hand it seems likely that the cost of coal will rise not only in Britain but on a world scale because of increased demand, due to the high price of oil and the difficulty of making further gains in productivity in strip mining. Although it is little more than a guess, a figure of 40p per therm in 2005 would seem reasonable and is consistent with Price Commission estimates.[20]

It is now necessary to subtract the cost of proving and extracting new reserves of gas. Here again it is only possible to make a guess but if the figure is put at 5p per therm the future rent that is being sacrificed becomes 35p per therm. If this is discounted at 5% p.a., which is the official rate, the depletion cost turns out to be 9½p per therm for 1978. When BGC's distribution costs are added in order to obtain the LRMC it appears that this was not very different from the renewal prices that industrial and commercial customers were being charged for firm and interruptible supplies, and although domestic customers were being charged less their elasticity of demand was probably low because gas was the cheapest fuel. It also appears that the gas component of the Corporation's LRMC (the extraction cost of 5p plus the depletion cost of 9½p) was approximately the same as the gas element in its SRMC, viz. the 12p per therm which was being paid for Frigg gas. Although my figure for the Gas Corporation's LRMC obviously depends on the number of hazardous assumptions it does suggest that BGC is pursuing a depletion policy which is broadly correct, namely a strategy of conserving the reserves in the southern part of the North Sea and placing maximum reliance on the northern sector. It would, however, be wrong at a time when, due to the rise in oil prices, the demand for gas is very high to restrict supplies if the price which consumers are prepared to pay exceeds the extraction and depletion cost of southern gas.

CHAPTER 3

Electricity

The British electricity industry has a more complex administrative structure than any of the other nationalised industries. In England and Wales electricity is produced by the Central Electricity Generating Board (CEGB) and distributed by twelve Area Boards, which also sell appliances and undertake contracting work. There is also an Electricity Council which is a federal body with certain planning and other central functions. In Scotland the South of Scotland Electricity Board and the North of Scotland Hydro-Electric Board are responsible for both production and distribution. However, these administrative distinctions will be ignored and the British Electricity Boards (BEB) will be referred to as if they were a single organisation.

PREVIOUS PERFORMANCE
AND POWER STATION CONSTRUCTION

In 1968 the electricity industry appeared successful and well managed. It was earning a substantial profit after depreciation at historic cost. This was, according to the Electricity Council's estimates, more than sufficient to meet its depreciation at replacement cost, although the position would have appeared less satisfactory if allowance had been made for interest during construction. During the preceding five years prices had been more or less stable and unit costs had fallen by nearly 10%. The most important reason for this was the large reduction in unit fuel costs due to the considerable increase in nuclear generation and the fall in coal and oil prices. There was also a considerable reduction in staff costs per unit of output as a result of a successful productivity deal in 1964–65 known

22

as the Status Agreement. It provided for staggered patterns of working and led to the elimination of systematic overtime. There was a reduction of eight hours per week in the hours worked by manual employees. The Agreement initially caused some rise in employment at power stations and the industry's labour force rose from 226,000 in 1963 to 238,000 in 1968. Nevertheless there was a substantial improvement in the efficiency with which labour was used. Between 1963 and 1968 OEW shot up by about 30% and, what is more conclusive, the total time worked by manual employees fell by 9% between April 1964 and April 1966 — the period during which average hours were cut back. During the preceding twenty-four months there had been, in contrast, a rise of 5%.

However, BEB's performance was less satisfactory than it appeared. A large increase in the quantity of capital in use coincided with a moderate rise in output. This had previously been growing rapidly but between 1963 and 1968 it increased by 23%, which was no faster than the rise in manufacturing production. Because electricity is so capital intensive total factor productivity grew by only 4%, and if the calculation is extended so as to embrace fuel the figure becomes 3%. This was a slow rate of advance by the industry's standards. What was even worse was that BEB had embarked on a massive programme of power station construction during the early 1960s which was turning out to be a costly mistake. Between 1955 and 1959 the CEGB and its predecessors authorised the construction of 9,000 MW of generating plant, but during 1960–64 the figure was stepped up to 25,000 MW. Ordering was then reduced, but a further 16,000 MW of new capacity was authorised between 1965 and 1973, all of which should have been completed by 1978.

Up to the late 1950s the electricity authorities assumed that the growth in peak demand, which is what determines the need for generating plant, would slow down because they considered that sales could not go on increasing indefinitely at their previous high rate. However, the pivotal estimate, which is usually made in the summer and relates to the sixth winter ahead, consistently turned out to be too low. Moreover during 1959–60 and the following three winters the maximum demand increased by around 9% p.a. when adjusted to standard weather conditions. (Henceforth all figures for peak demand refer to standard weather conditions.) As a result the Electricity Council, which was responsible for the final forecast, abandoned the view that the growth in sales would fall off and adopted progressively higher estimates of demand growth. By May 1962 it was basing its plans on the assumption that the peak load would rise by 7.9% p.a. which was slightly greater than the average increase over the preceding decade of 7.6% p.a. The adoption of a policy of faster economic growth led to even higher forecasts. The industry agreed, at the Government's request, to base its estimates on 4% economic growth and in 1964 it was predicting that peak demand would rise by 9.5% p.a.[1]

The winter of 1962–63 constituted a watershed for the electricity industry because thereafter peak demand increased relatively slowly. The upsurge had been primarily due to a massive increase in domestic demand, which is responsible for half the peak load. Between 1958 and 1963 total domestic sales shot up by 95% compared with 57% during the previous quinquennium and 27% during the period 1963–68. During the late 1950s and early 1960s there was a large rise in the electricity industry's share of domestic fuel consumption at the expense of solid fuel and, to a lesser extent, gas. The industry's proportion of consumers' expenditure on fuel, at 1963 prices, rose from 25% in 1958 to 38% in 1963, but during the following five years gas was the principal beneficiary from the continued decline in solid fuel and by 1968 electricity's share had only crept up to 42%. The Electricity Council would have required second sight to have foreseen exactly how demand would develop, and it is difficult to blame it for abandoning the assumption that the growth in sales would slow down after a succession of estimates had turned out to be on the low side and at a time when the growth in demand seemed to be rising. However, the industry's leaders, although sceptical as to whether 4% growth would be achieved, welcomed the opportunity to embark on a much larger plant building programme. They were very slow to recognise that the boom in sales was an aberration and that peak demand was now growing more slowly than it had in the past.

After 1964 the Council adopted progressively lower forecasts but it continued in most years to assume that demand would increase at a significantly faster pace than it had during the preceding decade. The civil servants who examined the industry's plans saw at the time that its forecasts were over-optimistic and fought a running battle in order that they should be revised downwards. For instance in the autumn of 1966 the Treasury and the Department of Economic Affairs prepared a forecast of future demand which implied that the peak load would only rise by around 6.7% p.a. However, in the spring of 1967 the Electricity Council adopted a figure of 7.3% p.a. for the period up to 1972–73, although there had been yet another winter in which the growth in peak demand had been very low, at less than 3%, and it had become known that huge quantities of natural gas would be available from the North Sea.[2] The Council's forecast has, like all of its predictions since 1960 turned out to be much too high. Peak demand increased by only 3.2% p.a. and was overstated by 27%, though it would be wrong to attribute all of this forecasting error to imprudence. Nobody could have forseen how slowly demand would develop. Nevertheless an industry which continues year after year to make forecasts which are patently too high is certainly open to criticism. In 1974 the Electricity Council was still forecasting that maximum demand would increase by 5.1% p.a. (between 1972–73 and 1979–80) but the Department was only expecting a rise of 2.9% p.a. (between 1974–75 and 1980–81).[3]

If the power stations which figured in the industry's plans had been constructed on time and functioned properly BEB would have had massive excess capacity. However it would have been able to make substantial savings by prematurely scrapping old plant and by running its high-cost stations less intensively. These savings would therefore have offset part or, because of the rise in energy prices, all of the extra capital charges which the construction of the unnecessary capacity has involved. In practice savings have been restricted and extra expenditure has been incurred because stations have not been completed on schedule and because serious operating problems have been encountered. This is partly explained by the quantity and the quality of plant that was ordered during the early 1960s. Most of the sets constructed during the 1950s were comparatively small and had a relatively low level of thermal efficiency, as judged by French and American standards. However, during the late 1950s and early 1960s there was a spectacular increase in the size of the units that were ordered. Between 1957 and 1960 the capacity of the largest sets that were included in the plant programmes was pushed up from 200 MW to 500 MW. This rise was desirable because there were substantial economies of scale and the large new units would have better thermal efficiencies. However, the movement from small to large sets was badly managed. Instead of making a jump, like the French, the industry took a series of quick steps and ordered units of 275 MW, 300 MW, 350 MW and 375 MW. This was pointless as the larger sets were designed before the CEGB had even had time to gain experience with its 200 MW units. As a result, and because of the huge amount of plant that was ordered, the design teams employed by the plant manufacturers were deluged with work which they did not have the resources to undertake. The number of top class designers was strictly limited and they were spread between eight major boilermakers and five turbo-generator firms. The CEGB was well aware that there were too many manufacturers and as early as 1961 its leaders were privately saying that rationalisation was necessary. However, they feared that if the Board forced firms to merge it would be accused of exercising monopoly power. The CEGB failed to act, the manufacturers were overwhelmed with orders and much of their design work was of a very low order.[4] They engaged in extrapolation when what they should have done was to make a new design.

The jerky movement from small to big sets, together with the large increase in the volume of plant ordered, led to serious delays in the completion of power stations. According to the Wilson Committee which investigated the problem there was, in particular, 'a cumulative series of difficulties [in the design, manufacture and erection of boilers]. Design information was not available on time, insufficient attention was paid to detailed design problems, and fabricated parts were delivered to site in insufficient quantities, often with faults and after severe delays'.[4] That the manufacturers were seriously overloaded and that completion times were not being met became apparent during 1964. Nevertheless the CEGB proceeded at the end of that year to authorise the construction of a further 5,590 MW of new plant and an additional 5,360 MW was scheduled during 1965 and 1966. The backlog of plant which should have been in operation steadily built up until at the beginning of 1970 it amounted to 13,600 MW, which was equivalent to about 30% of the CEGB's capacity. At that time units were being commissioned about eighteen months late, although the *planned* completion times were already a year longer than in the United States.[5] By the end of 1978 the backlog was somewhat smaller at 9,850 MW because stations had, in the fullness of time, been completed and relatively little new plant had been ordered. However, the delay in bringing stations into operation has grown longer. The fossil-fuelled generating units which are now in an advanced state of construction (Ince B, Grain and Littlebrook D) are expected to be around three years late and in the case of the nuclear plant (Dungeness B, Hartlepool and Heysham) the delay is about nine years.

The belated completion of the conventional stations appears to be mainly due to an escalation in industrial disputes at sites and a fall off in the already low level of productivity. Because of late starts and extended breaks, as little as three or four hours of productive work are undertaken per eight-hour shift.[6] It would be wrong to lay all the blame for this on the CEGB, although it has now assumed far more responsibility for the direction of sites. Low productivity and long delays are a general feature of large construction projects in the UK, but when the National Economic Development Office investigated a small number of large industrial projects, here and abroad, our power stations turned out to have particularly long completion times. It took around 90% longer to complete the UK generating stations than to construct the foreign stations, but for the other projects our completion periods were only about 40% greater.[7] The even longer delays which have been experienced at the nuclear stations have been due not only to labour problems at the sites but also to the acute technical difficulties which have been encountered. These have in turn been due to the adoption of the Advanced Gas-cooled Reactor (AGR).

In 1965 the CEGB opted for the AGR, which was sponsored by the Atomic Energy Authority (AEA), in preference to the American light water reactor (LWR). The British Magnox reactors which had been constructed under the first nuclear energy programme had turned out to be extremely costly but the CEGB concluded, after calling for tenders, that the AGR would produce slightly cheaper power than the LWR. The selection procedure was not impartial because the AEA, which was an interested party, helped the CEGB to choose; the scales were weighted against the LWR by ruling out the latest developments, although they were accepted for the AGR; the tender for the AGR was only based on a sketch design; the AGR's cost advantage depended on the dubious assumption that the generating sets would be operated continuously for two years; and the AGR was obviously the more risky choice because a 600 MW unit was being extrapolated from a 30 MW prototype whereas an LWR of 200 MW had been in commercial operation for a long period.[8] It was soon evident that there were serious design problems at the first AGR — Dungeness B — but the industry went ahead and ordered a further four, though long before the last was authorised it was known that the AGR could not be exported because it was too costly and that utilities throughout the world were plumping for LWRs. When the CEGB came to reassess the economics of ordering AGRs or LWRs in 1973 it concluded that power from the British reactor would be about 25% more expensive, and this was for second generation stations which would have been expected to be relatively free from problems.[9]

Serious operating problems have been encountered both at the two AGRs which have so far been completed and at the big conventional stations. The first AGR unit at Hinkley Point B was commissioned in September 1976 and the second in October 1978. During 1979–80 the station's production was equivalent to only 43% of its design capacity which, even allowing for inevitable teething troubles on the second unit, is a low figure. Moreover serious corrosion and vibration problems have been encountered and the level of utilisation will be permanently restricted at all the AGRs. To begin with, the availability of the 500 MW sets at conventional stations was very poor because of defects in their design and bad workmanship. During winter weekdays in 1974–75 only 75% of the capacity of the CEGB's 500 MW and two 660 MW units was available for use. The figure for sets of over 400 MW in France, Germany, Italy, Holland and Spain was 85% in 1974. Availability in Britain was also much lower than in America. During the whole of 1974–75, 56% of the capacity of the CEGB's big sets was available, whereas in the US it was 76% for units of between 390 and 599 MW in 1973. The Americans have a considerable number of gas-fired stations which have a very high level of availability. But even their big coal-fired units, which have the lowest level, achieved 67% during 1974.[10] The operating problems at the CEGB's big sets have gradually been overcome, although this has involved a considerable amount of expenditure and every one has had to be modified. By 1979–80 the annual availability of the 500 and 660 MW units averaged 70.9%. This was a great improvement but was still a little lower than the availability of 73.6%, which was achieved, during 1977, at conventional sets of 400 MW and above in other West European countries.[11]

Due once again to failures of design and manufacture the CEGB's big sets have failed to acheive the thermal efficiencies that had originally been planned. The 500 MW units at coal-fired stations were designed for an efficiency of 37.5% when operating on base load.[12] During 1974–75 the Board's 500 and 660 MW units, achieved only 33.5%. By 1978–79 the figure had improved slightly to 34.0%. Nevertheless the thermal efficiency at these stations, all of which were or could have been on base load, remained significantly lower than both their design level and the standards achieved by the better stations and more efficient undertakings abroad. It should, however, be pointed out that the average thermal efficiency of British fossil-fuelled stations (32.1% in 1978) now compares reasonably well with that of the United States (32.7% in 1977) and Germany (31%). Our thermal efficiency is still considerably lower than in France and Italy but they can draw on their extensive hydro-electric power at peak periods, which means that they tend to avoid the energy losses which occur when stations start up and close down.[13]

The cost to the community of the mistakes and errors which have marred the electricity industry's programme of power station construction has been enormous. First, the industry involved itself in unnecessary capital expenditure by selecting the wrong type of nuclear reactor. Estimates by the Nuclear Power Company and the CEGB show the AGR's construction cost as being 15–30% higher than that of the LWR, as represented by a pressurised water reactor (PWR).[14] Moreover, because the AGRs will not be able to achieve their design capacity they are even more expensive than they appear. By the spring of 1979 something like £700 million of extra capital expenditure had been incurred by opting for the AGR, and there is little or no compensating advantage. Second, the inefficient way in which power stations, both conventional and nuclear, have been designed and built has seriously inflated their capital costs. The late arrival of plant and equipment at sites has depressed productivity and made construction more expensive, and so has the need to undertake extra work because of defective components and design changes. Those conventional stations which should have been commissioned during the period 1964–79 have suffered increases in capital costs ranging from 8 to 36% and, exceptionally, over 50%.[15] This suggests that the economies of scale which the industry hoped to secure through the construction of big sets were never obtained (and probably explains why its increase in output per unit of labour and capital has been so small). Third, due to delays in completion, resources have been tied up for an excessively long period before starting to earn any return. This cost is reflected by the additional interest during construction which is incurred, or must be regarded as being incurred, during the period of delay. Although I have not tried to estimate this sum, it must be formidable. The CEGB's investment in projects which had not been completed stood at around £3,200 million in the spring of 1978. Hence if the rate of discount is taken to be 5%, a year's delay in its fructification would have given rise to £160 million of interest, ignoring interest on previous interest. Fourth, expenditure on the repair and modification of the big generating units has been exceptionally heavy because of their poor design and defective construction. Fifth, due to the late arrival and low availability of new plant, the industry has not been able to make the savings in operating expenditure that would otherwise have been possible. It has been necessary to retain old labour-intensive stations which might have been shut down and to produce more electricity at plants that have relatively high fuel costs. According to the Price Commission the timely commissioning of the AGR stations (and new oil-fired plant) would have enabled the CEGB to make savings in its fuel and labour costs of around £130 million during 1979–80. Although the sum involved is approximately 3 per cent to 5 per cent of the CEGB's costs it does not represent the full saving which might have been secured from nuclear plant, because allowance was made for the fact that the AGR has a low availability.[16] Sixth, when much of the capacity now under construction does belatedly arrive it will be of little use because it is oil-fired plant. Some of this was ordered before the rise in petroleum prices but 2000 MW of capacity was sanctioned in 1975–76. No comment on the wisdom of this is neccessary.

Output and Capacity

Between 1968 and 1978 BEB's output increased by 23%. However, as can be seen from Table 3.1, virtually all of this rise took place during the first half of the period and production fell back during 1974–75. Output would have risen faster but for the contraction in capital work and the sale and installation of appliances. Despite the enormous rise in the consumption of gas there has been some increase in electricity's share of the energy market. The usual basis of measurement is the proportion of the total thermal value of all fuel and power for which electricity is responsible. This, however, gives a misleading impression because electricity is a premium fuel and it is

TABLE 3.1 *British Electricity Boards: Output, Productivity and Finances*

	Output	Electricity production as % of capacity^a	Employment	Average weekly hours worked by manual workers, October week	Output per equivalent worker	Quantity of capital	Output per unit of labour and capital	Real unit operating costs^b	Real unit staff costs	Real staff costs per employee	Relative weekly earnings of manual men, October week	Real cost of fossil fuel per unit	Real revenue per unit	Revenue	Gross surplus^b	Gross surplus as % of revenue^b
	(1968=100)	(%)	(000)						(1968=100)					(£m, 1978 prices)		(%)
1963	81.4	46.9	225.8	48.8	76.6	75.8	96.1	109.8	108.2	93.0	112.7	119.0	101.4	3,682	1,305	35.4
1968	100.0	44.5	237.8	40.9	100.0	100.0	100.0	100.0	100.0	100.0	100.0	100.0	100.0	4,597	1,857	40.4
1969	105.7	44.9	224.2	40.6	112.5	104.5	104.2	95.5	93.3	103.6	100.1	96.4	93.8	4,614	1,832	39.7
1970	109.4	44.5	213.1	40.8	122.2	110.8	104.7	98.3	91.3	109.8	102.2	102.5	88.2	4,544	1,560	34.3
1971	111.7	42.5	203.4	40.7	130.9	120.1	101.7	100.9	92.2	118.0	114.6	104.2	88.7	4,659	1,511	32.4
1972	115.2	40.3	194.0	40.4	142.3	127.5	101.2	101.1	91.7	126.4	114.9	101.1	87.1	4,817	1,551	32.2
1973	121.2	41.7	190.1	40.6	152.3	132.5	103.6	98.5	87.9	128.3	114.0	99.5	81.1	4,651	1,288	27.7
1974	116.3	39.2	189.0	41.0	146.1	135.5	97.7	119.6	94.5	133.0	112.5	138.3	85.4	4,923	1,002	20.3
1975	116.0	39.3	188.7	39.2	149.7	136.1	97.6	121.4	96.6	137.1	117.4	144.8	92.3	5,182	1,212	23.4
1976	117.2	39.9	183.0	40.3	153.4	134.0	100.1	122.9	93.6	136.9	119.0	144.5	97.2	5,460	1,402	25.7
1977	119.8	41.7	177.8	39.5	163.3	132.2	104.3	123.7	87.7	134.6	116.2	148.2	98.4	5,630	1,448	25.7
1978	122.8	42.4	176.6	39.8	167.9	132.2	106.9	127.6	91.2	143.0	124.2	152.6	99.6	5,894	1,471	25.0

Note The output index includes eighteen weighted indicators: quantity of electricity supplied distinguishing between ordinary and off peak sales, number of appliances sold and contracting and capital work (expenditure on materials deflated). Revenue weights for 1968 (and 1963) were used for electricity itself; but this, contracting, and capital work were combined with net output weights. The per unit series were estimated using gross output, apart from capital work, at 1968 (and 1963) prices. The financial figures, employment and three output indicators were derived from financial year data. The CSO's figures for the gross capital stock were used as bench mark estimates for the quantity of capital in 1963 and 1978 as the CEGB's capital work in progress represented roughly the same proportion at both dates. BEB's generating capacity was used to interpolate the figures for the other years. A 1963 capital weight of 63.1% was used.

^a The plant load factor.
^b Amount written off nuclear stations' initial fuel has been excluded throughout.

preferable to use expenditure by final users at constant prices and to exclude transport where electricity scarcely competes. At 1973–74 prices electricity accounted for 39.1% of all such expenditure in 1968 (as against only 12.8% on a thermal basis). By 1978 its share had risen to 45.5% (or 16.7%).

However, BEB's showrooms have been losing business to their competitors. Between 1971 and 1979 the electricity industry's share of the joint revenue earned by showrooms and by private radio and electrical goods shops fell from 18% to 15.5%.[17] Surveys by the Consumers' Association show that the Boards' showrooms provide a wide choice of goods and that their staff are helpful and knowledgeable. However prices tend to be relatively high. Moreover, the Association's members report that the Boards are a little slower to deliver goods, and to remedy faulty ones, than other places. They also take longer to undertake repairs than independent repairers and retailers.[18]

As a result of the huge programme of power station construction that was launched during the 1960s there has been a large rise in BEB's capacity. This, together with the relatively small increase in sales, has led to a decline in the proportion being utilised. During 1963, when the industry was admittedly somewhat short of capacity, BEB had a plant load factor of 47%. In 1968 the figure was already lower, at 44½%, and during 1978 it was only 42½%, despite the withdrawal of a considerable amount of old plant. The reduction in the plant load factor has occurred during a period when it might, other things equal, have been expected to increase. The amount of capacity that the electricity industry requires is determined by the maximum demand that is encountered during the year. This has risen much less rapidly than the average load on the system. Between 1968 and 1978 there was an increase of 30% in the quantity of electricity supplied compared with a rise of only 15% in the peak demand which the electricity authorities in England and Wales have an obligation to supply. The slow growth in maximum demand has been partly due to the spread of gas fires and central heating and the declining use of electric fires, which once made a large contribution to peak demand. Moreover, arrangements have been made with a number of large industrial consumers whereby BEB supplies electricity at a cheap rate but can in return disconnect if this should become necessary.

Because the increase in peak consumption has been so small BEB has had little difficulty in meeting demand during the past decade, and this despite the delay in completing power stations and, until recently, the low availability of the big generating units. At no time has it been necessary to disconnect customers due to lack of capacity, although some voltage reductions occurred during the early 1970s and there were power cuts because of industrial action by electricity workers in 1970 and coal strikes in 1972 and 1974. If stations had been completed on time, and the big sets had not performed so badly, the electricity industry would have possessed far too much capacity. For instance, during the winter of 1972–73 the CEGB would have had over 65 GW of capacity but for commissioning delays. As the maximum demand was only 42.6 GW the Board's capacity would then have exceeded the peak load by well over 50%. A margin of 20% was regarded as necessary in order to allow for the possibility that the weather might be exceptionally inclement and for plant breakdowns. However the CEGB would nevertheless have had 28% more capacity than it required. During the winter of 1978–79 the Board would, in the absence of commissioning delays, have had 65.7 GW of plant in order to provide for a maximum demand of only 43.5 GW, after allowing for interruptible contracts. Capacity would therefore have continued to exceed peak demand by well over 50%. The reserve margin had, it is true, been increased to 28% for planning purposes, but this is unnecessarily high as the Board estimates that it can have 85% of its plant available at the time of maximum demand and it needs a reserve of only 6% in order to meet its objective for the security of supply: the disconnection of customers during one winter in thirty-three.[19] Moreover the industry could if it wanted secure a larger interruptible load and so reduce the size of the peak.

EMPLOYMENT AND PRODUCTIVITY

Between 1968 and 1978 BEB cut its labour force from 238,000 to 177,000 which was a reduction of more than a quarter. Over the period 1968–73 output per effective worker shot up by more than 50%. Between 1973 and 1978 progress was less rapid because output scarcely increased and the labour force declined more slowly. Nevertheless by 1978 OEW was two-thirds greater than it had been in 1968. The industry's performance appears much less impressive when allowance is made for the use of capital. Between 1968 and 1978 the quantity of capital in use rose by approximately a third due to the completion of stations which were begun during the period of optimistic growth forecasts and heavy plant ordering in the 1960s. As a result output per unit of labour and capital increased by only 7% over the period 1968–78, and the picture does not look any better if allowance is made for the amount of fuel that was used.

The rise in labour productivity has been partly due to the closure of old labour-intensive power stations and the introduction of big units which, because there are large economies of scale in generation, require relatively little manpower. The growth in OEW has also been due to the contraction of activities that are especially labour intensive, namely capital work and the sale and installation of appliances. Another factor has been the growth in sales of electricity as a large part of the labour force in distribution is engaged on work which is related to the number of customers or the size of the transmission system, both of which grew more slowly than consumption. Despite this it seems clear that there was a substantial improvement in the efficiency with which labour was used.

As we have seen, the Status Agreement of 1964–65 led to a large reduction in overtime through the introduction of staggered work patterns. The Agreement also contained a declaration that employees should cooperate in the adoption of the most efficient work practices and that flexible use could be made of labour, regardless of the old boundaries between jobs, provided that workers received the rate for the job and were not temporarily upgraded to craft duties. At a later stage the unions agreed to support the use of work study, which had hitherto been little used. As a result some progress was made towards the adoption of better working methods, but it was sporadic and tailed off. In September 1967 a new agreement was concluded. This affirmed management's right to make any changes in working arrangements that it considered necessary and spelt out the ways in which labour could be redeployed. The agreement also provided for the establishment of a central register of the best labour practices and for the introduction of manpower utilisation yardsticks by which progress would be jointly monitored. This concordat led to a dramatic improvement in efficiency. The size of work teams was reduced, craftsmen started to do work that had previously been undertaken by other craft grades or by those with less skill and there was also greater flexibility in the use of semi-skilled and unskilled workers. Jointing teams, for instance, were cut from three men to two, and craftsmen began driving themselves around and doing carpentry and other work where this was part of the job.[20] During 1968 a further and even more important agreement was concluded. It provided for the introduction of incentive payments based on work study. Bonus payments would commence when workers' performance reached 65% of the standard level and their size would increase until it reached 100%, at which point a maximum addition equivalent to one-third of basic pay would be received. As the general level of performance was still very low, at something under 65%, there was ample scope for improvement.[21] Relatively little progress was made with the introduction of the incentive payments until 1970 but after that progress was rapid and by 1973 the great bulk of all manual workers had been covered.

The Electricity Council has made estimates, based on activity yardsticks and on work study data, of the increase in the productivity of manual workers in distribution. These suggest that there was a rise of over 60% during the period 1968–77 and it appears from a survey that capital expenditure was responsible for only about 10% (and six percentage points) of this increase. The CEGB claims that even larger gains have been made at generating stations.[22] It is difficult to believe that the increase has been so large, but there is no doubt that there has been a marked improvement in efficiency, for which the industry deserves considerable credit. Many British industries use labour inefficiently but few have made a sustained effort to improve the situation and even fewer have had much success. That the electricity industry has succeeded has been due partly to the vision and persistence of its management and the good labour relations that had been fostered through joint consulation. However the *sine qua non* of success was the cooperative attitude of the electricity unions which were strongly committed to the cause of higher productivity, and mounted a determined campaign to persuade their reluctant rank and file to accept the agreements which had been negotiated.

International comparisons of the growth in labour productivity confirm that BEB has been fairly successful at improving the efficiency with which it uses its manpower. Between 1968 and 1978 there was a growth in electricity sales per man hour of 77% at BEB, 37% at the American investor-owned utilities, 83% in Germany (1968–77), 104% at Electricité de France and 112% in Belgium

(1968–77). However BEB continues to use labour less efficiently than the American private utilities. During 1978 the quantity of electricity sold per worker engaged on its production and distribution was nearly three times greater in the US than in Britain.[23] This, however, gives an exaggerated impression of American superiority, since there is a close association between sales per employee and sales per customer and the level of consumption is far greater in the US.

But high sales per customer are only an advantage for the distribution side of the industry. In production the quantity of electricity generated — or, what is preferable, capacity — can fairly be related to employment. If such a comparison is made it appears that during 1977–78 the number of workers per unit of capacity at power stations owned by the American investor-owned utilities was about 70% smaller than in Britain and that in France it was 50% lower.[24] These comparisons do not allow for any variation between the countries in average hours worked, the use of contract labour or other complications. However, a study of a Scottish station (Cockenzie) and a similar coal-fired generating plant in America (Will County), in which such factors were taken into account, showed that the number of equivalent workers per unit of capacity was about 45% lower in the US. The contrast was less great for two nuclear stations as the number of equivalent workers per unit was only 20% lower at the American plant (Dresden) than at the Scottish (Hunterston). Labour is also used somewhat more efficiently away from generating stations in America. In the investor-owned utilities there were 18% more customers per worker than in BEB, ignoring those employed at power stations, on capital work and (in Britain) on retailing and contracting (which are not undertaken by the American utilities).[25] However this almost certainly understates the Americans' lead and it is reported by a high ranking BEB official who has made an on-the-spot investigation that, where comparisons can be made, distribution manning levels are 30–40% higher in Britain. There are a number of reasons why American productivity is higher. At power stations there are fewer men watching machinery and dials because it is assumed that plant will function properly, there is greater flexibility of labour and it is reported that American maintenance staff get down to work more promptly. In distribution, too, less time is wasted because materials and parts are assembled overnight and are ready to be picked up by working parties.

Moreover some activities, such as overhead line work, are very efficiently organised and workers seem to be more highly motivated.

Costs Prices and Profits

Between 1968 and 1978 BEB's unit costs rose by 28%. During the first half of the period, when unit fuel costs were stable they were more or less constant. However, since 1973 there has been a spectacular increase in coal and oil prices and by 1978 expenditure per unit on these fuels was 53% higher than it had been in 1968. Since they already accounted for 45% of the industry's operating expenditure this naturally had a considerable impact on its (total) unit costs. The rise in fuel costs has to some extent been offset by a reduction in staff costs per unit of output. Between 1968 and 1978 they fell by 9%, due to the large rise in OMY, and despite an increase of 24% in the relative weekly earnings of the industry's manual workers. This rise has more than made good the (11%) fall which occurred between 1963 and 1968 as a result of the Status Agreement and the cutback in hours worked.

The rise in coal and oil prices would have had a smaller impact on BEB's costs if more electricity had been generated by nuclear power — as it would have been but for the serious delay in completing the AGR stations and the low level of output at the two which have so far been commissioned. Expenditure on fuel would also have been lower if the industry had imported more coal from abroad. During 1978–79 imports accounted for only 250,000 tonnes out of total coal deliveries of 78 million tonnes. A further 850,000 tonnes of foreign coal would have been taken under a contract for the supply of Australian coal but for a Government scheme to promote the use of British coal. As a result the CEGB, in the spring of 1979, was buying coal from the NCB at a price of around £22 per tonne — some of which was produced at a significant loss — and selling Australian coal, for which it was charged about £17 per tonne, to Electricité de France for around £13 per tonne. Although the CEGB was compensated for the loss that it incurred the Board has been prevented from buying any more cheap coal from abroad. In the autumn of 1977 it could have signed up a long-term contract for 3–5 million tonnes of Australian coal which would have cost £2–3 per tonne less than British coal, and cheap supplies have also been available from Poland. Although imports might over the years have been built up to a substantial level the direct saving would not have been enormous. However the NCB would have been under pressure to control its costs and it would almost certainly have been forced to close down its high cost pits.

Despite the steep rise in BEB's unit costs its prices were no higher during 1978 than they had been in 1968. Moreover during the intervening years they were lower and in 1973 reached a point nearly 20% below the 1968 level. Because of the divergence between costs and prices there has been a substantial fall in the industry's gross profits. During 1968 they totalled £1,850 million and represented 40% of revenue, whereas in 1978 they were £1,475 million which was a margin of 25%. However, during 1974 BEB's gross profit had been as low as £1,000 million, which constituted only 20% of its revenue. This was because unit costs had shot up, due to the steep rise in the price of fuel, but there was no compensating increase in charges due to the Government's policy of price restraint. BEB's gross profits appear huge. However when allowance is made for replacement cost depreciation, which amounted to £1,090 million, and for stock appreciation at £65 million the industry only had a net profit of £320 million during 1978–79. In England and Wales the return on capital employed — net profit as a proportion of net assets at replacement cost — was a mere 1%, and prices were 5–10% below the industry's long run marginal costs, as estimated with a real return of 5% on investment.[26]

Although the sale of appliances and installation work account for only a small part of the industry's turnover they are of considerable interest because they are the only area where BEB faces direct competition. If hire purchase interest is disregarded these activities sustained a net loss of over £8 million during 1978–79, after depreciation at historic cost and before allowing for stock appreciation. This represented a negative margin of 2½% on turnover. In England and Wales there was a small deficit on installation and servicing work, although major private contractors achieved a 4% margin.[27] In their retailing activities the Electricity Boards had a net margin of about 3½%, including hire purchase charges but excluding supplementary depreciation. The corresponding figure for Currys, which is the largest electrical chain store in the private sector, was about 5½%.

NUCLEAR OR COAL STATIONS?

Most of the debate about the electricity industry's future plans has until very recently had an air of unreality. The main issue under discussion has been whether BEB should build nuclear or coal-burning stations in order to meet the growth in demand. However, it will be many years before the industry will need to construct any new capacity for this purpose. The demand for electricity has only been growing at a modest rate and there is no reason to expect that it will accelerate. Between the winters of 1968–69 and 1978–79 the unrestricted maximum demand increased by 1.8% p.a. in England and Wales and the Electricity Council is now forecasting that it will only rise by 0.8% p.a. over the period from 1979–80 to 1986–87. The Department of Energy's long term forecast is that UK electricity sales will rise by 1.7% p.a. between 1977 and 2000 if the GDP grows by 2% p.a. and that, even with economic growth of 3% p.a., the consumption of electricity will rise by no more than 2.3% p.a.[28]

Moreover BEB will be able to avoid having to construct additional capacity by adopting measures to restrict the growth in peak demand. It is believed within the industry that if a suitable tariff were to be introduced the interruptible load could increase from 1,800 MW to as much as 4,000 MW. The peak load could also be cut back by temporarily disconnecting domestic electrical appliances. This can be achieved by means of an impulse conveyed via consumers' television sets, and this system of control is already being used by one of the German electricity companies. There are a substantial number of appliances, including water heaters and freezers, which consumers might be willing to have disconnected for short periods if offered a suitable financial incentive; and it is believed that in this way it might be possible to shave 3,000–6,000 MW off the peak load.

During 1978–79 the unrestricted peak load totalled 45,000 MW in England and Wales and if it increases by as much as 1.7% p.a. it will rise to around 59,000 MW by the mid-1990s. However, if a modest allowance is made for interruptible loads (6,000 MW) and external supplies (1,000 MW) the figure is reduced to 52,000 MW. In order to meet this load the CEGB will, allowing for a margin of reserve plant of 24%, require a capacity of about 64,500 MW. The Board's planning margin has now been raised to 28%, but 24% should be adequate as the Board needs a margin of only 6% in order to meet its objective for security, and it estimates that 85% of its plant should be available at the time of peak demand.[19] During the spring of 1979 the CEGB had 56,100 MW of plant, and over 14,800

MW of capacity was under construction, including the new coal-fired units at Drax. However, by the mid–1990s the Board, if it follows its past practice and retires plant when it reaches forty years of age, will have scrapped nearly 7,000 MW of existing capacity. This means that the Board should have, without embarking on the construction of any more plant, about as much capacity as it will need, and not until the late 1980s will it be necessary for the CEGB to start work on any new stations.

However, this applies only to the construction of capacity to meet the possible growth in demand and to enable the CEGB to retire plant when it is 40 or more years old. The real question is whether plant should be built to replace the oldest and most expensive coal-fired capacity as soon as possible. The CEGB believes that if it builds pressurised water reactors it is desirable to embark on a programme of replacement. The total cost of the additional nuclear power including capital charges, as estimated with a 5% rate of interest, would be smaller than the reduction in the avoidable cost of operating its existing stations. Expenditure would decline not only because the Board would be able to dispense completely with some high cost plant but also because it would need to use its other fossil-fueled stations less intensively. Nuclear power, which has very low running costs, would account for more of the base load and those conventional stations with the lowest fuel costs would at each stage take over part of the work previously undertaken by stations that have higher short-run marginal costs. Early in 1979 the CEGB made some estimates which showed that it would be desirable on cost saving grounds for the Board to replace at least 3,300 MW of old coal-burning capacity as soon as possible, and even the third of the 1,100 MW replacement stations which the Board considered turned out to be well worth while. It was still desirable when attention was confined to the reduction in fuel costs and staff savings were ignored, and some scrapping continued to be justified even when the cost of the nuclear island, which accounts for half of the capital expenditure on a nuclear station, was doubled *or* it was assumed that new plant would take an extra five years to construct. Moreover the CEGB's estimates were based on what was being charged for coal (£1 per gigajoule) and, although the most expensive coal is priced about 10% above the average, the cost of producing it is far higher. Hence the saving in costs through closing down old coal-fired stations should be considerably greater than it appears.

There seems, therefore, to be a well nigh impregnable case for replacing a substantial slice of coal-burning capacity as quickly as possible. However it cannot be taken for granted that the new plant should be nuclear. If nuclear stations are built the CEGB will make large savings in fuel costs, but will incur heavy capital charges. Whereas if coal-burning capacity is installed there will be a much smaller reduction in expenditure on fuel but capital charges will be much less onerous. Which type of plant it is desirable to construct therefore depends on the comparative total costs of generating electricity at nuclear and coal-fired stations. Such estimates of costs have been prepared by the Department of Energy and Mr M.J. Prior. It is impossible to embark on a full description and discussion of Prior's assumptions and methods but they seem reasonable and the CEGB does not disagree with his estimates, though it does question the mildly anti-nuclear conclusion at which he arrives. According to Prior, if a 5% discount rate is used nuclear power from an LWR becomes cheaper than coal-fired generation when the price of coal rises above £1 per gigajoule (GJ), which is equivalent to about £23.60 per tonne.[29] The Department of Energy's estimates show nuclear power from a pressurised water reactor as having a slight cost advantage over electricity from a coal-burning station using a discount rate of 7% and with a price of coal which begins (in Profile 4) at £1.05 per GJ and rises to £1.30 in 2010.[30]

If anything, the Department's study probably shows nuclear energy in a slightly too favourable light because no allowance is made, as in Prior's investigation, for a lower initial availability at nuclear stations and because it is assumed that they would operate at a load factor of 65% whereas coal stations would only achieve 55%. This assumption might be justified on the ground that coal-fired units would be pushed down the CEGB's merit order for generation by the subsequent construction of nuclear stations, which have very low running costs, or coal-burning capacity of a more advanced type. However if nuclear power is more expensive no further stations of this type should be built and very little scope remains for achieving higher thermal efficiencies at coal stations. It may therefore be preferable to evaluate coal and nuclear plant at a common high load factor, such as Prior's 65%, although there is some American evidence which suggests that ultimately the level of availability becomes significantly better at nuclear than at coal stations.[31] However the most important and interesting point about the studies by Prior and the Department is that they both suggest that nuclear power is to be preferred on grounds of cost if the price of coal is above about £1 per GJ.

In mid-1980 the CEGB was paying an average of about £1.10 per GJ for British coal, but this does not necessarily mean that it should opt for nuclear power. If, as seems likely, the Board can arrange suitable long-term contracts for the importation of cheap foreign coal it might be desirable for the electricity industry to begin building coal stations on coastal sites. However the industry already has ample coal-burning capacity and its best course of action may therefore be to use most of the cheap foreign coal which it can purchase at its existing stations (though it would be necessary to construct additional port facilities in order to raise imports beyond about 5 million tonnes). The question therefore remains of whether the electricity industry should use nuclear energy or burn British coal. Although its price now appears to be above the break-even point this is not necessarily the case because the (real) cost of constructing power stations has risen substantially since Prior, the Department and the CEGB made their estimates. There appears to be a tendency for construction costs to increase over time and since nuclear power is capital intensive this would, other things equal, raise the threshold price at which coal ceases to be economically attractive. It is therefore a moot point whether the cost of coal is above or below this point.

The electricity authorities would reply that what is relevant is not the present price of coal but the future cost, and this will be very much higher than at present. According to the Electricity Council 'there is a general expectation ... that world prices for oil will at least double in real terms by the end of the century. It seems inevitable that market considerations will result in comparable increases in real terms in the price of coal'.[32] This is nonsense because oil is becoming a premium fuel which, as a result of the latest rise in oil prices, is no longer in serious competition with coal for the purpose of heat raising. The alternative to coal at generating stations is not oil but nuclear power, and this will gradually replace coal unless the NCB and other producers can keep their prices just below the level at which nuclear stations become more attractive than coal-fired capacity. Whether they will be able to do this depends, of course, on their costs.

There seems little doubt that the NCB's costs will tend to increase. When the Department of Energy made its comparison between coal and nuclear power station costs the NCB's estimates of the price that it would need to charge (viz. Profile 4) showed an increase of 1% p.a. over the period 1977–2010.[30] Moreover the Board appears of late to have become more pessimistic and is now forecasting that there will be an increase of about 50% by the late 1980s, which is about 5% p.a. The CEGB's estimates suggest that the figure will be even higher at 7% p.a. Although the increase may turn out to be lower, and there should be some respite once the NCB's investment programme begins to bear fruit, it seems unlikely that the Board will make sufficient savings to counterbalance the increase in its capital charges. However, even if there is a substantial rise in the price of coal this does not mean that there is a conclusive case for building nuclear stations. The cost of constructing nuclear stations could turn out to be so high or escalate so fast that nuclear power remains as expensive as coal-fired generation. This, after all, is what has happened in the past.

Nevertheless there appear to be three extremely powerful arguments for constructing a series of LWR stations. The first is that they would displace coal which is being produced at a cost that is very much higher than the price charged by the NCB. Hence it is necessary when considering the rival merits of nuclear and coal-fired generation to base the financial estimates for coal stations on the cost of the most expensive coal which the NCB supplies to BEB. During 1978–79 the CEGB was buying a substantial tonnage from high cost pits which were losing money. It may be said that the pits at which this coal is mined will already have been closed by the time that LWR stations could be entering service. However it will be many years before all the NCB's high cost mines have been shut and the Board is, as we shall see, now engaged on extending the lives of unprofitable pits so that it can produce as much coal as possible. Moreover, by the time that all the existing high cost pits have been eliminated other mines, which are now profitable, will have turned into loss makers because their best reserves will have been exhausted and their productivity will have fallen, or at least have risen more slowly than real wages. The second reason for constructing LWR stations is that this will put some much-needed pressure on the NCB to raise its efficiency and control its costs. In the third place, and this is an argument which weighs greatly with the industry itself, it is undesirable that electricity should be so dependent on coal. On grounds of risk reduction it is sensible to increase nuclear generation.

At the end of 1979 it was announced that the industry was to embark on the construction of a series of nuclear stations, which would include PWRs. However, Heysham and Torness, which are being started in 1980, are AGRs and the first stations under the new programme will also be of this type, although they will be expensive and a PWR could probably be built more quickly because it would require 10–15% fewer man hours of site work.[33] Both the Government and the industry were reluctant to construct AGRs but there seemed no choice because it would take the Nuclear Installations Inspectorate, which lacks the necessary staff, years to give the PWR safety clearance. It was believed that meanwhile the concerns engaged in the construction of nuclear stations would have languished through lack of work. Hence due to the folly of having failed even to plan PWRs, for which the last Government and the CEGB must take the blame, the electricity authorities are now embarking on the construction of more high cost nuclear capacity.

CHAPTER 4

The Coal Mines

Over the decade up to 1968 the Coal Board had to contend with a huge contraction in demand. It met this challenge by reducing its capacity, raising its productivity and cutting its prices.

Between 1958 and 1968 the Board's deep-mined production, which had been more or less stable until 1957, was reduced from around 200 million tonnes to about 160 million and its output dropped by 28%. This reduction was necessitated by the decline in demand which was in turn largely due to the availability of cheap oil and of gas produced from cheap oil. Over the period 1954–68 the price of fuel oil to industrial users was reduced by a quarter relative to that of coal; and this despite the imposition of a tax which was equivalent to about 40% on the delivered pre-tax price. Industry, gas works and domestic consumers each used about 15 million tonnes less coal in 1968 than they had a decade earlier, and BR's consumption fell by 10 million tonnes. Only at power stations was there an increase (of 27 million tonnes).

Employment was reduced by almost 50% from 765,000 to 400,000 and output per equivalent worker rose by almost half. A large part of the reduction in manpower was brought about by the closure of collieries and this was how the Board managed to cut its capacity. However, only 15% of the increase in output per manshift between 1963–64 and 1968–69 was due to colliery closures. A larger contribution was probably made by the completion of the pit modernisation projects which had formed part of the investment programme that the NCB had launched in 1950. But what was even more important was the mechanisation of mining and in particular the installation of cutter-loaders and self-advancing pit props. During the early 1960s the output per manshift (OMS) of underground workers was about

70% higher at pits where cutter-loaders were in use than at other collieries, but this gives a rather exaggerated impression of their importance because they were introduced first at the best pits. Moreover at those faces that were equipped with the most widely used type of cutter-loader the OMS was 50% greater where self-advancing pit props were in use. Between 1958 and 1968 the proportion of output that was simultaneously cut and loaded by machine was pushed up from under 30% to over 90%, and by the end of the period about two-thirds of all output came from faces with self-advancing pit props, compared with a negligible proportion in 1958.

Because staff costs represent such a large part of the industry's expenditure the rapid rise in productivity brought unit costs down and enabled prices to be reduced (in real terms). Between 1958 and 1968–69 unit costs declined by 12% and prices fell by 9%. Moreover, as costs dropped by more than prices, the gross margin improved slightly from 6½% in 1958 to approaching 9% in 1968–69.

Although the Coal Board, under the direction of Lord Robens, had acted with commendable vigour, it had only managed to keep its problems in check and formidable difficulties lay ahead. There was every prospect that the decline in demand would continue. The official forecast, put forward in the White Paper on *Fuel Policy*, was that domestic consumption, which amounted to 167 million tonnes in 1968, would fall to 120 million tonnes in 1975; a prediction that turned out, despite a number of unforseen developments, to be remarkably close to the actual figure of 122 million.[1] This meant that pit closures would have to continue and this was doubly necessary as a large part of the Board's output was already being mined at a loss. During 1967–68 those pits where book depreciation was not being covered accounted for 60 million tonnes of production. It does not necessarily follow that they were all candidates for immediate closure because some of them would have been covering their short-run avoidable costs. However, frequent injections of capital are necessary if pits are to be kept open and mining machinery usually has an alternative use, and hence an opportunity cost, because it can be transferred from one colliery to another.

Hitherto the Board had, by phasing the closure of collieries and redeploying workers, been remarkably successful in avoiding unemployment, and the National Union of Mineworkers (NUM) had cooperated over the shutting of pits. However, this might change and there were strong signs that the miners were becoming restive at the decline in their relative earnings (which was the other reason, apart from higher productivity, why unit costs had fallen). The mine workers had accepted the argument, which Lord Robens put so forcefully and persuasively, that higher wages meant fewer jobs, only to find that employment contracted in any case. Another danger was that the growth in productivity would slow down now that the introduction of power-loading and self-advancing pit props was almost complete. However, as we shall see, the Board had good reasons for believing that OMS would continue to increase at a rapid rate.

PRODUCTION AND CAPACITY

Although the year 1968 constitutes a watershed in the development of the coal industry there was no change in the rate at which production was declining. Between 1968 and 1973 the deep-mined tonnage fell from 159 million to 119 million and the weighted output fell by 27%, compared with a reduction of 21% during the previous five years. By 1978 there had been, as Table 4.1 shows, a further fall although it was smaller than before: the tonnage was down to 107 million and output was 36% lower than it had been in 1968.

Over the period from 1968 to 1978 UK coal consumption dropped by 47 million tonnes (a figure which differs from the fall in deep-mined production because of opencast mining and changes in stocks). Eleven million tonnes of the reduction was attributable to the gas industry which still had some carbonisation plant at the beginning of the period. There were also sharp reductions in sales to industry, to coke ovens and to domestic consumers, each of which had absorbed 23–25 million tonnes in 1968. Industrial consumption fell by 14 million tonnes, household usage was reduced by 13 million tonnes because coal was replaced by gas, and at coke ovens there was a decline of 10 million tonnes because of the fall in steel production and energy saving during iron making. Power stations were the only place where consumption increased. They used 74 million tonnes in 1968 and 81 million in 1978.

The greater part of the decline in coal consumption took place before the enormous rise in oil prices at the end of 1973. Nevertheless UK coal consumption, which stood at 133 million tonnes in 1973, declined by a further 13 million to 120 million in 1978. (Although during the following year consumption bounced back to just under 130 million tonnes as a result of the further rise in oil prices, which led to a large increase in the coal burn at power stations.) The reduction over the period 1973–78 was due both to the decline in total energy consumption and to a slight fall in coal's share of the market. Its proportion of energy consumption, which had slumped from 53% in 1968 to 38% in 1973, slipped to 35% in 1978 (as measured on a coal equivalent basis). There was a rise in coal's share of fuel used at power stations (from 66 to 69%), but a decline in its proportion of domestic consumption (from 28 to 19%) and in its share in general industrial consumption (from 16 to 12%).

At first sight it seems surprising that coal has not increased its penetration in the general industrial market. Before the dramatic increase in oil prices at the end of 1973 coal was more expensive than heavy fuel oil, but since then oil has been considerably dearer. For instance, during 1978 large industrial consumers were paying an average of 12.6p per therm for heavy fuel oil as against 8.9p per therm for coal. Moreover coal has from 1974 been cheaper than gas. But despite coal's price advantage, which to begin with was not very great in comparison with gas, it was the latter fuel which picked up the business that oil lost. The reason is that oil burning equipment can readily be switched to gas but not to coal. Gas supplies, as we have seen, have been restricted, but coal's price advantage over oil has been far too small to induce firms to replace oil-fired boilers with coal burning equipment. This has even been the case where new plant is necessary because the price of coal needs to be 3–4p cheaper than that of oil to offset the greater expense of installing and operating coal burning equipment.

Price considerations also explain why the NCB only exported something over 2 million tonnes of coal in 1978. During the previous year the other Common Market countries imported 22 million tonnes of coal from third countries for use in their power stations. The NCB therefore has a large potential market but its prices are uncompetitive. As we have seen the CEGB could have obtained coal from Australia at a lower price than the NCB charges and the cost of BSC's imports from Australia and the US is about £10 per tonne lower. Moreover much of the Board's output is very expensive to mine and is sold at a large loss. The Board produces at a loss for the domestic market but is reluctant to supply coal abroad on this basis.

The fall in deep-mined production since 1968 has been partly due to the closure of collieries and partly to a fall in output at those

TABLE 4.1 NCB Collieries: Output, Productivity and Finances

	Output	Tonnage	Employment	Average number of shifts per week per wage earner	Output per equivalent worker	Output per worker	Quantity of capital	Output per unit of labour and capital	Real unit operating costs[ab]	Real staff costs[abc]	Real staff costs per employee[abc]	Relative weekly earnings of miners, October week	Real prices[a]	Revenue[a]	Gross surplus[ab]	Gross surplus as % of revenue[ab]
	(1968=100)	(tonnes m)	(000)			(1968=100)	(1968=100)		(1968–69=100)	(1968–69=100)	(1968–69=100)	(1968=100)	(1968–69=100)	(£m, 1978 prices)	(£m, 1978 prices)	(%)
1958	138.6	202.1	766.0	4.51	67.1	72.7	..	..	113.1	125.4	90.0	113.8	110.4	3,621	236	6.5
1963	126.1	191.2	588.7	4.23	84.2	86.0	..	..	104.9	112.0	96.4	106.6	109.1	3,201	394	12.3
1968	100.0	158.7	401.7	4.13	100.0	100.0	100.0	100.0	100.0	100.0	100.0	100.0	100.0	2,276	201	8.8
1969	91.5	145.7	360.4	4.09	102.9	102.0	98.2	100.8	100.3	98.8	99.7	96.4	98.2	2,057	140	6.8
1970	85.0	135.9	337.8	4.02	103.5	101.1	95.9	100.2	105.5	102.6	103.0	93.6	104.9	2,079	172	8.3
1971	83.9	135.7	332.8	4.12	101.5	101.2	94.0	98.8	131.3	121.5	97.2	98.2	112.1	1,742	−118	−6.8
1972[d]	66.9	108.4	317.9	3.47	97.8	84.5	92.0	91.5	121.5	120.3	118.8	100.8	112.3	2,063	28	1.4
1973	73.1	119.4	308.1	3.90	99.9	95.3	89.5	95.7	145.4	144.3	111.2	96.6	105.3	1,428	−369	−25.9
1974[d]	61.5	99.4	295.7	3.59	93.9	83.5	87.2	88.1	147.1	147.7	134.8	108.5	136.1	2,200	32	1.4
1975	70.8	116.8	299.6	3.99	97.7	94.9	86.4	94.1	164.1	165.1	146.7	117.0	158.6	2,426	137	5.7
1976	66.3	109.7	294.1	3.93	94.5	90.6	86.9	90.2	162.4	159.9	141.5	113.8	161.7	2,423	204	8.4
1977	64.3	106.5	292.1	3.93	92.2	88.4	88.7	87.4	169.1	165.2	143.4	112.9	165.7	2,420	167	6.9
1978	63.8	106.9	287.8	3.90	93.4	89.0	92.3	87.3	180.8	180.1	156.2	123.1	166.5	2,436	24	1.0

Note The output index comprises seven indicators (tonnes delivered to different types of consumer) combined with 1968 (and 1963) revenue weights. Allowance was made for the overall change in stocks. The per unit series were estimated using an index for the value of production at constant prices calculated with the wholesale price index for coal. The quantity of capital is the gross capital stock, as estimated by the CSO. Its figures contain some investment which has not yet fructified but must, in 1968, have contained capital at pits that had been closed prematurely. The gradual removal of these assets as their normal lives have expired should exert some downward bias on the estimates. A capital weight of 19.8% was used.

[a] Financial year (April–March) beginning during year shown, except for 1958 which is the calendar year.
[b] Pension fund deficiency payments and 'social costs' have been disregarded.
[c] Staff costs for all NCB employees.
[d] There were prolonged industrial disputes during the first quarters of 1972 and 1974.

collieries which have remained open. Between 1968–69 and 1978–79 production at those pits which were still open at the end of the period fell from 124 to 104 million tonnes, which means they accounted for 20 million tonnes of the overall decline of 50 million. Moreover, if the potential output of each continuing colliery is deemed to be what it produced during 1968–69, the NCB had a substantial amount of unused capacity. It may be objected that in the absence of large scale expenditure on reconstruction and modernisation a pit's output will slowly decline because the best seams tend to be mined first, travelling times increase as coal is mined outwards from the pit bottom, and underground haulage systems become longer and more complicated. On the other hand, the introduction of better equipment and improved methods of working should have tended to raise output. It therefore seems unlikely that there has been any great decline in the potential production of those collieries that have remained open. In 1968 the Board believed that it would be able to produce up to 130 million tonnes during 1978 without having to invest in additional capacity; and in 1974 a working party consisting of representatives from the NCB, the NUM and government departments estimated that it should be possible to produce about 130 million tonnes.[2] The large gap between output and potential production is largely explained by the decline in productivity.

EMPLOYMENT AND PRODUCTIVITY

Between 1968 and 1973 employment fell from just over 400,000 to just under 310,000 and by 1978 the number had slipped to a little under 290,000; which meant there was an overall reduction of 28%. The drop in output was somewhat greater and output per man year (OMY) fell by 11%. However, there was a significant reduction in the number of shifts worked per week and if allowance is made for this productivity declined by 7%. During the earlier part of the period there had been a small rise and in 1970 output per equivalent worker was over 3% higher than in 1968, but from 1971 to 1977 there was a steady decline, ignoring 1972 and 1974 which were affected by the national coal strikes. However 1978 saw a slight recovery. The reduction in total factor productivity during the decade has been even larger than the fall in labour productivity. During 1978 output per unit of labour and capital appears to have been

13% lower than in 1968.

Since 1968 some of the sources of productivity growth, which had made such a large contribution during the previous decade, have dried up. Between 1958 and 1968 the Board had the benefit of the large post-nationalisation programme of modernisation and reconstruction but by 1968 expenditure on major projects had fallen to a very low ebb. For instance, during 1973–74 it amounted to only £14 million. Since then there has been a spectacular increase but relatively few schemes have been completed. And, as we have seen, cutter-loaders and self-advancing pit props, which had played such a large part in raising productivity, had already been introduced on a high proportion of all faces by 1968. Nevertheless the Board was anticipating that productivity would go on increasing at a rapid rate. In mid-1969 it forecast that OMS would increase from 42.5 cwt in 1968–69 to 75 cwt in 1975–76, which is an increase of over 75%.[3] (During 1975–76 it was scarcely higher than it had been in 1968–69, viz. 44.8 cwt.) There was probably an element of wishful thinking, and even propaganda, in the NCB's estimate and the Ministry was doubtful whether the rise would be as great. However, even they were expecting a substantial rise (55%) and the Board did have solid reasons for believing that productivity would continue to grow. A number of possible sources of productivity growth had been identified including retreat mining, new forms of mechanisation, and improved versions and better use of existing equipment.[4]

Under the advancing system, which is normal in Britain, coal is extracted outwards in a series of strips parallel to the roadway along which the face was commenced. With the retreat method tunnels are driven out and linked with a face. The coal is then extracted back towards the main roadway. With the advancing system progress is often interrupted because faults or other geological difficulties are encountered on 30% of faces. Under retreat mining this does not happen because the panel of coal is proved before extraction commences. Moreover it is unnecessary to maintain the tunnels in the region from which the coal has already been extracted: a task of some difficulty on an advancing face because of the need to hold up the sides on which the coal has been removed. On advancing faces it is usually necessary to cut holes, known as stables, at each end to accommodate the coal cutter when it has finished a traverse, but under the retreating system the tunnel can be used instead. Consequently while an advancing face usually has a complement of eighteen to twenty men per shift, as few as eight men are required on a retreat face, though this gives a slightly exaggerated impression because it ignores preparatory work on the retreating face.[5] Moreover in September 1968 the daily output per face was 35% higher on retreat than on advancing faces. Some progress has been made with the introduction of retreat mining, but it has been less rapid than the Board had hoped. The proportion of output so obtained has increased from 4% in September 1968 to 20% in September 1978. However, by September 1978 only 14% of all faces were using the retreat system, although geological conditions would permit 25–30% of faces to be switched to retreat mining.[6]

This technique was expected to account for only part of the coming rise in productivity. Further mechanisation was planned because, despite the use of cutter-loaders and self-advancing pit props, mining had only been partly mechanised. A considerable amount of labour was absorbed in cutting stable holes, driving tunnels and supporting their sides with stone packs. It was planned that the work would be mechanised by, for instance, using an extra power-loader to cut the opening. In 1968 the new methods had been applied to a very limited extent, but by March 1976 traditional stables had been eliminated on over 70% of all advancing faces and by 1978 the ripping of side tunnels had been mechanised at one or more of the ends of a third of all faces.[7] Even more progress had been made with the introduction of machines to drive the tunnels for retreat faces and the roadways to new advancing faces. Despite this the average daily advance has not increased and there has been a decline in the distance cut per manshift devoted to this activity. The slow rate at which tunnels are driven explains, incidentally, why retreat mining has not been introduced more rapidly.

During the period 1968–78 a considerable amount of face equipment has, as planned, been replaced by superior machinery. Far more powerful cutter-loaders have been introduced and the new types of self-advancing pit props can be shifted forward more rapidly. Conveyor belts which have a much greater capacity have been put in, and underground bunkers have been installed at pits where there is insufficient shaft capacity. The Board hoped that by such means it would be able both to increase cutting speeds and reduce the amount of time that face equipment was out of action. There was obviously considerable scope for improvement since in March 1966 cutter-loaders ran for only two hours and six minutes

out of a shift of seven hours and fifteen minutes.[8] Although this
excludes winding time, it includes travel underground and the meal
break, and some delay is unavoidable at the end of each traverse.
Nevertheless cutter-loaders were only being operated for a small
proportion of the time that was available. A substantial amount of
time was wasted because equipment broke down. It cannot be
expected that machinery will function perfectly under the adverse
and highly varied conditions that are encountered in a mine. However breakdowns also occurred because maintenance procedures
were defective and the machines were not being operated correctly.
Another important source of delay was that the advance of the face
was retarded. This might happen because coal could not be conveyed away sufficiently fast; because the support system started to
lag behind; because the side tunnels were being driven forward at a
slower rate; or because the stable holes were not ready to accommodate the coal cutter.

The NCB has tried to tackle the problem of machine delay not
only through mechanisation and better equipment, but also by
improving training, tightening up maintenance, adopting new techniques and carefully planning operations at each face. During 1967,
in an attempt to show what was possible, nineteen 'spearhead' faces
were selected and carefully planned for high levels of output. The
experiment was a great success and an attempt was made to apply
elsewhere the lessons that had been learned. In spite of this a sample
inquiry showed that cutter-loaders ran for an average of only one
hour and forty-six minutes per shift during the early part of 1976.
Even when allowance is made for the time (29 minutes) spent at the
face ends, machines were only operated for 42% of the time that was
available (319 minutes) excluding travelling, refreshment and preparation time.[9]

Why is machine running time still so short? One possible explanation is that underground travelling times have risen due to the
growing distance between the face and the pit bottom. Between 1968
and 1974 there was a reduction of eighteen minutes in the time that
faceworkers spent at their place of work, although there appears to
have been little change since then. However running time would not
have been reduced by the same amount partly because of the practice of cutting only two strips per shift and partly because machines
only cut for one-third of the net time. Moreover travelling time
obviously cannot explain why this proportion is so low.

One reason is that some obvious and remediable causes of delay have been neglected. The face study in 1976 showed that thirty-seven minutes were lost as a result of difficulties with the armoured flexible conveyor (AFC) onto which the cutter-loader deposits the coal and on which it is mounted. According to one of the Board's Area Directors the AFC and related equipment 'represent only 6% of the total face installation costs and statistics show that 20% of lost production can be attributed to them. Improvement in design to reduce the delays due to AFC difficulties is long overdue'.[9] It is also noteworthy that thirty-eight minutes were lost as a result of coal clearance delays, which seems a surprisingly high figure as the equipment is relatively simple. What has happened is that attention and capital expenditure have until recently been concentrated on the face and that coal handling has to some extent been neglected.

However, it seems clear that there are other and more fundamental reasons why machine running time is so short and why so little coal is cut even when the cutter-loaders are working. In 1979 OMH was no higher than in 1976 when the Chairman of the Coal Board told the NUM:

> we are not yet achieving the improvement in productivity which our massive investment programme would lead us to expect. Of course, a large part of the investment will take some time to materialise. But a good part is also spent on meeting current needs with the supply of adequate quantities of up-to-date machinery and equipment. Many pits have performed remarkably, but our overall performance is poor.[10]

There is little doubt that miners have lacked motivation, and the same may be true of managers. The Board has found that cutter-loaders are frequently stopped for no apparent reason, and managers report that often an excessively long period is taken to sort out the difficulties that do occur. Motivation would have been higher, and effort greater, but for the switch from piecework to time rates, though this has at long last been reversed. The dropping of incentive payments was due to the National Power Loading Agreement of 1966, and took place as new faces were introduced. Piecework was disliked by both the NCB and the NUM because there were wide differentials between districts which were not related to effort. The Board had proposed as far back as 1958 that an incentive system should be introduced for those on faces equipped with cutter-loaders which would, through the use of work study, provide equal pay for equal work. However most areas within the NUM were bitterly opposed to the use of stop-watches to measure the time that miners took to perform a given task, though a highly successful incentive scheme, based on work measurement, was operated in Nottingham.[11] The deadlock was ultimately broken by the Board's proposal to replace piecework by a day wage. The NCB believed that the pace of work was no longer determined by effort but by the machine, and that faceworkers would go on receiving disproportionately large wage increases so long as they were paid by results.

Both these arguments are hollow, as Searle Barnes pointed out, though others including myself accepted somewhat uncritically that the abolition of piecework was a step forward. Over the decade preceding the Agreement the earnings of day wage and pieceworkers increased by about the same proportion, and the percentage differential appears to have narrowed during the period's latter years. The introduction of cutter-loaders and self-advancing pit props had made certain tasks far easier but others, such as the ripping of tunnels, still involved considerable drudgery. And the efficiency with which the new machines were operated depended crucially upon miners' motivation. However, the case in favour of retaining piecework may not at that time have seemed very strong. In Scotland, where there were no incentive payments, there had been a rapid increase in OMS at the face, and in Yorkshire there was not much difference in productivity between piecework and day wage faces.[12]

At first the National Power Loading Agreement did not have any visible effect on face productivity, which continued to increase at a rapid rate. However, this may well have been because the widespread introduction of self-advancing pit props was pushing productivity up. Searle Barnes who made some detailed investigations in Nottingham found clear evidence that the Agreement was having an unfavourable impact, although it may have been more serious here than in other coalfields. When seventeen day wage faces were matched up with piecework faces it was discovered that there was only one day wage face which had a performance as good as that of its piecework counterpart. On the remaining sixteen day wage faces OMS was lower, often by a substantial amount, because their manning was greater and their output was almost always smaller. The Agreement appeared to have had an even more damaging effect on the productivity of those faceworkers who were engaged on advancing the headings at either end of the face and there were reports from several other coalfields that their performance was being seriously impaired.[13] Nevertheless the Board concluded a further agreement in 1971 by which those employed on other tunnelling were transferred from piecework to day work. This led to a reduction in their performance despite the widespread introduction of machinery.

By the end of 1971 the NCB had come to the conclusion that an incentive payment scheme was needed for faceworkers. However there was resolute opposition within the NUM. Its leadership, which had become far more militant, was determined to secure a large wage increase on a national basis. The NUM's swing to the left was partly due to accumulated resentment at colliery closures and partly to the way in which miners had dropped down the earnings league. As a result of the National Power Loading Agreement the position of faceworkers, who play a key role in the Union, had deteriorated particularly sharply.[14] The ending of piecework also increased faceworkers' sense of solidarity since they were now unable to increase their earnings through greater effort or their skill in negotiating improved rates for their teams. This was the background to the national coal strikes of 1972 and 1974 and helps explain why, in a national ballot in October 1974, the miners rejected a scheme for pit-based incentive payments. After this, wage restraint blocked any further attempt to introduce a proper incentive system, and it was not until early in 1978 that incentive payments were introduced through local negotiations, the miners having again rejected the proposal in a national ballot.

Between 1977 and 1978 there was only a small rise in productivity and the following year did not see any increase in the level of OMS. It would however be premature to conclude that incentive payments are ineffective or that productivity would have been no higher even if they had been introduced earlier. OMS appears to be rising now and there may have been special reasons why incentives did not lead to the expected growth in productivity. The industry has, due to the reduction in the age of retirement, been taking on a large number of new and inexperienced workers. It has also been reported that in some places the advance of the face has been retarded because of difficulties with the new heading equipment that is being installed. Moreover it appears that higher productivity at the face, where the incentive payments are received, has for some reason been offset by poor results elsewhere.

In any case there was probably another factor besides the absence of incentives that was and still is depressing efficiency, namely the cessation of colliery closures except in cases of exhaustion. Up to 1970 a large number of pits were shut each year because they made substantial and persistent losses. Moreover, major investment projects were only sanctioned at those pits that were listed as having good long term prospects and a pit with a poor financial performance was unlikely to be included. Hence managers and men had a powerful incentive for efficiency, as was shown time and again by the improvement which took place when pits were told that their future was in jeopardy.

The closure of pits on financial grounds more or less came to an end during 1970 when considerably more coal could have been sold if it had been available, and the Board also had production difficulties during 1972–73 and 1974–75 as an aftermath of the national strikes. What was more important was that the NUM, as a result of its leftward swing, began to oppose any closure that was not due to exhaustion, and it has over the years gained experience in mining engineering and become more skilful at arguing its case. The Board also become less willing to press closures because, as a result of the rise in energy prices, some unprofitable pits started to make more money. Moreover it is difficult to combine an extremely optimistic attitude towards the industry's prospects with the closure of pits on the ground that they are grossly unprofitable.

Although, considered in isolation, the NCB's productivity performance looks very poor it does not seem quite so bad when viewed in the light of what has been happening in other European countries. Poland and the USSR are the only major producers to have made large gains in productivity since 1968. Between 1968 and 1979 there appears to have been a rise of 73% in OMS underground in Poland, though this figure is a little suspect. On the other hand, there was an increase of 28% in France, of 21% in Belgium and of 15% in Germany. The corresponding increase in the UK was 7%. Although the NCB was at the bottom end of the range, it should be borne in mind that Poland has been investing very heavily and that the continental countries had at the start of the period made less progress with the introduction of cutter-loaders and self-advancing pit props. Moreover in Germany and Belgium productivity has been stagnant or falling since the early 1970s. However, international comparisons also suggest that the Coal Board has considerable scope to improve its performance. During 1979 the output per man hour for underground workers was 46% greater in West Germany than in Britain, although our geological conditions are slightly more favourable.[15]

Costs, Prices and Losses

Since 1968 there has been, as can be seen from Table 4.1, an enormous rise in the NCB's unit operating costs and their growth has been almost continuous. By 1978–79 collieries' unit costs were about 80% greater than they had been during 1968–69. The increase has been so large partly because OMY has slumped and partly because of the substantial rise in the average weekly earnings of mineworkers relative to those of workers in manufacturing. Up to 1973 earnings in coal tended to rise less rapidly than in manufacturing, despite the national coal strike of 1972 and the large wage award that miners received as a result of the Wilberforce Inquiry. Early in 1974, after the second national coal strike, miners received another massive wage increase. This produced a more permanent rise in their earnings and during 1978 these were boosted still further by incentive payments. Between October 1968 and October 1978 mineworkers' earnings rose by 23% relative to manufacturing.

The massive rise in the Board's unit costs has led to a huge increase in its prices. By 1978–79 the price of coal was 66% greater than in 1968–69, though most of this increase took place during 1974–75 and 1975–76. In 1968–69 collieries earned a gross surplus of £200 million but because prices increased less rapidly than costs there was a gross deficit of around £10 million in 1978-9, after allowing for £35 million of stock appreciation. The size of the industry's gross surplus depends on the way in which deficiency contributions to pension funds and what are termed 'social costs' are treated. In the NCB's accounts they are included in operating expenditure, although the Board receives a subsidy which covers part of the cost. However, they are best disregarded because they do not form part of the cost of producing coal during the year to which they appear to relate and would not be avoided if production were curtailed. Indeed social costs are the expenditure which the Board incurs when it eliminates uneconomic capacity, such as the amounts paid to pension and superannuation funds to meet the extra cost of early retirement benefits awarded to redundant mineworkers. This is clearly a transfer payment rather than a resource cost. (It should be noted that the costs of closures and deficiency contributions have been disregarded not only here but wherever they are recorded as having occurred within the nationalised sector.)

On the other hand, it is necessary to allow for replacement cost depreciation which has hitherto been ignored. The Board's estimates suggest that it amounts to about £185 million. If so, collieries had a net deficit of nearly £200 million during 1978–79. This was a particularly poor year but at no time since 1968–69 has the NCB managed to both cover its depreciation and provide for stock appreciation; and in most years there have been large losses. It may be objected that, during the early years of the period at least, the Board had surplus capacity and misallocation would have resulted if depreciation had been met. If excess capacity exists prices should be based on avoidable costs, which appears to mean that depreciation will not be recovered. The charge will in any case be excessive if depreciation is being provided in respect of surplus assets that will never be replaced. However, allowance has been made for this because capital has been written off and, as we have seen, mining machinery usually has an opportunity cost. What is even more important is that coal is an increasing cost industry, i.e. the greater the output the higher costs will tend to be as mines where the geological conditions are increasingly unfavourable have to be brought into production. It follows that even if the Board's high cost pits only earn sufficient revenue to meet their avoidable costs, its low cost mines will show a large gross surplus (or rent). This would more than cover its replacement cost depreciation.

But what happens is that the Board sustains a huge loss at its high cost pits. Instead of closing them and basing its prices upon its marginal costs the Board practises cross-subsidisation and charges somewhat less than its average cost of production. The Board does not even have to recover the full cost of producing its deep-mined output because it is able to draw upon the handsome profit which it earns on its opencast production. This has always been relatively profitable but has, during the past few years, turned into a bonanza. Due to the rapid escalation in coal prices there has been a large absolute increase in the revenue per tonne which has not been matched by a corresponding rise in the absolute cost per tonne, primarily because this was considerably lower to begin with. During 1978–79 the NCB earned a net profit of about £95 million from its opencast output (before stock appreciation). On the other hand a huge loss was incurred at those of the Board's pits that were unprofitable. I have roughly estimated from colliery output and employment data that the pits that made gross losses incurred an aggregate deficit of £180 million during 1978–79. In addition their retention must have necessitated a substantial amount of investment, both directly in order that they might continue operations, and indirectly because the NCB was put to the expense of purchasing equipment for its profitable pits which could instead have been transferred from loss-making collieries.

Plans For Coal

In mid-1974 the NCB published *Plan for Coal*. It was argued that, due to the massive increase in oil prices, the industry's prospects had greatly improved and stated that by 1985 demand might range up to about 150 million tonnes, although the Board omitted to mention that its estimates showed that consumption might be as low as 120 million tonnes. It was hoped that the NCB might be almost able to meet a demand of 150 million tonnes by creating 43 million tonnes of capacity to offset the exhaustion of existing reserves, through the better use of existing capacity and by stepping up opencast production from 10 to 15 million tonnes.[16] During 1976 the NCB, the Government and the mining unions made a joint review of the industry's plans and prospects, the results of which were embodied in *Coal for the Future*. There was no longer any talk of demand being as high as 150 million tonnes and it was declared that the NCB should aim to produce something over 135 million tonnes in 1985. Although the production target was lower and pits were being closed less rapidly than had been planned it was still believed that about 43 million tonnes of replacement capacity would be necessary. The explanation was that output was dropping and the Board's effective capacity was declining. But this was not spelt out and the 8–9 million tonnes of additional coal through the fuller use of capacity was simply forgotten. However it was admitted that the cost of the programme would be far greater than the sum which was originally mentioned, though the extent of the increase was not revealed.[17] When the plan was announced the cost was said to be £2,600 million, but the Government was later told that £4,100 million of expenditure was involved, excluding the additional projects which were now included. A large part of this escalation of 55% arose because projects had been under-costed and because the original figure (£1,400 million) was at September 1973 prices, and not at March 1974 prices as repeatedly stated.[18]

What was far more worrying than the increase in the cost of the Board's investment programme was the change in its composition. It had originally been planned that by 1985 Selby and other new collieries would be producing 20 million tonnes, but it soon became evident that this was over-optimistic. In *Coal for the Future* the figure was revised down to 10 million tonnes and it will turn out to be even lower.[17] *Plan for Coal* already included 9 million tonnes of replacement capacity from the life extension of pits that would otherwise exhaust and, due to the shortfall in output from new pits, it was decided to include more projects of this type. Because of the reduction in the amount of low cost output from new mines, a number of schemes which were designed to keep costs down were also included in the Board's revised plan. As a result the new investment programme covered forty more pits and provision was made for £200 million of capital expenditure on the additional projects.[18]

The life extension projects were almost all at collieries which had previously been candidates for closure because it was known that the best seams were almost worked out. Consequently they had been starved of capital and in many cases relatively large amounts of replacement investment were necessary if production were to continue. Moreover the prolongation of the collieries' lives meant that inferior reserves would have to be opened up and that in some cases productivity would fall while in others a low grade of coal would be produced. The Coal Board began by sanctioning projects at pits where productivity was above average but has gone on to invest in pits where it is below. The Board was able to claim in *Coal for the Future* that productivity, at the mines at which major projects had been authorised, was 24% higher than average but subsequent schemes have depressed the figure to 9%.[19] This can only mean that OMS is less than the industry average at those pits where major projects were sanctioned between 1976 and early 1979. It would be wrong to jump to the conclusion that none of these supplementary projects are justified because it is expected that productivity will on completion be around 20% higher than average. This however is an overall figure and in coal there is always a wide dispersion around the mean.

Some of the life extension and modernisation schemes appeared to show moderately good returns even with a discount rate of 10%. But many of them were not likely to be very profitable and in some cases the internal rates of return were negative and it was anticipated that the pits would, like Cynheidre in South Wales and Haig at White-haven, go on losing money. Such investment was justified on the ground that the coal, which might be of a special grade such as anthracite or coking coal, was necessary if the market was to be satisfied; that it was desirable to retain labour so that it could eventually be transferred to neighbouring collieries where output was being expanded; or that it would reduce or eliminate losses at pits which were not going to be closed. It is the Board's practice when calculating the return on investment to assume that a loss eliminated is the equivalent of a profit earned. Hence capital expenditure which leads to a reduction in losses often appears to be highly desirable, though all that is relevant unless it is impossible to close the pit is the positive profit that will be earned. The Board tries to guard against investing in projects which appear to have a high return but where the pit will end up making little or no profit by examining whether they will have a positive cash flow after the investment has been made. However, it must be difficult in an industry where it is hard to close collieries and where cross-subsidisation is being practiced not to be impressed by projects that show a high rate of return because a loss will be avoided.

Although part of the NCB's investment programme is of a dubi-ous nature it would be quite wrong to conclude that the whole, or even the bulk, of the projects are ill-judged. At those collieries where production is being expanded the additional output will be pro-duced relatively cheaply. Shafts and other facilities are already in existence and by no means all mining employment can be regarded as a variable cost. As a result both capital and labour costs will be comparatively low per tonne of incremental output. Indeed it was stated in *Coal for the Future* that the average internal rate of return for projects of this type had been estimated at 30%, although this is likely to be an overstatement if only because of the failure to allow for any increase in real wages.[20] The Board's new drift mines are also attractive projects. Productivity is or will be high and, because shaft sinking is avoided, the capital cost per tonne is low and construction time is short.

The £500 million pit complex at Selby is a more borderline project because, although productivity will be high and operating costs will be low, it will take at least thirteen years to construct the mine and build production up to the full rate of 10 million tonnes. The Board's initial calculations, which were based on its standard assumptions that there would be no increase in the price of coal or in real wages, showed that the internal rate of return would be less than 10%. Moreover no allowance was made either for possible over-optimism about the level of OMY, which is forecast to be five times higher than the general average, or for possible delays in the completion of the project, which has already fallen two years behind schedule.

In supplementary calculations a more cautious view was taken about productivity and it was assumed that there would be a substantial rise in the prices of coal and oil, but that the benefit would be partly offset by an almost matching increase in miners' earnings. It turned out that if this happened the rate of return would be in the low teens. Thus at first sight Selby appears to be a somewhat risky venture because it seems almost inevitable that there will, over the years, be a considerable rise in miners' earnings. However, it seems unlikely that the industry will make sufficient gains in productivity to both cover the rise in miners' earnings and meet the capital charges on the huge programme of investment which is being undertaken. If so, the price of coal will rise and, as we have seen, this is what the NCB expects. Such a rise will make Selby more profitable and only in the somewhat unlikely case of stable coal prices but rising earnings will Selby turn out to be an unjustifiable investment, unless of course its output and productivity have been greatly over-estimated. However, a rise in coal prices will restrict the amount of coal which can be disposed of at a profit and put a question mark against other investment projects which the NCB is planning to undertake.

The Coal Board and the Government have taken a highly optimistic view of the industry's long term prospects. *Coal for the Future* declared that it would need to equip itself to produce around 170 million tonnes by 2000, of which at least 150 million tonnes would have to be deep-mined. After allowing for the working out of existing pits, this would mean that the NCB would have to create 60 million tonnes of new capacity beyond that being provided under *Plan for Coal*. The great bulk of this would have to be at new mines.[21]

It is extremely doubtful whether the market for British coal will be anything like as great as the NCB anticipates. The electricity industry used nearly 90 million tonnes of coal in 1979 and the Board is hoping that it will require around 85 million in 2000. This seems improbable. According to the Department of Energy's latest projections power stations' fuel consumption will by then amount to 163 million tonnes of coal equivalent (mtce) if the economy grows by about 2% p.a. (and will be only 23 mtce higher with 3% growth).[22] Our discussion of the relative merits of coal and nuclear generation suggests that it is desirable to use nuclear stations to meet the base load, unless cheap coal can be purchased abroad. The base load, as derived from the minimum demand encountered during the year, represents about 40% of all electricity supplied. However, maintenance and overhaul can be undertaken during the high summer when demand is at its low ebb and, if the minimum demand during a typical summer night is taken to represent the base load it forms around 60% of total demand. This suggests that nuclear stations should by 2000 account for some 95 mtce, which is about the same as the Department estimates (viz. 88–95 mtce). The Department predicts that oil-fired stations will only use 10 mtce in 2000. If so, the electricity industry's (residual) requirement for British coal will amount to only about 60 million tonnes, although its total consumption would be greater if stations using imported coal were to be constructed in place of some of the nuclear plant. It is questionable whether the growth in the demand for electricity will be as high as the Department expects. In this case a smaller amount of new capacity will be required to meet the growth in demand but coal consumption at power stations would nevertheless fall to around 60 million tonnes, due to the retirement of old coal-fired capacity. It would only be higher if replacement stations using British coal were to be constructed and this will be uneconomic until the NCB eliminates all those collieries which are losing money on the coal which they supply to the electricity industry.

The NCB forecasts that in the year 2000 domestic and commercial consumption will amount to about 20 million tonnes and that coke ovens will absorb around 23 million tonnes. They used only 12 million tonnes of British coal in 1979 and the NCB's estimate assumes a steel production of nearly 40 million tonnes.[21] This now seems ridiculously high and, as we shall see, imported coking coal has a considerable advantage over indigenous production on grounds of both price and quality.[23] It would therefore be unwise to assume that more than, say, 5 million tonnes of British coal will be used at coke ovens in 2000. The NCB's forecast for domestic and commercial consumption rests on the belief that the production of natural gas will have begun to decline by 2000 and includes coal for the manufacture of substitute natural gas. However, as we have already seen, supplies of natural gas are likely to be maintained up to 2000.[24] The Department's estimates suggest that in this case domestic and commercial users will burn only about 5 million tonnes of coal in 2000.[25] However, domestic consumption has held up remarkably well in the face of competition from gas and the rise in its price will help the NCB to retain business that might otherwise have been lost. Moreover about 5 mtce of fuel oil is used within the domestic and commercial sector and it might be possible for coal to pick up some customers here. It therefore seems possible that coal consumption, which amounted to something over 15 million tonnes in 1979, will be maintained at about the same level.

General industry, which is the NCB's final market, only consumed 9 million tonnes during 1979 but the NCB anticipates that the figure will shoot up to around 40 million tonnes by 2000.[21] Although this appears on the high side coal does have great expectations provided that the price of oil is maintained at such a level that coal has a price advantage over heavy fuel oil. Whether this will hold is in the lap of the OPEC gods who seem firmly committed to a policy of restricted supply and high prices. The position may alter during the fullness of time and, although it is difficult to see why it should, it is never easy to identify the springs of change. However the most reasonable assumption for planning purposes is that by 2000 industrial users will have largely switched from fuel oil to coal. During 1978 general industry consumed nearly 20 mtce of fuel oil and, allowing on the one hand for an increase in energy consumption and on the other for oil retaining some customers, this seems to be about the amount of extra business which coal might secure by 2000. If so, general industrial consumption could be around 30 million tonnes at the

turn of the century, and the Department's estimates suggest a figure
of only about 25 million tonnes if industrial gas consumption is
maintained.[25]

It must therefore be concluded that the home demand for coal is
unlikely to exceed about 110 million tonnes in 2000. Four points
must be made about this figure. First, it does not purport to be a
sophisticated estimate. It is merely a back of an envelope calculation
to discover whether the NCB's target of around 170 million tonnes is
realistic. Second, it is not a prediction of what will actually happen,
but a 'guesstimate' for use in policy formation. The quantity of
British coal consumed by the electricity industry may well turn out
to be greater than 60 million tonnes because the construction of
nuclear stations and/or the use of foreign coal is held back. Third,
my figure for demand is not a target and this helps to explain why it
is so much lower than the projection given in the 1978 Green Paper
on *Energy Policy*. It was suggested in this document that even if coal
production were stepped up to 170 million tonnes there would be,
with 3% economic growth, an unsatisfied need for 50 mtce at power
stations by 2000, which it might not be possible to meet by additional energy imports.[26] This scenario of shortage was adopted
because the planners were afraid that Britain would not be able to
achieve faster economic growth if the energy industries failed to
provide sufficient capacity. Their projections were not based on
what they thought the demand for energy would be but on what they
believed it should be. They were engaging in targetry. The Department's figures were too implausible to survive for long and at the
end of 1979 it had another shot in its *Energy Projections*. The estimates
based on 3% growth have been downgraded and equal prominence
is accorded to those based on 2%. However, the demand for coal is
still put at 128–165 million tonnes in 2000 as a result of the continued assumption that natural gas will have started to run out by
2000. And every tonne of indigenous energy still appears to be
necessary for Britain's economic survival because the planners by
massaging the reserve statistics, have reduced their estimate of
North Sea oil production in 2000 by a third![27]

The final point about my 'guesstimate' of the future demand for
coal is that it does not allow for possible imports for the domestic,
commercial and general industrial markets. There is little doubt
that in the short and medium term substantial quantities of coal
should be imported. A considerable part of the NCB's output is

being produced at a large loss and, as we have seen, the Board is engaging in some questionable investment in order to keep almost exhausted collieries in production. The obvious answer is for the NCB to reduce its output and to start closing those collieries which are unprofitable and nearly worked out. As a result coal imports would rise. This suggestion will no doubt be criticised on the ground that it will deprive miners of work and that it will impose a strain on the balance of payments. The latter objection is, in reality, an argument in favour of closing loss-making collieries. Due to North Sea oil the pound is now very strong and it is difficult for British manufacturers to export or to meet competition from imports. In consequence workers are being thrown out of jobs and factories are being shut. This must, in part, be regarded as the price of maintaining unprofitable pits in operation and of preserving jobs in coal. If loss-making collieries were closed and more coal were imported the pound would (temporarily) weaken and our hard-pressed manufacturers would find it easier to compete.

It may be replied that the Government should pursue expansionary fiscal and monetary policies in order to stimulate home demand and restore full employment. This would lead to additional imports, the pound would weaken, exports would be stimulated and foreign coal would become somewhat less attractive. However, as the Government feels unable to pursue expansionary policies because of the likelihood of greater inflation, the maintenance of employment in coal, or in any of the other nationalised industries, is likely to result in more unemployment in the rest of the economy. Unemployment is high because of the need to moderate wage demands and if the rate is low for the nationalised industries it will have to be greater elsewhere. In this case consumers will be deprived of private sector products which they value sufficiently highly to be prepared to pay a price that reflects their costs of production and will be provided instead with public enterprise products at a price which does not.

However, let us assume for the sake of argument that the economy can be returned to full employment and reasonably stable prices, or at least a stable level of inflation. In this situation it might seem desirable for the NCB's unprofitable pits to remain open because they are concentrated in areas where there are few alternative jobs and because their workers are not prepared to move elsewhere. If loss-making pits were closed society would be deprived of the coal they produced without there being any commensurate increase in production elsewhere in the economy. If so, the wage that miners receive exceeds the opportunity cost of their labour — the value of the production being forgone elsewhere — and their continued employment does not show that misallocation is occurring.

However, by no means all of the NCB's unprofitable pits are situated in districts where unemployment is high. During 1978–79 there appear to have been about 60 collieries in the central coalfields which failed to earn sufficient revenue to cover their operating expenditure. They produced 25 million tonnes and had nearly 65,000 workers on their books. If the Board does not accelerate the closure of loss-making collieries it will not be able to raise its production at those mines where expansion schemes have been, or are being, carried out. In this case, no additional output will be obtained by continuing to employ workers in areas of high unemployment. The coal they contribute will simply take the place of output that would have been produced elsewhere. Moreover the incentive to produce efficiently is likely to be reduced if it is known that pits will be retained even though they are grossly unprofitable and if low cost mines which could expand their output are held back.

There appear to have been during 1978–79 around fifty-five grossly unprofitable pits in Scotland, Wales and the other outlying coalfields where unemployment is relatively high. They had an output of over 15 million tonnes and employed 50,000 workers. However most of these pits are within travelling distance of other pits and the NCB should therefore be able to find alternative work for many of their employees. Hence it seems likely that if the closure of grossly unprofitable collieries were carefully planned only a relatively small number of workers would not be able to transfer to a new job at another colliery and some of the remaining workers would obtain local jobs or move to another part of the country where employment prospects are better. The continued operation of grossly unprofitable pits means that young and potentially mobile workers have to be taken on to cover natural wastage. This has been particularly high because the age at which miners can retire has been progressively reduced from 65 to 60. As a result the oldest and least mobile workers have been leaving the industry and it would have been particularly easy to close unprofitable pits. Unfortunately the opportunity has been allowed to slip by and the Board is recruiting a large number of workers who could have been employed more productively elsewhere in the economy. These workers, as they age and take on the characteristics of the coal miner, will become less and less mobile. Hence their earnings potential will be reduced in later life and it will be necessary to recruit still more workers if they are to continue to be employed. Thus the opportunity cost — the output foregone — by absorbing them into the coal industry exceeds the wages they are paid by the NCB, and to this extent the Board's losses understate the social cost which is incurred through the continued operation of unprofitable pits.

It may be replied that if they are shut their workers may refuse to accept jobs at neighbouring collieries and, even if they do accept them, may simply deprive other workers of employment. If the latter fail to move in search of jobs the community will have sacrificed output in coal for nothing. This argument is almost certainly too pessimistic because many workers are prepared to move in search of work. However, if it is true that workers are now very immobile, the Government must bear much of the blame for having made unemployment too attractive and adopted housing policies which discourage mobility. These are large issues and this is not the place to discuss them. But what is clear is that mistaken policies will not be abandoned so long as unemployment is hidden because unprofitable pits and plants are kept going. That the closure of loss-making collieries should be accelerated is recognised in Whitehall and the Coal Board. Although little has been said about the problem in public, it was reported by a tripartite committee that 'a study by Treasury and Department of Energy economists of the economics of the [South Wales] coalfield on the basis of resource costs (taking account of rates of unemployment and balance of payments) suggested that this approach offered no escape from the need to consider a major restructuring of the coalfield'.[28]

It must be concluded that the Coal Board's policies and plans have serious weaknesses. A large part of its output is being produced at a loss and, though many of the schemes which figure in its short term capital expenditure programme are worth while, it has embarked upon some dubious projects. The Board's long term programme is based on a wildly over-optimistic estimate of the likely demand for coal and this obviously places a question mark against the huge programme of investment which it is planning to undertake.

PART 2

Transport and Communications

CHAPTER 5

British Rail

By 1968 the attempt to restore British Rail to profitability seemed to have failed, although more progress had been made than appeared to the naked eye. During the early 1960s the Government, which had hitherto been passively financing the mounting deficit, placed Dr Beeching in charge, instructed him to make the railways cover their costs, broke up the old Transport Commission and placed BR under a separate Board. (The British Railways Board also controls shipping services, hotels and other subsidiary activities, but these we shall ignore.) In 1963 Beeching published his report. It was a far more positive document than is usually supposed for it initiated Freightliners, and proposed a switch from wagon to trainload working and the introduction of company trains. However, it was mainly a plan for rationalisation.

Between 1963 and 1968 four-fifths of freight stations were closed, the wagon fleet was cut by nearly 45% and freight train mileage was reduced by a third. A quarter of the passenger route was closed but because it was very little used the number of passenger train miles declined by only 15% and the Beeching cuts appear to have reduced passenger traffic by only about 3%. Because of the drive for greater efficiency which Beeching launched, and due to the replacement of steam, there was a substantial improvement in productivity. In 1963 it was not much higher than it had been during the mid 1950s but between 1963 and 1968 output per equivalent worker rose by about a third. This was entirely accounted for by the reduction in employment, which was cut by a third. Output fell by nearly 10%. There was a considerable reduction in freight traffic, despite BR's success in obtaining a large amount of new business from the oil companies and some from the cement and car industries.

Regrettably the rise in productivity by no means eliminated the rail deficit. In 1963 BR had a gross loss of about £100 million, which was equivalent to 6% of revenue. By 1968 this had been reduced to around £50 million, or 4%. The fall would have been larger but for a considerable increase in the relative earnings of railwaymen (9%) and a substantial decline in BR's prices (11%) because of the large reduction in freight rates. What seems to have happened, at least in oil and cars, is that BR cut its rates because it was anxious to gain new traffic. By the end of the period it may well have been under-pricing some of its services.

One well-worn explanation for BR's continuing losses is that it was not permitted to withdraw all the passenger services which had been submitted for closure. However, this accounted for only a small part of its deficit. The real problem was that the Beeching Report was inadequate and over-optimistic. It forecast, for instance, that Freightliners would produce a profit of £35 million in 1968, although they turned out to have a loss of £9 million after interest. The report ended with a seemingly impressive list of financial benefits, but no allowance was made for the rise in railwaymen's real earnings. It was not recognised that the general level of railway costs was too high and that the chief need was to drastically reduce the labour force. Beeching was too preoccupied with those lines and activities on which the most spectacular losses were being incurred and, perhaps because he came from ICI which is extremely capital intensive, his principal aim was to improve the utilisation of equipment rather than to use manpower more productively.

Nevertheless, there was a great improvement in efficiency and the Beeching Report was only intended as the first stage of railway reform. Early in 1965 *The Development of the Major Railway Trunk Routes* was published. This proposed to reduce both track and train costs by concentrating traffic on selected routes. It was implied that, with the exception of some suburban lines and isolated stretches of heavily used freight route, the rest of the system should be either closed or reduced to single track. Such medicine was far too strong and unpalatable for the Labour Party, which had recently assumed power. Moreover Beeching's successor, Sir Stanley Raymond, strongly urged that BR needed a period of stability. Early in 1967 the government and the Board agreed that a basic network of some 11,000 route miles should be retained out of the existing 13,200 miles.

No real attempt was made to discover whether all the lines in the basic network were worth retaining. Although Barbara Castle, who was the Minister of Transport, was prepared to sanction individual closures, she was ideologically committed to a large rail system. The departmental view was that it would be several years before the lines that did not form part of the basic network had gone through the closure machinery by which time the commitment to preservation would have lapsed. The Ministry was just completing a study of three rail closures and 1,100 former regular users.[1] It showed that although there was some reduction in travel among the minority who had only made the journey once or twice a week,

> The great majority of travellers making the rail journey five times a week before the closure continued to make the same journey by an alternative means of transport . . . . In terms of increases in cost and times of journeys no widespread hardship resulted from the closures. About half the former regular travellers reported lower or unchanged costs, and about two-fifths reported shorter or unchanged journey time. Average increases in cost and time were small.

The decision to stabilise the size of the system meant that BR would have to be provided with permanent financial support. However, Barbara Castle wanted to eliminate open-ended subsidies and impose financial discipline on the Railways Board. The solution adopted was to identify those passenger services that were losing money and to cover their estimated deficit through a subsidy. This arrangement was embodied in the 1968 Transport Act which also helped the Board by writing off a large part of its capital and hiving off two unprofitable activities: National Carriers and Freightliners. The Government regarded the new passenger subsidy and the financial reconstruction as a full, fair and final settlement of the railways' claim for assistance and declared that the Board's profit and loss account would 'become a fair measure of the success or failure of the industry's management'.[2]

With the assistance of a subsidy of £220 million BR managed to cover its much reduced interest charges during 1969. The government was hopeful that the deficit would not re-emerge. BR had provided the Joint Steering Group (JSG), that paved the way for the Act, with forecasts which showed that by 1974 it would have eliminated its working deficit. This did not allow either for the passenger subsidy or for the financial reconstruction and when they were taken into account it appeared that BR would be able to meet its financial

TABLE 5.1 *BR: Output, Productivity and Finances*

	Output Passenger	Freight	Total	Employment	Average weekly hours worked by manual workers [a,b]	Output per equivalent worker [a]	Real unit operating staff costs [a]	Real unit staff costs [d]	Real staff costs per employee [e]	Relative weekly earnings of manual men, autumn	Real revenue per unit Passenger	Freight	Total	Revenue	Gross surplus [c]	Gross surplus as % of revenue [c] (%)	Net deficit [f]
	(1968=100)			(000)					(1968=100)					(£m, 1978 prices)			(£m, 1978 prices)
1963[g]	106.0	112.9	110.3	458.0	45.7	75.6	114.9	112.3	83.9	90.5	101.3	121.0	112.8	1,742	−103	−5.9	...
1968	100.0	100.0	100.0	307.2	47.0	100.0	100.0	100.0	100.0	100.0	100.0	100.0	100.0	1,402	−53	−3.8	...
				239.4	48.3									1,350	1	0.1	330
1969	104.8	98.7	101.4	221.9	49.0	108.2	99.0	96.4	104.8	101.2	100.9	99.7	100.2	1,373	20	1.4	311
1970	108.6	94.0	100.5	213.6	49.6	110.5	101.5	100.2	111.7	100.2	100.8	103.6	102.3	1,387	14	1.0	317
1971	106.9	90.1	97.6	209.2	48.3	111.7	102.5	102.6	113.8	101.7	107.9	94.6	100.8	1,331	−17	−1.3	347
1972	102.1	82.6	91.3	203.5	48.1	107.8	109.4	109.2	117.8	99.9	109.8	93.3	101.2	1,244	−99	−8.0	427
1973	102.4	85.9	93.3	198.1	47.4	114.3	106.6	109.0	122.6	93.9	108.9	89.2	98.5	1,234	−102	−8.2	432
1974	105.1	79.3	90.8	197.3	48.1	110.5	118.8	115.6	126.4	107.5	98.0	83.7	90.8	1,104	−342	−30.9	676
1975	102.8	75.6	87.7	197.0	48.0	107.1	124.3	123.1	129.5	110.4	104.3	82.7	93.6	1,098	−365	−33.2	703
1976	95.7	70.9	81.9	190.7	47.5	104.2	130.0	125.6	125.7	103.1	114.6	94.2	104.5	1,138	−284	−25.0	622
1977	98.1	67.0	80.8	184.5	47.8	105.7	127.5	120.7	122.2	102.3	116.7	100.0	108.7	1,165	−209	−18.0	566[f]
1978	103.3	65.4	82.3	182.2	48.4	107.9	128.1	121.3	126.1	101.1	119.9	103.1	112.3	1,224	−180	−14.7	527[f]

Note The output index comprises twelve indicators (passenger miles and freight tonnes) combined with 1968 (and 1963) revenue weights, except that payments to NCL were excluded. Separate tonnage figures were used for wagon and train load traffic. If anything failure to allow for changes in average hauls has probably imparted an upward bias because, over the period 1968–78, they fell for two of the three commodity groups distinguished — solid fuel and general traffic — and remained the same for iron and steel. If workshop staff — disregarded because of increasing capital and outside work — are included OEW increased by 5.6% between 1968 and 1978. The per unit series were estimated using gross output at 1968 (and 1963) prices.

[a] Workshop staff excluded below line/ from 1968. [b] Adult men only below line average of spring and autumn weeks. [c] Benefits to retired staff and pension fund deficiency payments have been disregarded. Excludes expenditure of a capital nature which has been charged to revenue account since 1975. [d] Staff costs include amounts charged to capital etc, from 1963 to 1975, but exclude them from 1975 to 1978. [e] Staff costs, as previously defined, divided by total rail employment, including workshops. [f] Gross rail surplus plus net receipts from related activities (the average for 1975–78) now charged to revenue account. Allows for stock appreciation of £20m depreciation and £145m of expenditure of a capital nature less £208m of replacement cost depreciation and £9m in 1977 and £9m in 1978. [g] Index numbers for 1963 and figures above line include freight sundries (National Carriers) and Freightliners.

obligations. Whether BR would succeed in doing this would obviously depend on the traffic it obtained and on its success in cutting its costs.

TRAFFIC

Rail traffic fell away sharply during the recession in the early 1970s as can be seen from Table 5.1. There was only a slight recovery during the subsequent boom and in 1973 BR's output was 7% lower than in 1968. Between 1973 and 1976 traffic slumped and during 1978 output was 18% below the 1968 level. This fall was wholly attributable to freight which declined by about a third.

One reason has been the decline in wagonload traffic which has only been partly compensated for by an increase in trainload work. In 1968 wagonload traffic still accounted for around 70% of general freight revenue partly because receipts per tonne were approximately 70% greater than for trainload traffic. Between 1968 and 1978 wagonload work fell from 119 million tonnes to only 26 million. This has been due partly to the slow and unreliable service which BR provides, partly to the decision to slough off unprofitable work and partly to a switch from wagon to trainload working which, due to the avoidance of marshalling, is far less costly. Meanwhile trainload traffic increased from 91 million tonnes to 144 million. As the bulk of the rise in the trainload tonnage was in coal it is evident that BR did not succeed in obtaining much new business. However there was, over the period 1968–78, some rise in the tonnage of other trainload traffic (18 million). Part of this would have been former wagonload work, but the major part was new and was attributable to the rise in Freightliner carryings (+ 5 million tonnes), oil traffic (+ 2½ million tonnes) and the movement of quarry products (+ 4½ million tonnes).

The reduction in BR's freight was also due to the contraction of those industries and undertakings from which the railways receive most of their business. During 1968 coal and steel traffics provided BR with more than two-thirds of its freight revenue. Between 1968 and 1978 carryings of iron and steel fell from 39 million tonnes to 25 million. British Rail obtains almost all its work from BSC, and rail traffic has declined by about the same proportion as the Steel Corporation's requirement for transport, as measured by the tonnage of materials it used and the quantity of products it dispatched.

BR's coal traffic fell from 125 million tonnes to 94 million, but disposals of home-produced coal declined slightly faster. Between 1968 and 1978 carryings of petroleum products increased from 14½ million tonnes to 17 million, but there was very little increase in total deliveries and BR's position strengthened.

Although they are very small in terms of tonnage, BR's carryings of parcels, letters and newspapers contribute a substantial part of its revenue. This section of its freight has also been declining. British Rail's parcels service has lost about a third of its traffic over the past decade and there has been a substantial reduction in the work which BR undertakes for the Post Office. This has been due to the decline in the number of letters and parcels that the Post Office receives and to the way in which the sorting of parcels has been concentrated at a small number of depots. Within most of the new parcels districts neither the distances nor the flows of traffic are large enough to make rail economic because of the extra loading and unloading that is usually involved. Between the depots road is both cheaper and faster where distances are short but, where they are long, Freightliners provide the best service if they are available.

Between 1968 and 1978 BR's share of the total tonne mileage by road and rail fell from 23½% to only 17%. This suggests that there must be a considerable volume of traffic which it could have secured if it had made the most of its opportunities. Although the major part of road freight consists of the movement of small loads for short distances, heavy goods vehicles with a carrying capacity of over about 19 tonnes moved nearly 600 million tonnes in 1978. But only 44 million tonnes travelled more than 190 miles. This is the minimum distance over which BR can have any hope of competing where the traffic has to be collected and delivered by road as transhipment is very expensive. During 1979 Freightliners' break even distance was between 200 and 230 miles.[3]

If the places between which the traffic is passing happen to be rail connected BR may be competitive even though the haul is a short one, but only where the traffic is regular and moves in trainload quantities. Wagonload working is usually uneconomic due to the expense of marshalling and the light loading of the trains that pick up and deliver wagons at private sidings. Just how little road traffic is suitable for rail conveyance was shown by a survey in 1974 that was conducted by the Freight Transport Association in conjunction with British Rail and the Department of the Environment. It was found that the 100 large undertakings which cooperated in the inquiry had 2¼ million tonnes of potential rail and Freightliner traffic. If private sidings were constructed there was a further 8¼ million tonnes. However, not all of this could be moved in trainloads and some of it has already been obtained by BR as a result of the construction of sidings with government assistance. Under the Railways Act of 1974 the Ministry covers up to 50% of the cost of building sidings where it is considered that the project is commercially unattractive but that environmental benefits will result. By the end of 1977 schemes involving the movement of 5 million tonnes of additional rail freight per year had been sanctioned.

In an attempt to compete for wagonload freight that can be moved between private sidings BR has launched Speedlink which is a network of fast services using high capacity air-braked wagons. Blocks of wagons are shifted between trains at intermediate sidings, but conventional marshalling and the big yards are avoided. During 1979 Speedlink carried only 3 million tonnes and by no means all of this was new business. The plans for Speedlink were first formulated in 1970 and if it had been launched earlier more traffic might have been retained or captured. However, the Board believes that there is only 11 million tonnes of road traffic where the flows are sufficiently heavy to make rail competitive.[4] Not all of this could have been secured, and the Board's figures are notoriously over-optimistic. Moreover it is questionable whether an extended network of services could be made to pay.

It may be concluded that the decline in rail freight has been largely inevitable and that there is remarkably little traffic which BR can hope to secure. Nevertheless a little extra traffic might have been obtained if the railways had provided a better quality service. Certainly its standards leave something to be desired even in the case of company trains. Poor time-keeping is sometimes the customers' fault but the Post Office has long been concerned about the late running of mail trains, there is dissatisfaction within the newspaper industry about the interruptions that occur in train services and BR has been partly to blame for the extensive cancellation of Freightliner trains.

BR's passenger traffic appears to have been slightly higher in 1978 than in 1968. There was a slight decline in the number of passenger miles travelled on the London and South Eastern services and the local provincial services. Although there was a rise of 25% in

Inter-City passenger miles, there was a substantial decline in the number travelled at the full fare (−15%). Allowing for the shift from full to reduced fares it appears that Inter-City output only increased by something like 12%. Between 1968 and 1978 BR increased it fares by 20% (and even the revenue per passenger per mile, which allows for the greater availability of reduced fares, rose by 15%). BR estimates that the price elasticity is 0.3 for commuter traffic and 0.75 for Inter-City.[5] The increase in fares has been so large that traffic could have been depressed by something like 10%.

The volume of rail travel is responsive not only to variations in price but also to alterations in journey speeds. An investigation by Ian Jones of traffic flows between London and seventeen major provincial towns, covering the period from 1970 to 1976-77, suggests that every 1% reduction in journey time led to an increase of around 0.6% in traffic.[6] Although there has been some increase in speeds, it would have been considerably greater if the High Speed Train (HST) and Advanced Passenger Train (APT) had been introduced when BR intended. In 1968 BR hoped that introduction of the APT would begin about 1974, but it will be some years before any significant number can be brought into service.[7] Although the HST was introduced in 1976 it was behind schedule and during 1978 it performed only a quarter of the mileage which had been envisaged in 1971 for both trains.[8]

There has been an enormous divergence between the traffic forecasts that BR has made since 1968 and what has happened. Although the estimates that it prepared for the JSG turned out to be too high, they were reasonably cautious and some decline in revenue was envisaged. However, by 1970 the Board had become far more hopeful. The Second Corporate Plan took a less bullish view, but was still unrealistic, as the officials in the Department recognised. They concluded that 'there was considerable risk that the overall rate of growth foreseen in traffic and revenue on Inter-City passenger services would not be achieved'. They took the view that the freight traffic forecasts were at the upper end of the range of possibilities, and that it was much more likely that the actual result by 1977 would be 10%, or about 20 million tons, lower than forecast. By 1973 BR had adopted a more realistic attitude to its freight prospects, but the Inter-City forecast remained improbably high. The Board's over-optimism helps to explain why it has not made greater progress in cutting employment and raising productivity.

EMPLOYMENT AND PRODUCTIVITY

Between 1968 and 1973 British Rail's labour force was reduced from 239,000 to 198,000, excluding the workshops. It was maintained at about this level until 1975. During 1976 and 1977 a further reduction took place and in 1978 BR had 182,000 staff, which was 24% less than in 1968. Over the period 1968–73 there was a rise of 14% in output per equivalent worker, although most of the increase took place during the earlier years when falling employment coincided with more or less stable output. After 1973 the combination of stable employment and falling output led to a swift reduction in OEW. Although there was some recovery in 1977 and 1978 productivity was, during the latter year, only 8% greater than it had been a decade earlier and no higher than in 1969.

Even if the period since the energy crisis is ignored it is clear that the growth in BR's productivity has slowed down. Between 1963 and 1968 OEW increased by 32% but from 1968 to 1973 it rose only 14%, though the decline in traffic was no greater than it had been during the earlier period. By the late 1960s the switch from steam to diesel and electric traction had been completed and the easiest savings in manpower had been secured. Nevertheless, BR has had considerable scope for reducing employment and raising productivity. At the time of the JSG it was envisaged that the length of running track would be reduced to about 18,000 miles by, for instance, reducing some lines from double to single track.[9] However, the programme for the elimination of surplus track capacity was only partly carried out and during 1978 BR still had about 22,200 miles of running track. If its original plans had been implemented the reduction in its track mileage would have been more rapid over the period 1968–78 than it was between 1963 and 1968. The financial forecasts which BR prepared for the JSG appear to have been based on the assumption that it would reduce its labour force (including the workshops) to no more than 200,000 by 1974. And a new estimate by BR's work study staff in 1969 confirmed that it would be possible to slim down to 201,000 by 1974.[10] At the end of 1978 BR still had 218,000 workers, despite the fact that its traffic was much lower than had been anticipated. In mid-1976 the Board announced that it was planning to reduce the rail labour force (excluding the workshops and corporate staff) from 190,000 at the beginning of 1976 to 150,000 by 1981, which is an average of 6,700 per year.[11] BR cut its manpower by 7,200 during the course of 1976 but it managed to make a saving of only 4,500 in 1977, and there was no reduction whatsoever during 1978 and 1979.

British Rail does not even seem to have scaled its employment down in line with its workload. Between the end of 1968 and the end of 1978 there was a fall of 7% in the length of running track per worker engaged on the maintenance of track and signalling. During this period there was some increase in the intensity with which the track was used, trains became faster and axle loads grew heavier. On the other hand, continuously welded rail, which needs substantially less maintenance than jointed track, increased from 15% to 43% of all running line. Moreover, since 1968 there has been a considerable extension in the mechanisation of track maintenance and more efficient machines have been introduced. Although wagonload traffic has slumped, possible economies have not been made and, to quote BR, there is 'substantial excess capacity in the "conventional" wagonload system (particularly marshalling capacity)'. There has, during the course of the decade, been a considerable fall in the number of drivers and guards (−13%) but it has been considerably smaller than the reduction in the time that locomotives and multiple units are away from depots and stabling points in the charge of a driver (−29%).

The productivity of BR's train crews is very low by the standards of most European railways, especially on the freight side where the number of train miles per man hour is only about a third as great as in France, Belgium, Holland, Sweden and Norway.[5] A large reduction in train staff could have been secured by renegotiating manning agreements, adopting more efficient operating practices and by investment in new wagons, which would then have shown greater returns. Under the manning agreements of 1965 and 1968 there has to be a second man in the locomotive when certain time and distance limits are exceeded and while the engine is running light. The number of second men has been reduced from 12,200 in 1968 to 6,400 in 1978. However, it is unnecessary to carry firemen on diesel and electric trains and the existing manning arrangements are unduly restrictive. British Rail now concedes that it needs only 2,000 second men who would be required for the purpose of training.[12]

At present all trains carry guards. They could often be dispensed with on empty passenger trains and on those few where the carriages have sliding doors. But the main scope for their removal is in freight working. Guards are necessary on trains where the wagons do not have power brakes and there is a danger that the rear part of the train might start to roll backwards if a coupling snapped. The guard would then apply the hand brake in the guard's van. However, if the wagons are fitted with power brakes these will be applied automatically and there are no guards' vans on fully fitted trains. Thus guards could have been almost wholly dispensed with if BR had, like other West European railways, got rid of loose-coupled wagons. In France and Germany they had been eliminated by the mid-1930s but, at the beginning of 1967, 80,000 out of BR's 180,000 wagons did not have power brakes.[4] Their survival is partly due to the selection of the wrong braking system back in the 1950s and partly to the fact that extensive expenditure on wagons has never, since that time, appeared financially attractive. It might well have done if one of the benefits had been the removal of guards and if the utilisation of wagons had been better and fewer new wagons had been required to replace the old unfitted stock. During 1978 BR's wagons averaged only about 73 miles per week, excluding empty running, and made only forty-six loaded journeys in the whole of the year. Even the new and very expensive air-braked wagons which Speedfreight uses make only eighty loaded journeys each year.[13]

The continued existence of so many unfitted wagons helps to explain why British freight trains travel so slowly; though this is also due to the large number of short-wheelbase wagons, which are restricted to 45 mph. It was proposed in the First Corporate Plan to modify those which had vacuum brakes so that they could travel at 60 mph, but this was never carried out, even though the cost would not have been very great.[14] Because so many wagons had low maximum speeds, and due to the operating difficulties which this caused, freight trains averaged only 22½ mph during 1973.[15] Although there seems to have been some improvement this means that BR has to employ an unduly large number of drivers.

The figure is inflated still further by the small number of hours which they drive. Until recently the amount of driving time averaged only about three and three-quarter hours per eight-hour turn of duty, and the corresponding period for guards is also very low. The amount of productive time would be higher if the agreements which determine drivers' duties were less restrictive and if drivers' route knowledge were more extensive. BR seems to think that it is possible to push up the amount of driving time to four and a half to five hours but this does not allow for the possible introduction of split shift working.[16] Where BR has to employ two drivers — one to operate a morning peak train and another for its evening counterpart — it would be possible to use only one and there would still be a saving equivalent to three-quarters of a man even if their working week were reduced to four days.

While the scope for saving manpower is exceptionally great in the case of train crews, substantial economies could also be made in staff engaged on ticketing. At suburban stations manned barriers should have been replaced by automatic turnstiles which are relatively inexpensive, and were successfully introduced in Chicago by the Illinois Central Railroad as long ago as 1966. Inter-City passengers have their tickets checked before they board and again on the train, and collection usually takes place where they alight. This involves an excessive amount of manpower without being particularly efficient. BR should have adopted the continental system of confining inspection and collection to the train. Here the guard could, if the tickets were on display, make repeated checks.

If the railways' manual work force had been slimmed down in these and other ways it would have been possible to make large savings in salaried staff since a high proportion are occupied on work, such as the payment of wages, that depends on the number employed. Even without a faster reduction in manual staff BR could have made a large economy in its white collar employment. BR itself concedes that 'our system is over administered . . . we do have too many administrative staff.'[17] In an attempt to correct the situation the Board proposed in 1971 to cut out a tier of management in order to reduce the number of salaried staff by 4,500 – 6,500. However the scheme was abandoned in 1975 primarily because it would have meant that some white collar workers would have had to move house. The Board now believes that it can make a similar reduction in staff by other means. Although some pruning has already taken place it is obvious that progress could and should have been faster.

Some idea of the number of workers that would be required to run the present railway system, if opportunities for saving manpower had been taken, can be obtained from detailed calculations which I made in 1975. I estimated that BR ought to be able to prune its labour force to 136,000. (The figure, as originally published, was 153,000 but this includes the workshops.) At the end of 1978 BR had 182,000 workers. My estimate related to 1981, and BR's freight tonnage and passenger train mileage are lower than I was forecasting. The figure of 136,000 may, therefore, be about right, although it should be recognised that because BR has been moving so slowly it would be unrealistic to suppose that it can now be attained by 1981. It should also be noted that BR would have had to invest considerably more in new wagons. However its total investment need not have been correspondingly greater as a considerable amount of its capital expenditure has been misdirected. BR has probably spent too much on colour light signalling and new Inter-City carriages, and investment has been wasted on locomotives for unprofitable freight traffic, suburban electrification and new commuter systems in the provincial conurbations.[18]

Why has British Rail failed to make the savings in manpower for which it has had scope? The possibility that it was unaware of the opportunities can be dismissed. BR told the Prices and Incomes Board as far back as 1966 that it did not need guards on fully-braked freight trains and has now conceded that almost all of the steps that have been advocated above are practicable.[19] However rail officials offer the excuse that it would have been difficult or impossible to persuade the unions to agree to changes in the manning agreements. While the National Union of Railwaymen is a fairly cooperative and moderate union, ASLEF, to which most footplate staff belong, is at once militant and conservative. Its leadership is fighting to maintain membership in order that the Union shall retain its power and identity, and has been waging a campaign for the partial reinstatement of a second man in the cab. The HST and APT were initially designed to be single manned but a ban was imposed until the Board agreed that a co-driver should be carried.

Nevertheless the intransigence of ASLEF and its members, who have sometimes refused to abide by the present manning rules, does not excuse the Railways Board for not having tried to renegotiate the agreements by which it is bound. The fact that ASLEF is so obdurate means that the process should have started years ago, but the Board has only recently begun to raise the issue. There are, moreover, other less contentious ways in which BR might have reduced its labour force, e.g., the introduction of automatic barriers. It is significant that progress has been very slow and that BR has so framed its plans for their installation in the London area that very little labour will be saved.[20]

The underlying reason why the railways have not been managed better and why the unions have not been more cooperative is that there has been very little pressure due to the availability of subsidies. As we have seen, it was the Government's intention at the time of the 1968 Transport Act to pay BR a limited and closely controlled subsidy which would increase, and not weaken, financial discipline. However, according to Dr Stewart Joy, who as a consultant to the Ministry of Transport was closely involved in the work of the Joint Steering Group, BR's attitude was very different:

> Beeching had failed to shake the belief of BR management that the Nation wanted to have a comprehensive railway service, regardless of its cost . . . In effect, in 1967, the Board was again saying 'this is the railway the Nation wants, but our annual deficits show that they do not seem prepared to pay for it; if we can somehow put the deficit on a regular and more automatic basis, all will be well.' In brief, and this was the most common attitude of the BR representatives on the JSG, they thought its purpose was to 'whitewash the deficit'.[21]

This was an understandable reaction since virtually no attempt was made to discover whether the services that were to be subsidised were worth retaining. The moral to be drawn from the 1968 Act was that, as the Government was prepared to subsidise those parts of the system where traffic was sparse and costs greatly exceeded revenue, it would support the main lines if they too became unprofitable. The railways were not slow to grasp the message. The Act had scarcely taken effect before BR's Chairman was suggesting that the railway's unprofitable freight services should also be subsidised.[22]

In 1971 the Railways Board, despite its subsidy, made a loss after interest and its deficit swiftly mounted. The Government's response, which was embodied in the 1974 Railways Act, was to write off another slice of the Board's capital and to provide BR with a general passenger subsidy. The story of how this policy came to be adopted is complicated and I have told it elsewhere.[23] However, the vital point is that the Government rejected the idea of putting pressure on BR to cut its costs, although this was what the civil servants proposed and the Minister was well aware that BR was over-manned. Mr Peter Walker, recalling the period when he was in charge of the DoE, says:

> It seems a pity that the protective attitude of railwaymen meant that they were unwilling to accept some of the necessary manpower chan-

ges . . . It was depressing that a Freightliner train with no guard's van and no fire . . . had under union agreements to have both a guard and a fireman, neither of whom had any particular role to perform. I visited a Freightliner depot in London and asked why a second person was joining the driver . . . only to be told that it was a great advantage to have two men rather than one in the event of a crash. A little later a further man joined them, making three in all. I asked the vice-chairman of British Rail why there were now three men there and he said with a smile that in the event of a crash it was probably better to have three men there than two.[24]

Mr Walker does not explain why, if he knew that BR was inefficient, he opted for a policy of massive subsidy; thereby committing the incoming Labour Government which, because of its pro-rail stance and intimate connection with the railway unions, could not appear less generous than the Tories. However, he no doubt wished to avoid becoming too intimately involved in rail management especially as this carried the risk of a confrontation with the unions. This would not win any support or popularity whereas financial assistance for the railways would appeal to those who, like Mr Walker himself, favoured railways on environmental grounds.

Moreover it was not realised how far and fast BR's financial position would deteriorate once it was provided with an open-ended subsidy. This was partly because BR, although it said that its employment was to be reduced, promptly launched a recruitment drive. As a result the rail labour force increased by over 6,000 between the end of 1973 and March 1975. However in June the Government, which was now alarmed at the growth of the rail deficit and was trying to bring public expenditure under control, announced that there must be no further rise in the real level of passenger support. The Board, which was pressing for a freight subsidy, was also instructed to start to make its freight operations pay. It had forecast that they would show a deficit of £21 million in 1975, but had then, to the Government's consternation, suddenly revealed that there would be a deficit of £110 million before interest.[25]

The Board was now once again under some financial discipline. By 1978 the (visible) freight deficit had been eliminated, although the Board had previously said that it was incurable. And between the spring of 1975 and the end of 1977 rail employment was reduced by 19,000. This was accomplished by tightening up efficiency and eliminating the slack which had been allowed to accumulate.

Although this is all to the good it does mean, to quote Mr C.A. Rose, the Board member responsible for industrial relations, that BR has 'not really got to grips with productivity'.[26] However, at the end of 1979 BR at long last placed on the negotiating table a long list of proposals — including the single manning of fully-braked freight trains and the withdrawal of ticket checkers from Inter-City platforms — which it had previously criticised as visionary or impracticable.

COSTS, PRICES AND LOSSES

Because the growth in productivity has been so slow there has been a large rise in BR's unit costs. Between 1968 and 1973 there was a rise of only 7% because, although unit staff costs rose sharply, there was little or no increase for other forms of expenditure. However by 1976 BR's unit costs had shot up to a point 30% above 1968 because a further large rise in unit staff costs was now accompanied by a substantial rise in expenditure on fuel and other purchases. Since then BR's unit costs have fallen back slightly due to a reduction in unit staff costs. This, in turn, has resulted partly from the upturn in productivity, and partly from the continued loss by railwaymen of the gain in relative earnings that they had made because of the large award by the Railway Staff National Tribunal in 1974.

Rail prices were relatively stable between 1968 and 1973 because the rise in fares was offset by a reduction in freight charges. There was then a sharp fall and during 1974 BR's prices appear to have been 9% lower than they had been in 1968. Passenger fares fell back due to price control but it seems doubtful whether this was the sole reason for the decline in freight charges to a point approximately 15% below 1968. This reduction may in part have been due to the fact that two-thirds of BR's tonnage was carried under long-term contracts which provided for the adjustment of prices once every twelve months. As BR received no compensation for the rise in prices which occurred during the intervening period its charges naturally tended to lag during an inflationary period. Since the beginning of 1975 the Board has insisted that freight rates are adjusted at least every six months and has been trying to charge what the market will bear. There have also been large increases in fares, and by 1978 the overall level of rail prices was 12% higher than in 1968, with fares 20% greater and freight charges if anything slightly higher than they had been at the start of the period.

In 1968 BR's revenue was just sufficient to cover its operating costs when Freightliners and National Carriers are excluded. And during 1969 and 1970 there was a small gross surplus, although there was a net deficit of something like £300 million. In 1971 BR's revenue was insufficient to meet its operating expenditure and by 1973 — with its prices stable and its unit costs increasing — the gross loss had risen to £100 million. In 1974 the deficit shot up due to a massive increase in unit costs in combination with a large fall in prices. In the following year, when BR's finances were at their nadir, there was a gross loss of £365 million and a net loss of £700 million, which was equivalent to 64% of revenue. After this the position improved somewhat because unit costs were more stable and there was a large increase in charges. By 1978 the gross deficit had fallen to £180 million and the net loss to £525 million, or 43% of revenue.

Where is BR's huge loss occurring? Freight appears to have had an operating surplus of approximately £27 million in 1978. However, depreciation at replacement cost seems from the Board's estimates to have amounted to around £110 million and too little of BR's expenditure on infrastructure and general administration (at £680 million) has been attributed to freight and parcels (£165 million). Disregarding expenditure on freight only routes and the Southern Region (SR), a mere 11% of BR's expenditure on infrastructure was assigned to freight in 1976.[27] Yet freight trains must be responsible for a substantial proportion of spending on infrastructure because they are heavy and slow. During 1976 they accounted for about 45% of total traffic, as measured by gross tonne miles, and the Board has to maintain slow tracks and duplicate routes. In addition there is a considerable mileage of route which, although it is open for passenger services, is primarily maintained for freight work.

Nevertheless the great bulk of BR's deficit is incurred on the passenger side. The SR is the only part that comes anywhere near to covering its costs. During 1978 its revenue, including what little it earned from freight, was just about sufficient to meet its operating expenditure including infrastructure and regional administration.[28] However, this ignores depreciation, which can be roughly estimated at £30 million, and some small part of headquarters and other general expenditure was presumably incurred on the Region's behalf. The remaining commuter services in London and the South East appear to do no more than cover their direct costs, which consist in the main of expenditure on running trains and operating stations. The provincial stopping services are even more unprofitable and sustained a direct loss of nearly £50 million; equivalent to 56% of their revenue.

In contrast the Inter-City services, including those in the SR, produced a net revenue of £153 million after deducting direct costs. Nevertheless there seems little doubt that Inter-City makes a large loss. It seems reasonable to assume that administrative and general expenditure for BR's stopping services outside the SR bears about the same relationship to direct expenditure as that which prevails in the Southern Region (after treating the SR's share of headquarters' cost as part of its administration). On this basis the stopping services accounted for about £85 million of general and administrative expenditure and freight appears, according to BR's own estimates, to have been responsible for something over £50 million.[29] This leaves around £110 million of general and administrative expenditure for Inter-City. This figure may well be on the high side because BR has probably assigned an unduly small part of its general overheads to its freight operations. However it is difficult to believe that the burden of administration is less onerous for the Inter-City services than for the Southern. Administrative and general expenditure represents an addition of 27% to the SR's direct expenses, and on this basis the administrative overheads for Inter-City work out at £50 million. Hence Inter-City must be debited with between £50 million and £110 million of administrative and general expenditure. In addition it is necessary to allow for its depreciation, which BR estimates at £38 million, and for interest charges and the deficit on train catering, which together amounted to about £20 million.[30] It is therefore doubtful whether the Inter-City services make any significant contribution towards the heavy infrastructure costs for which they are responsible.

Inter-City's disappointing performance appears to be largely explained by the provision of too much capacity. Between 1968 and 1970 traffic grew but there was little increase in Inter-City train mileage and the average load — as measured by passenger miles per train mile — rose to about 160. However the period 1970–78 saw a large increase in train miles (19%) but only a small growth in traffic (8%) and during 1978 the average load was only around 145, although this was a somewhat better figure than in 1976–77. There has also been some increase in the length of trains and the load factor for Inter-City is only about 38%. There is surprisingly little variation in average loads between routes, probably because BR restricts capacity where traffic is light and puts on so many extra trains, where traffic is heavy, that loadings are depressed. However there is a marked variation in loads over the course of the day. There is a heavy flow into London of Inter-City traffic which leaves provincial centres between 7.00 and 9.30 and a large reverse movement between 16.00 and 19.00. It seems clear that some of the trains which travel at other times of the day or move in the opposite direction are very lightly loaded. Moreover there will probably be some train units which, although they make a number of journeys, do not help to carry either of the peak flows and transport relatively few passengers throughout the day.

It may be replied that the break even load for an Inter-City train is relatively low. However it is only worth while providing those train units which generate sufficient traffic to cover the additional costs which they involve. It seems clear that many of the trains that BR runs divert passengers from other trains and that their withdrawal would not involve any significant loss of traffic. Mr Ian Jones has examined, by means of regression analysis, various possible factors, including the frequency of departure, that may help to explain the change in Inter-City traffic between London and seventeen towns over the period between 1970 and 1976–77. Most of the routes enjoyed substantial increases in departure frequency and although speed and frequency were sometimes increased simultaneously this was by no means always the case. Mr Jones found that there was no significant relationship between changes in frequency and traffic.[31] Officials at the Department of Transport have become concerned that BR might be running too many Inter-City trains: a charge to which the Board has found it difficult to reply if only because of its failure to investigate the separate effect of frequency on traffic.

SHOULD BR BE SUBSIDISED?

The fact that BR has a massive deficit would appear to indicate that resources are being wasted. They are used inefficiently because costs are unnecessarily high, and they are misallocated because of the divergence between the costs of operating the railways and the value which marginal rail users place upon the service they receive, in terms of the price they are prepared to pay. In other words the railways produce too much at too high a cost. This conclusion will be resisted by those who believe that British Rail should be subsidised on welfare grounds. It is impossible, due to lack of space, to examine the arguments for subsidy in detail. Nor is it necessary, since it is evident that government financial support has led to inefficiency and high costs. The benefits from subsidisation would therefore have to be very large if they were to outweigh the negative consequences. Thus all that needs to be established is that the gains are unlikely to be very great.

The classic case for subsidising railways is that they have heavy fixed expenditure, principally on infrastructure, but can carry extra traffic at a low cost. If prices merely reflect a railway's variable costs a large loss will be sustained but it is wrong to charge anything over and above the avoidable cost because this is all that will be saved if traffic is choked off. Although this argument may appear convincing it has a number of serious weaknesses. First, the money for the subsidy will have to be found. If this means additional indirect taxation the prices of the products involved will be raised above their costs of production. On the other hand if the taxation is direct the choice between work and leisure is distorted because leisure is tax free. In either case misallocation will occur. Second, by paying a subsidy the Government is redistributing income in favour of rail users and there is no reason to suppose that they are a particularly deserving section of the community. Third, the once and for all costs of railway construction — expenditure on permanent assets such as cuttings and embankments — have long ago been written off. Fourth, only a small part of a railway's infrastructure costs are fixed in the sense that they remain the same whatever the volume and type of traffic which is carried. Obviously BR does bear certain costs which are inescapable so long as a route remains open. These include all or most of BR's expenditure on fencing, embankments and cuttings, together with that part of the cost of maintaining a single line of track that is due to the passage of time and to natural causes and not to the movement of trains. The available information suggests that the minimum cost of maintaining BR's present route system is some £80 million out of the £475 million which BR spent on its infrastructure during 1978. This estimate does not include any expenditure on signalling. If there were very few trains none would be necessary, but it would be possible to provide a simple signalling system at very little expense, either by radio control or by two aspect signals controlled automatically through track circuiting. Although the initial fixed element cannot account for more than a fifth of BR's expenditure on infrastructure there are other cost steps which have to be surmounted if extra blocks of traffic are to be carried or speed bands are to be entered. Hence it is always possible to argue that once total expenditure has been raised to a higher level the cost of running extra trains will be relatively low. If, however, the Government is prepared to meet the railways' semi-fixed costs what will almost certainly happen is that the quantity (and quality) of rail output will be pushed to a point where the total cost of carrying an extra tranche of traffic (or of improving the quality of service) exceeds the value which rail users derive, as measured by the total amount that they would be prepared to pay for the service in question. The final weakness of the argument that BR's fixed costs should be covered by a subsidy is that BR is able to differentiate its prices. It should therefore be possible for BR to recover its fixed costs by charging marginal consumers the marginal cost and intra-marginal consumers something over average cost.

A related argument for providing BR with a subsidy is that its unprofitable lines and services would be able to cover their costs if each rail user could be made to pay as much as he were prepared to. If so, the value that consumers place on the service will exceed the costs involved. This is, in economic language, the familiar argument that the withdrawal of passenger services involves hardship because of the frequent absence of any satisfactory alternative; in which case rail users will be willing to pay more than BR charges. In 1978 the direct costs of those provincial stopping services which run outside the PTEs were nearly 80% greater than their earnings and it is not uncommon, when services are considered individually, for specific costs to exceed revenue by three or more times. It seems highly improbable that rail users would be prepared to pay sufficient to meet the enormous losses which these services are incurring. Cost-benefit analysis confirms that there is no justification for maintaining a large number of BR's services. In the various studies that have been undertaken the additional amount that rail users would be prepared to pay is, in effect, measured by the estimated value of the time which they save by travelling by train rather than by bus, and allowance is made for various other benefits which are not reflected in BR's revenue, e.g., the cost of the road accidents and road congestion that are avoided. When the results of the six major cost–benefit studies were revised and put on a standard basis they gave similar figures for the benefit per passenger mile. During 1973–74 about fifty out of BR's two hundred provincial stopping services had specific costs per passenger mile which exceeded the average benefit per passenger mile.[32] This, however, gives an exaggerated impression of the number that are worth retaining as specific costs only include train costs and expenditure on those facilities that were used exclusively by the service in question.

The final argument for providing BR with a subsidy is that this keeps traffic off the roads. This is held to be desirable on the ground that they are excessively used because the cost that the marginal road user has to bear is less than the cost he imposes on society. Private and social costs may diverge (a) because road users do not pay sufficient by way of fuel duty and other taxation that varies with road use to meet the cost of providing the road system; (b) because cars and lorries cause noise and other disamenities for which the driver is not charged; and (c) because, where roads are congested, the presence of an extra vehicle will slow down other road users.

Estimates by the DoE show that private road users pay more than sufficient in transport taxation (£2,365 million in 1978–79, excluding car tax and car licences) to cover government expenditure on roads (£1,670 million, including construction, maintenance, police and accident costs borne by the health service). Apart from buses, the only type of vehicle that fails to meet its share of road costs is the heavy lorry with four axles. The shortfall in taxation for such vehicles during 1979–80 represented approximately 2% of the revenue which they earned.[33] However during 1978 the loss that BR sustained on its freight, after replacement cost depreciation but before interest, and with only partial payment for infrastructure, was equivalent to 16% of revenue. Moreover Speedfreight, which competes most directly with the heavy lorry, barely covers its direct costs. Hence the divergence between prices and costs in the field of freight transport appears to be much greater for rail than for road. Appearances could be deceptive because the figures which have so far been quoted do not allow for the lorry's environmental effects. Although, when expressed in terms of money they add up to a substantial sum, it is relatively small in relation to the total amount that is spent on road goods transport.[34] Moreover an investigation by consultants for the DoE of the environmental effects of transferring specimen flows of traffic from road to rail (and vice versa) showed a cost per vehicle mile that was less than the amount of fuel tax that heavy lorries were then paying.

Motorists pay far more in fuel tax (£1,455 million) than their estimated share of expenditure on roads (£1,030 million). The bulk of the road system is not congested and government expenditure includes the cost of constructing new roads and improving old roads in order to prevent or alleviate congestion. There is therefore no case for subsidising BR's rural or interurban passenger services. The case for providing its commuter services with financial support is stronger. In London and some of the provincial conurbations congestion is serious and it would be very expensive to increase the capacity of the road system. However the losses incurred by some of BR's commuter services are so large as to make it seem likely that the divergence between prices and costs is often greater for rail than for road. This is the more probable because there is also a congestion problem on BR. When an extra passenger gets on a crowded rush hour train this will reduce the welfare of those who have already boarded.

Even if the subsidy that BR receives for its commuter services does lead, on balance, to an improvement in welfare it is unlikely to be large. Unless the subsidy is wholly absorbed by an increase in rail costs, road users will gain as a result of the diversion of traffic to BR and the consequent reduction in road congestion. However this benefit will be at least partly offset by the reduction in welfare that will arise because rail services are being supplied at a price that does not fully reflect the cost of the resources they use. The loss in welfare will be equivalent to that part of the cost of carrying the extra rail passengers that they would not be willing to pay because they do not value the service sufficiently highly. The fact that there is inevitably some reduction in welfare on the railways shows that subsidies are very much a second best solution. The optimum solution is to discourage motorists from bringing their cars into crowded city centres by making them buy a supplementary licence or by introducing road pricing. Rail subsidies divert attention from such policies although they are by no means impracticable.

It must be concluded, to quote the *Consultation Document* on *Transport Policy*, that 'social, environmental and economic considerations do not seem to justify the large subsidy which railway users now receive'.[35]

CHAPTER 6

The National and Scottish Bus Groups

There are two road passenger transport undertakings in national ownership: the National Bus Company (NBC) and the Scottish Bus Group (SBG), which is owned by the Scottish Transport Group (STG). NBC and the Scottish Transport Group, which came into existence at the end of 1968, took over the bus companies that had previously been under the control of the state-owned Transport Holding Company. Some of these undertakings had long been in public ownership but it had only just taken over Midland Red and the other companies in the British Electric Traction Group. At the end of 1969 London Transport's Green Line Services and Country Buses were transferred to NBC. This and the acquisition of the British Electric Traction companies served to increase employment within the state bus sector by 90%. During 1978 National and Scottish accounted for 43% of all stage bus receipts and outside London and the larger towns they are responsible for the vast majority of all stage bus services. Moreover this type of work accounted for 88% of their passenger revenue.

PERFORMANCE AND PROBLEMS PRIOR TO 1968

It was already clear when NBC and STG came into existence that the bus industry had entered a difficult period. Between 1963 and 1968 the undertakings which they came to control lost 10% of their traffic (as measured throughout by passenger revenue at constant prices) and, although there was some reduction in employment, output per effective worker fell by 6%. The vehicle mileage was only cut back slightly at a time when traffic was falling and the amount of traffic per vehicle mile appears to have declined by 7%. However, in Scotland — the one place for which there are reliable statistics — the average passenger load, as measured by passenger miles per bus mile, fell by 14% over the period 1964–68.

As a result of these adverse developments there was a rapid rise in unit costs and over the period 1963–68 fares were raised by 7%. Despite this the gross profits of the undertakings which NBC and STG acquired fell from about £75 million in 1963 to around £55 million in 1968, though it should be noted that the tax rebate on bus fuel has been added back onto their costs. This remission, which was introduced in 1964, was the first brick in the edifice of financial support.

Government assistance and large fare increases would not have been necessary if more had been done to cut costs and raise productivity. One way of doing this would have been to reduce the amount of capacity provided and match it more closely to the available demand. Another approach would be to use labour more efficiently. The most obvious step was to switch to single man operation. It was legally necessary to have a conductor on a double decker until 1966, but single deckers constituted over half the fleet. An agreement that driver–operators should receive a bonus of 15% was negotiated centrally in 1960. However, largely due to union opposition, particularly at a local level, the removal of conductors was a slow process. Between 1963 and 1968 the proportion of the stage mileage that was single manned only increased from about 8% to 18%. There were various other ways in which productivity could be raised. As the Prices and Incomes Board discovered restrictive practices were widespread, and it found that in the case of maintenance workers only one of the fourteen undertakings it visited had made proper use of work measurement and related systems of payment.[1]

It is clear that the bus groups which passed into the hands of NBC and STG were inefficient. Their management was complacent, inward looking, inbred and amateur. This is illustrated by the failure to develop costing systems in order to find out which services were unprofitable. The position was made worse by the uncooperative and restrictive attitudes of the work force. These weaknesses were largely attributable to the licensing system. Under the Road Traffic Act of 1930 bus operators were protected against competition, and allowed to charge prices which enabled them to earn a

TABLE 6.1 National and Scottish Bus Groups: Output, Productivity and Finances

	Output	Vehicle miles in service	Output per vehicle mile	Employ-ment	Average weekly hours worked by manual workers, October week [a]	Output per equivalent worker [b]	Quantity of capital	Output per unit of labour and capital	Real unit operating costs [c]	Real unit staff costs	Real staff costs per employee	Relative weekly earnings of manual men, October week [d]	Real fares	Revenue	Gross surplus [d]	Gross surplus as % of revenue [d]	Net surplus
	(1968 = 100)			(000)					(1968 = 100)					(£m, 1978 prices)	(£m, 1978 prices)	(%)	(£m, 1978 prices)
1963[a]	110.6	103.3	107.1	112.8	48.6	106.5	..	..	86.1	86.5	90.7	97.6	93.6	546	76	13.9	..
1968[e]	100.0	100.0	100.0	107.0	49.5	100.0	100.0	100.0	100.0	100.0	100.0	100.0	100.0	550	57	10.4	12
1969	98.1	98.4	99.7	104.1	49.8	100.2	103.4	99.4	102.8	100.6	101.4	101.1	98.6	529	32	6.0	−14
1970[f]	88.0	92.4	95.3	102.5	47.0	96.0	106.0	93.8	119.3	117.1	107.6	98.2	104.6	510	−8	−1.6	−54
1971	85.5	91.2	93.7	97.0	47.2	98.2	107.8	94.8	123.4	123.1	115.9	106.0	114.5	542	22	4.0	−25
1972	84.5	87.3	96.8	89.4	46.8	106.2	108.6	100.7	123.1	119.8	121.1	101.9	111.9	525	26	4.9	−22
1973	85.1	86.1	98.8	85.0	47.8	110.4	109.0	103.9	118.4	120.1	128.7	104.7	107.8	511	14	2.8	−34
1974[f]	81.2	83.9	96.8	83.4	47.8	107.4	109.5	100.6	126.7	126.6	131.8	106.9	105.8	475	−32	−6.8	−83
1975	76.3	84.8	90.0	84.8	46.6	101.5	111.1	94.6	142.9	148.0	142.5	112.7	119.1	500	−37	−7.5	−89
1976	71.9	81.6	88.1	83.5	46.4	97.5	112.8	90.2	146.3	150.5	138.7	109.1	127.9	501	−17	−3.5	−70
1977	68.1	78.8	86.4	79.9	47.4	94.7	115.9	86.7	148.6	147.5	134.5	109.1	129.5	482	−18	−3.6	−71
1978	67.0	77.7	86.3	77.6	47.7	95.4	117.7	86.5	152.5	148.1	136.8	106.7	134.1	493	−11	−2.2	−65

Note Output was estimated by deflating passenger receipts (excluding subsidies except in respect of concessionary travel) with the official price index for 'other operators'. The quantity of capital was derived from the CSO's figures for road passenger transport by calculating, year by year, the gross stock per vehicle and multiplying by the number possessed by National and Scottish. If alternatively this number had been used to represent the quantity of capital, total factor productivity would have been shown as having fallen by 7% between 1968 and 1978. A capital weight of 15.1% was used.

[a] Road passenger transport, excluding London Transport. [b] Estimated using average hours in previous column. [c] Includes during latter years payments in respect of leased assets, although these were relatively small. [d] After deducting payments in respect of leased assets. [e] Includes British Electric Traction and London Country Buses. [f] Affected by industrial dispute.

normal profit, in return for practising cross-subsidisation and providing extensive and frequent services.

TRAFFIC AND CAPACITY

Since 1968 there has been a spectacular decline in traffic. As Table 6.1 indicates, it fell sharply between 1968 and 1971. During the next three years traffic was more or less stable after allowing for the effects of strikes and the loss of territory. From 1975 traffic once again declined sharply and by 1978 it was a third lower than it had been in 1968. Of this reduction 2–3 percentage points was due to the loss of services to the Passenger Transport Executives in Manchester (1972) and the West Midlands (1973). Between 1968 and 1973 traffic and bus mileage declined by about the same percentage, but after this the reduction in vehicle mileage did not keep pace with the fall in traffic. By 1978 traffic per vehicle mile was approximately 14% lower than it had been in 1968.

The decline in traffic has been largely due to the spread of car ownership. The National Travel Survey of 1972–73 showed that car-owning households spend only about a third as much on stage bus travel as those who do not have cars but are on the same income level. The survey also shows that expenditure on buses tends to rise with income for both car and non-car-owning families.[2] This suggests that although increasing affluence leads to more car ownership and a decline in bus travel, it also results in greater expenditure on the part of those who have already acquired cars. However, it seems doubtful whether this is the case as the increase in bus travel as incomes rise is almost wholly due to higher expenditure on journeys to and from work. This is not the consequence of extra income but the cause of extra income for it is evident that households with high incomes tend to contain more earners and these have to get to work.

Although the decline in bus patronage has been partly the ineluctable and direct result of rising car ownership, this has not been the only factor at work. A considerable contribution has been made by the rise in bus fares, which increased by a third between 1968 and 1978. In the bus industry the volume of traffic does not seem to be very responsive to alterations in price and the elasticity seems to be around 0.5.[3] However the rise in fares has been so large that it must have had a substantial impact on NBC and SBG carryings. This is confirmed by the way in which price and volume have moved over the period 1968–78. During the years 1971–74 when there was a considerable decline in fares traffic was more or less stable.

The reduction in traffic would probably have been less sharp if National and Scottish had been more flexible and competitive. Although stage traffic has been in decline, not all types of work have been contracting. Between 1968 and 1978 the number of journeys on vehicles that were operated under contract or for private hire increased by over 60%. This field of activity, that consists largely of works and school buses, is dominated by the private operator, and the state undertakings carried no more traffic in 1978 than they had in 1968. Private firms are also responsible for the bulk of all excursions and tours. Whereas they have maintained their business, there has been a reduction in the number of journeys on NBC and SBG.

Though the state concerns have been trying to increase their tour business they have made very little effort to compete for contract and private hire work, and have failed to introduce services that meet the need for which works buses now cater. This is probably partly because NBC and SBG are inflexible and regard their job as the provision of conventional stage services. However it also seems likely that their costs are much higher than those of private operators. During 1978 the average revenue per vehicle mile which NBC and SBG earned from contract and private hire work was 50% higher than the amount that private concerns received. Moreover the average revenue per vehicle mile that NBC and SBG received for their contract and private hire work (53p) was lower than their average costs for the whole of their operations (58p per mile excluding conductors and capital charges). NBC and SBG cannot therefore have been making enormous profits on their contract and private hire business.

Although there has been a large overall decline in traffic on stage services the reduction has been less marked in some parts of the country than in others. For instance within NBC, Eastern Counties and the City of Oxford Motor Services (COMS) have had some success in maintaining their carryings. Between 1968 and 1973 COMS' traffic declined by the same proportion as in the rest of NBC, but over the period 1973–78 the number of journeys on COMS fell by only 8% whereas there was a reduction of 23% in the other NBC companies. COMS has been helped by the measures that have been taken to restrict the use of cars in Oxford, but its success has also been due to the introduction of limited stop services to London and Birmingham and to various marketing initiatives, including cheap return tickets which can be used by shoppers during off peak periods for a day.

Most NBC and STG subsidiaries have failed to promote the use of their services through well-devised arrangements for discount fares and have until recently done too little to recast their services in order to make better provision for the available demand. There has, since about 1975, been a considerable growth in discount fares which are now fairly widely available. However most of the schemes appear to be perverse because they are not restricted to off-peak periods when the elasticity of demand is likely to be relatively high and the cost of carrying extra passengers is low. Indeed, as we shall see, they are often tailored to meet the needs of those who travel at peak times. Although timetables have from time to time been amended, insufficient effort has *until recently* been devoted to re-routing and rescheduling services. The market research which has been undertaken at Midland Red and at COMS has revealed that a considerable number of alterations need to be made and that there is some scope for the introduction of new services. In particular it has been found that there are opportunities for excursion services for shoppers and that inter-urban services need to be speeded up and extended. This can be achieved not only by reducing the number of stops and putting on more through services but also by making timetables tighter. An investigation in Cheshire has shown that running times on such routes are frequently the same as in the 1930s when buses were restricted to a maximum of 30 mph and their performance was greatly inferior. The average speed is only 17 mph and the County transport department believes that an improvement is possible on about half of the routes.[4] In urban areas buses almost always run to a fixed timetable although running times could usually be cut during off peak periods and at week-ends: a step which would obviously tend to make buses more attractive. It is also evident, as passenger surveys in the Midlands have shown, that greater efforts need to be made to provide potential passengers with information about services.

EMPLOYMENT AND PRODUCTIVITY

There has over the years been a considerable decline in employment within the nationalised bus sector. In 1968 NBC and SBG had

107,000 workers. By 1978 they employed only 78,000, which means there was a fall of 27%, though it should be observed that nearly 2,500 staff were transferred to PTEs. The most notable feature of the reduction was that it was very largely accounted for by the elimination of conductors. Between the end of 1968 and the end of 1978 the switch to one-man operation was responsible for three-quarters of the total decline in employment. Nevertheless there were still nearly 10,000 conductors during 1978. Conversion to single manning has been impeded by manufacturers' failure to supply sufficient new vehicles and there has been some opposition from staff, especially in Scotland.

There was a temporary reduction in output per equivalent worker during 1970–71 but by 1973 it was approximately 10% higher than it had been in 1968. This was entirely due to conversion to one-man operation. After 1973 OEW fell and in 1978 it was some 5% lower than it had been in 1968 and total factor productivity appears to have declined by 13%. The fall in OEW was partly due to a reduction in the efficiency with which drivers, maintenance workers and other staff were used. Between 1968 and 1978 there appears to have been a decline of around 12% in the number of vehicle miles per driver hour, only part of which can have been due to the loss of flexibility which resulted from the change, which took place during 1970, in the regulations on drivers' hours. For workers apart from drivers and conductors there was a fall of about 15% in the number of miles *per capita*. About half of them are engaged on maintenance and it has been argued that the decline in the number of vehicle miles per employee has occurred because front engine vehicles have fewer problems than the rear engine models, which have been introduced so that passengers can board at the front and pay the driver. Moreover buses have become more difficult to service because they are now equipped with such features as power doors and better heating. On the other hand the Leyland National buses that have been purchased in large numbers were designed for easy maintenance and, as we have seen, NBC and SBG had scope to improve the efficiency of their workshops. The principal reason for the fall in the number of vehicle miles per worker is almost certainly that buses are serviced at regular intervals, and these have stayed more or less the same though there has been a substantial decline in the average mileage per vehicle.

Although very little information is available, there appear to be substantial variations within the nationalised bus sector in the efficiency with which labour is used. In 1978 the number of drivers per million vehicle miles was 8% lower in the Scottish Bus Group than at NBC, and at COMS it was 20% lower than in the rest of National Bus. Moreover there was a considerable variation in the cost per vehicle mile within NBC (from 55p at East Midland Motor to 76p for Potteries Motor Traction). Some of these and the other contrasts may be partly or wholly due to the differing characteristics of the areas being served. However it seems unlikely that this would explain why the number of administrative workers per bus was 38% smaller in the Scottish Bus Group than it was at NBC. On the other hand the number of maintenance workers per million vehicle miles was 19% lower at National Bus than at SBG, although their buses are the same size.

That National and Scottish could have done more to rationalise their operations and raise their productivity is evident from the progress which has already been made in some parts of the state bus sector. Between 1968 and 1978 there was a fall of 2% in the number of journeys per employee at COMS compared with a fall of 15% for NBC as a whole. As the average length of journey rose these figures do not have any absolute significance but the comparison is instructive. It is also notable that the number of vehicle miles per worker rose by 50% at COMS to a point 35% greater than in the rest of NBC. Oxford's superior performance has been due to a number of factors including the virtual elimination of conductors and its success in introducing new services and gaining new traffic. It has also rationalised its route system by integrating its town and country services. There used to be one set of services which carried passengers within the built-up area, and another which began at the centre and penetrated into the countryside but did not carry those whose journey was restricted to the town. With the decline in patronage this method of operation became less and less efficient. The merger of the two networks has led to considerable economies in buses and staff, the quality of service has improved and traffic has increased. Elsewhere separate town and country services often survive, though this is sometimes because the urban services are operated by a municipal bus undertaking.

In Oxford progress has been gradual but in Midland Red a systematic attempt has been made to reshape services and cut costs.

The transfer of services in the Birmingham area to the Passenger Transport Executive had put the Company in a difficult financial position, and it was found that fare increases were producing diminishing returns. Large demands for support were made to the Shire Counties, but they were only granted in part and with considerable reluctance.[5] As a result Midland Red established its Viable Network Project in 1976 'with the main aim of getting the Company into a position where it could finance a known level of service from the farebox and thus be potentially independent of the financial support of central government and local authorities'. The whole of Midland Red has been surveyed and so has COMS. Moreover NBC has decided that all of its companies should progressively be covered and project teams are now at work in each region.

It has been found through the detailed market research which has been carried out in the Midlands that there is considerable scope to rationalise and reform the route network. Routes which cover much the same ground could sometimes be replaced by a single service and in other places too many extra buses were being provided during peak periods. At Midland Red depots the vehicle fleet could typically be reduced by around 30% and costs could be cut by 20–25%. This was largely due to the reduction in the number of buses and drivers and to the removal of conductors because of the freeing of suitable vehicles. However the general tightening up of efficiency also played some part and a small contribution was made by pruning the most unprofitable services. Although the service revisions were expected to lead, on balance, to some loss in revenue, the reduction was estimated at only about 5%. At COMS, which is an exceptionally well run undertaking, the projected savings were considerably smaller. But even here the Market Analysis Project, as it has now been renamed, disclosed that the bus fleet could be cut by 14% and that, after allowing for some loss of revenue as a result of service revisions, it would be possible to close the existing gap of around 9% between the Company's costs and revenue. In Midland Red and Oxford the planned changes have, with the cooperation of the unions, already been put into effect and are proving effective.

Despite the comprehensive nature of NBC's investigations the project teams have neglected one important area: namely greater flexibility in the use of staff. When Professor Graham Rees and Mr Richard Wragg investigated transport in rural Wales they found that because of flexibility the independent firms had significantly lower costs than Crosvilles, which belonged to National Bus. In 1972 the (unweighted) average cost per vehicle mile at eight of Crosville's Welsh depots was about 45% higher than the (unweighted) average for nine small private concerns for which they obtained details. Only one of the latter had a cost per mile in excess of that of the Crosville depot with the lowest costs per mile. The discrepancy in costs was only partly explained by differences in the type of route operated and in costing procedures. According to Professor Rees, 'independent operators have a greater flexibility in the use of labour, employing part-time staff for periods when work is available, as well as being able to use staff for various roles such as drivers, cleaners, mechanics, etc. Crosville, on the other hand, employ only full-time staff for specialised functions — a driver can only be employed as a driver, even if there is not sufficient work to keep him fully occupied.'[6]

There is a considerable need for flexibility because traffic is highly peaked. During the working week demand is very heavy between 8 a.m. and 9 a.m. and again between 3.30 p.m. and 6 p.m. On the other hand National and Scottish run very few services before 7 a.m. and provide a much reduced service after 7 p.m. Drivers are legally permitted to be out on the road for ten hours per day, but this can be spread over a period of fifteen and a half hours on three days of each week and over fourteen hours on other days. National and Scottish are therefore able to operate on the basis of one driver per bus for their services between 7 a.m. and 7 p.m. However this method of operation is only possible if drivers and unions are prepared to allow work to be spread over the full period. At some depots this is possible but at others it is not, but even where there is no restriction on spreadovers the peaky nature of traffic may mean that drivers are used inefficiently unless they can be employed on other available work or engaged on a part-time basis. In many NBC Companies part-time staff are taken on to cover seasonal requirements and they are sometimes employed to drive at weekends. However they are seldom used on a regular basis during the working week. At some depots drivers help with work which is normally undertaken by garage staff, e.g., shifting buses. But they do not engage in maintenance or clerical activities, though such workers sometimes drive if no driver is available. Some flexibility therefore exists, but it does not extend to the point where any considerable number of drivers can be regularly employed for part of their day on other work.

As a result, there is a tendency to provide a level of service during off peak periods that will utilise the number of drivers available. This can be justified in the name of marginal cost pricing. If there is no alternative work for the drivers who have to be employed to provide the peak hour services, it will pay to put on extra buses so long as the additional passenger revenue exceeds their avoidable operating costs. These are restricted to the cost of fuel, on which no tax is paid, and to expenditure on tyres and maintenance. During 1977 these items averaged only 14½p per vehicle mile for NBC and SBG. As their revenue averaged around 3½p per passenger mile they only needed an average load of about four passengers in order to cover these avoidable costs, though this ignores the possibility that some of the passengers would still make the journey by bus even if the service were less frequent; and it appears that the number of passengers only rises by about 0.5–0.7% for every 1% by which the vehicle mileage is increased. There is therefore little doubt that services during off-peak periods are more frequent than would be warranted if the National and Scottish Bus Groups were able to use their labour in a truly flexible manner.

Moreover the present restrictions on the use of labour help to explain why scheduled speeds are sometimes unrealistically high during peak periods but unduly low at other times. Obviously bus undertakings try desperately to restrict the number of drivers required during the rush hours because there is not enough work for them at other times. On the other hand there seems little point in speeding up buses during the rest of the day when management already faces the problem of how to provide work for the drivers who are available.

This line of argument will be met with the reply that NBC and SBG cannot use their labour flexibly because, as the opposition to spreadover duties shows, workers will not agree. However, no attempt has ever been made to negotiate the type of flexibility that is so evidently needed, viz. the employment of some workers both as drivers and on another activity during the period while they are on duty. It is difficult to see why drivers would complain since it would reduce the need for spreadovers and enhance their status. The people who would object would be the maintenance and clerical workers who would say that drivers were depriving them of jobs. Whether it would have been possible for NBC and SBG to have secured more flexible working arrangements it is impossible to know for certain. However some progress would probably have been made if they had tried sufficiently hard.

COSTS, PRICES AND LOSSES

The past decade has seen a spectacular increase in the state buses' operating costs. Between 1968 and 1973, when the modest increase in productivity kept the growth in staff costs in check, there was a rise of 18% in unit operating costs, though they had been higher during the early 1970s when productivity was depressed. During 1974 and 1975 unit costs soared because productivity fell back and there was a considerable increase in the relative earnings of busmen. By 1975 staff costs per employee were 43% higher than they had been in 1968, compared with a rise of only 24% in manufacturing. Since 1975 the growth in unit operating costs has been much slower because, although there has been a further fall in productivity, staff costs per employee have declined and busmen have lost some of the gains which they had made relative to manufacturing workers. Nevertheless by 1968 unit operating costs were over 50% greater than they had been in 1968.

It is therefore scarcely surprising that NBC and SBG have made large price increases. Between 1968 and 1978 fares rose by a third. Fares were not increased steadily. After having been pushed up by 1971 to a point 14% above 1968, they fell back until 1974 when they were only 6% higher than in 1968. As we have seen falling fares led to a stabilisation in traffic, but this was at the expense of a serious decline in profitability. Between 1968 and 1975 the gross margin fell from +10% to −7%. During recent years there has been some improvement in the state bus companies' financial position and in 1978 the gross margin was −2%. This amelioration occurred because the growth in unit costs had slowed down and large fare increases were made.

During 1968 NBC and SBG more than covered their depreciation at replacement cost, but in the following year there was a loss, and by 1975 the net deficit had risen to about £90 million. During 1978 they still had a net loss of £65 million, which was equivalent to 13% of their earnings. This includes the £25 million of fuel tax which was refunded to National and Scottish because it has been regarded as their contribution towards the cost of providing and maintaining the road system. Although NBC make a large loss overall some of its constituent companies — COMS, East Midland Motor and three Yorkshire concerns — show profits (after interest but before allowing for full depreciation or adding back fuel tax). And 40% of the loss is accounted for by four companies which are responsible for only 17% of NBC's mileage. It is also noteworthy that NBC manages to lose money on National Travel, which operates most of its express coaches. There is a huge variation in the profitability of different services with some showing large profits in relation to revenue and others making enormous losses. From costing studies at a limited number of depots it appears that NBC's inter-urban routes are the most remunerative. The cost per bus mile tends to be low because speeds are relatively high, there is relatively little dead time at the end of the trips and extra buses are seldom required during the peaks. Despite the large variation in costs and loadings NBC and SBG have fare structures which are uniform within large districts, though because charges are tapered revenue per mile tends to be low for the inter-urban services.

Costs also vary over the course of the day. At some Midland Red depots it was found that, when fixed costs were attributed to the peaks and other costs, including crews' wages, were allocated in proportion to bus hours, the cost per passenger was around 20% lower than the average level between 9 a.m. and 3.30 p.m. and the cost was in general much above average up to 9 a.m. and after 6 p.m. The difference in costs may have been exaggerated if only because vehicle maintenance and some other items that were regarded as fixed vary, or at least should vary, according to the mileage that is run. Nevertheless there does appear to be a case for having lower fares during the inter-peak period. Some NBC companies do charge a lower price, mostly by offering off-peak return tickets. However most companies provide discounts for peak travel in the form of season tickets which are available to adults and scholars travelling between fixed points; and the past few years have seen the widespread introduction of period tickets which provide for unlimited travel within a specified area. According to NBC they are 'geared largely to commuters'.[7]

THE SYSTEM OF SUPPORT

During 1978 National and Scottish were not only refunded £25 million of fuel tax, but also received over £30 million of revenue support from local authorities and were provided with a government contribution of £27 million towards the cost of buying new buses. This system of subvention had small beginnings and it was never envisaged that the call on public funds would become so large. The foundations were laid in the Transport Act of 1968. First, the Act provided for a large increase in the size of the bus fuel grant, which had hitherto been modest; although there was a Government declaration that, 'It would be wrong to exempt stage bus services entirely from taxation on the fuel they use . . . In economic terms it is right that bus operators should meet a charge at least as high as the cost of providing the track which they use'.[8] This did not prevent the next Labour Government from entirely exempting stage bus services from fuel duty. Second, in order to speed up the introduction of one-man operation, the Act provided for a 25% grant towards the cost of new buses. This was increased to 50% — incredible as it may seem, the decision was made in a hurry one afternoon so that London Transport could avoid having to make a fare increase. Third, the Transport Act enabled local authorities to subsidise rural bus services with the assistance of a 50% government grant. It was not expected that the total cost would rise above £13 million, not all of which would be received by NBC and SBG.[9]

The Government's intention was that National and Scottish would, in consequence, be able to pay their way and NBC was given the target of maintaining its profits at about the 1968 level. National Bus made it clear that it did not regard this objective as attainable and was soon pressing for subsidies for its urban services. In the autumn of 1970 local authorities were informed that a large number of rural services would be withdrawn unless they made a contribution towards their costs. At this point two official Steering Groups were set up to study rural passenger transport needs in West Suffolk and Devon. The market research that they commissioned showed that stage bus services played a very small part in rural transport. The Groups concluded that where demand was insufficient to warrant a conventional bus service the needs of the small minority that did not have access to a car could be met by such means as organised lift giving, which even on an informal basis was more important than the local bus.[10]

Nevertheless the Government was so impressed with the seriousness of the transport problem and so wedded to the belief that buses were a social service, that in the Local Government Act of 1972 the

Shire Counties were given the duty of promoting the provision of a public transport system that would 'meet the needs of the county', and were empowered to make grants to the undertakings involved. What precisely the Government's intentions were at this stage it is impossible to tell since the clause in question was never debated, but it is noteworthy that the public expenditure projections published in December 1972 did not contain any provision for additional bus subsidies. The Act came into force in 1975 and this was the year when, partly because action was deferred in the expectation of higher subsidies, NBC experienced a financial collapse.

County Councils were encouraged to provide subsidies by the new machinery for the finance and control of their transport expenditure which came into operation during 1975. There had previously been a system of specific grants, e.g., for road maintenance and bus support. These were replaced by a general Transport Supplementary Grant. This meets 70% of that part of transport expenditure that is approved by the Department and is above a minimum level. What happens each year is that the nationalised bus undertakings have to negotiate with the County Councils before the latter submit their transport programmes to the government, and then re-negotiate when the counties have been told what level of expenditure will qualify for Transport Supplementary Grant. The operators then have to submit any changes in services and fares to the Traffic Commissioners, besides having to secure the agreement of the unions to any alteration in schedules. The process of negotiation is complicated by the rapid shifts which take place in the policies of both central and local government. Under such conditions efficient management becomes extremely difficult, as NBC is well aware.

Although the Department simply announces that a certain sum will qualify for grant purposes it has told County Councils that it is favourably disposed towards expenditure on rural and other local bus services that are in need of support. In the 1976 *Consultation Document* on *Transport Policy* the Government declared that public transport is 'a basic community need' and asserted that without subsidies it would be impossible to maintain an adequate network of bus services for the large section of society that does not have access to a car.[11] General statements of this type, and they are all that have been vouchsafed, gloss over the problems of how the concept of need is to be interpreted and what level of service is considered adequate. These are not simply academic questions, for once it is decided to reject the market test a political decision becomes necessary.

A detailed examination of the way in which County Councils have approached the task has been prepared for the National Bus Company by consultants. They found that 'very little clarity and a great deal of confusion exists in the definition of the objectives of rural transport policy. Objectives are only expressed, if at all, in the most general of terms and the policies of the authority are often put forward as objectives.' Moreover 'in the absence of specific objectives for rural transport, there is often no real indication of any rigorous approach having yet been employed in deciding on the extent or direction of financial support. Many counties are at present simply striving to maintain existing levels of service as far as financial resources will permit.'[12] Twenty-one of the thirty-eight counties on which information was obtained had failed to adopt any specific criteria to help them to decide which bus services were worthy of support. Decisions were therefore left to the judgement of members and officers, or in some cases, where the counties merely fix an overall level of support, to NBC. Ten of the authorities where yardsticks were employed placed the emphasis on a financial test which generally included a requirement that the revenue from a service should cover a certain proportion of its costs. This was sometimes 50% — the minimum figure on which the Government used to insist when making grants under the 1968 Act — but several had adopted a more flexible approach, which in practice probably meant that the threshold had been reduced.[13]

Although financial tests have the merit of providing some restriction on expenditure they suffer from the obvious weakness that there is no way of knowing whether the services that qualify for support yield a benefit that outweighs their cost. Very little use has been made of cost–benefit analysis and it is difficult to see how it can be employed since the rural bus has no close alternative. It would be grossly misleading to work out the cost of using taxis as these provide a high quality service but charge a price higher than many bus passengers would be prepared to pay. Moreover, those who regard buses as an essential public service always refuse to recognise that if a route is withdrawn a considerable proportion of former users will probably arrange lifts.

ARE SUBSIDIES DESIRABLE?

Those who advocate subsidies will reply that, whatever the weaknesses of the present support system, it is preferable to a situation in which large sections of the community are rendered immobile. According to the *Consultation Document* it is already the case that 'mobility has been reduced for those without a car'.[14] In fact, there has over the years been a considerable increase. During 1937–38 individuals over the age of three in working and lower middle class families averaged only three miles per week by public transport, excluding journeys to work. In both 1965 and 1975–76 the corresponding figure for those in households without cars was around sixteen miles but their mileage in the form of lifts increased from seven to nine. As younger and more mobile families were buying cars over this period the stability in the distance by public transport is very remarkable. The available evidence also shows there has been a large rise in the mobility of those members of car-owing households who are unable to drive.[15] Nor, in view of television, the spread of telephones, and the introduction of meals on wheels, can it plausibly be maintained that the need for mobility has increased.

Mobility might, however, be curtailed if the withdrawal of bus subsidies were to lead to a large part of the bus network being abandoned. However there are a number of reasons for believing that this would not, or at least need not, happen.

1. A large part of NBC's loss is incurred by a small number of companies and about 40% of the stage vehicle mileage is accounted for by undertakings which are profitable or where the loss (as previously defined) is no more than 3.7% of revenue. 2. Even at one of the most unprofitable undertakings — Crosville — it has been found that a viable network composed of the most profitable routes would include 45% of the existing bus mileage and carry half the traffic.[16] Allowance was made for conversion to one-man operation, due to the release of suitable vehicles, but no attempt was made to reshape services. 3. NBC believes that traffic falls by half the percentage by which bus frequency is reduced. This means that instead of withdrawing unprofitable services it is often possible to reduce

their frequency. 4. As the Market Analysis Project has shown there is considerable scope to reorganise services and cut costs. The depots at Evesham and Stratford-upon-Avon, where the Project was implemented first, have become financially self-supporting, although previously they were both incurring large losses. This has been achieved without any great reduction in the volume of traffic. 5. There are obvious ways in which NBC and SBG could improve their efficiency. They could make a saving of £45 million simply by completing the switch to one-man operation and reducing the number of administrative and maintenance workers per bus mile to the 1968 level. 6. Because demand is relatively inelastic it should be possible to reduce losses by raising fares.

However it must be recognised that some routes are wildly unprofitable. At Midland Red there are a few services which operate throughout the day where fares meet less than a quarter of the cost. In some cases, as private operators have shown, it might be possible to substitute an off-peak service to meet the needs of shoppers. These could often be provided in conjunction with school buses. The small private firms which operate most of these buses often find it difficult to employ the vehicles, or even the drivers, during the rest of the day. With this in mind the Oxfordshire County Council, which is one of the few authorities that has refused to subsidise NBC, has decided to invite tenders for the joint provision of a school bus and an off-peak service and to encourage the latter by providing a small subsidy. Although four contracts have been let the County's efforts have so far been largely frustrated by COMS, which has refused either to put in a bid or relinquish its unprofitable services, and by the Traffic Commissioners who have, in a splendidly splenetic judgement, refused to grant licences where they would mean that COMS would be subjected to competition.[17]

It is difficult to believe that any great hardship would result if grossly uneconomic routes were abandoned or reduced to an occasional bus for shopping. Hardly anyone travels on them. The average number of passenger miles per bus mile on rural routes is only about seven and on those which are grossly unprofitable it is only around three.[18] Stage bus services now have a very limited role in country areas. During 1975–76 only 22% of those who lived in rural areas were in non-car-owning households and local buses accounted for only 5% of the mileage (and of the journeys) travelled by those who lived in rural areas, compared with 81% by car and 3% by works and school buses. It seems probable that even in families that do not own cars the mileage by car is greater than that by stage bus. During 1975–76, 34% of the passenger mileage for those in non-vehicle-owning households was by local bus and 30% by car. However this is for all parts of the country and local surveys suggest that lift giving is particularly widespread in rural areas. The studies of twenty-four rural parishes in Devon and West Suffolk, made for the official Steering Groups, showed that there were more lifts than local bus journeys. According to the Steering Group for Devon:

> The absence of buses is compensated for by increased use of cars and by getting lifts. A greater proportion of people in the poorly served areas get regular daily lifts . . . where there is a good bus service (east of Tiverton) the elderly make slightly more journeys than average, i.e. they were more mobile, but not a lot more mobile. In other areas the relative frequency of bus services did not seem to make much difference to how often they travelled. In the areas worst served by buses, the survey showed that the elderly were able to get many lifts, and lifts formed a much larger proportion of their journeys than of those for other age groups. This suggests that relatives and friends are prepared to help out.[19]

Another study covering the Malvern Hills area revealed that the number of shopping journeys per week from non-car-owning households was virtually the same in the larger parishes, which mostly had a reasonable bus service, as in the smaller parishes where it was very limited. The number of journeys made by obtaining a lift was considerably greater in the latter (0.5 per week) than it was in the larger parishes (0.2 per week).[20]

These inquiries suggest that the withdrawal of those bus services that are hopelessly unprofitable would be at least partly compensated for by an increase in lift giving. What is wanted, as the Steering Group on West Suffolk observed, is the establishment in each village where public transport is inadequate of a rudimentary clearing house system to bring those who need lifts and those who are willing to provide them into contact.[21] The Oxfordshire County Council has tried to organise lift giving clubs in a few villages but has not had much success. However, the withdrawal of bus services might well provide the necessary impetus and they will be easier to arrange now that the Government has made it legal to pay for lifts. The village bus experiments, which have been organised by local committees, show that community action of this type is by no means out of the question. These community buses, which are now running successfully in Norfolk, Clwyd and Suffolk, are serviced by National Bus but operated by unpaid volunteer drivers. Where a journey of some importance has to be made a lift can probably be specially arranged. More than fifty social car services are already being operated by the WRVS in cooperation with local authorities. The cost per trip is relatively high because drivers are usually provided with a mileage allowance to cover their costs, but this would seem a much better use of limited public funds than the indiscriminate subsidy of buses that may not run to the right place or at the right time.

CHAPTER 7

The National Freight

Corporation

The National Freight Corporation (NFC) came into existence at the end of 1968. It inherited British Road Services (BRS) and the other road haulage concerns that had been controlled by the Transport Holding Company and it took over National Carriers and Freight-liners from British Rail. The latter retained a 49% holding in Freightliners and reassumed full control in the summer of 1978.

NFC's INHERITANCE

NFC inherited serious problems, the most acute of which were in parcels, which accounted for about 45% of its revenue. During 1968 National Carriers (NCL) sustained a net loss of about £60 million, which was equivalent to half its turnover. This activity had been identified in the Beeching Report as a heavy loss maker and a National Sundries Plan was implemented. The number of places at which traffic was handled was cut from 950 in 1961 to 180 in 1968, and there was a substantial reduction in staff. But traffic fell by a third between 1964 and 1968 and there was no decline in the deficit. The size of the network and the use of rail for the trunk haul meant that there was a large amount of transhipment and that the quality of service was very poor. Parcels were only moved two or three times a week between some of the main depots and, if anything, the standard of service deteriorated because of the disruptions which rationalisation involved. Roadline, or BRS Parcels as it was then known, was in a much healthier condition, but was running into difficulties. Between 1963 and 1968 traffic and parcels per worker fell (4% and 9%) and revenue per parcel rose (7%). Despite this the net surplus fell (after depreciation at historic cost) from £7½ million in 1963 to less than £2 million in 1968, which was only 2.7% on revenue.

Provision was made in the Transport Act of 1968 for NFC to receive a subsidy while National Carriers was restored to profitability. However it was restricted both in amount and duration and vigorous action was clearly necessary. One possibility would have been to merge National Carriers and Roadline. While they remained separate their collection and delivery rounds would inevitably overlap. The length of these rounds could therefore be reduced in those places where they both maintained depots either by closing down one, or by dividing the town into two districts and serving each district exclusively from one. However, a parcels system with a large number of depots has the disadvantage that, although its collection and delivery rounds will tend to be short, its trunking operations will be complex and costly. If a parcels network contains 100 depots, like Roadline in 1968, and every branch is provided with a direct link to every other branch, there will have to be 4950 trunk haulage routes. As there will obviously be very little traffic between many of the branches any undertaking with a large number of branches will have to use indirect links. Hence it will be put to the expense of transferring and re-sorting parcels and its delivery times will tend to be slow and unreliable.

Only in the unlikely event of it being possible to handle the combined traffic of Roadline and National Carriers from the number of depots possessed by the concern where they were most numerous would it have been possible to avoid an increase in the cost and complexity of trunking operations. And although the merger of Roadline and NCL would have provided scope for the rationalisation of local delivery rounds it seems doubtful whether the gains would have been very large. They were to some extent engaged in different types of work: National Carriers, unlike Roadline, was not involved in household delivery and handled heavier packages. This means that rationalisation might not have led to any great rise in the number of parcels dropped off at each stop. Moreover investigations by the Post Office indicate that for every 10% by which parcels traffic increases there will be a reduction of only 2% in the amount of delivery time per parcel.

Not only were the arguments in favour of merger much weaker than they appeared but there were powerful arguments against. The merger of Roadline and National Carriers would almost certainly have led to a loss of business, because customers do not like to become too dependent on a single supplier. This would have accentuated the already formidable problems of integrating two large concerns — with staff in different unions — and would have diverted management from more important tasks. Both carriers were probably already beyond the optimum size and the private concerns which have been gaining business at their expense have decided not to expand their networks beyond about twenty branches. Although there was considerable opposition to a merger within NFC, studies appeared to show that considerable economies would be secured. An attempt was made to create a joint management structure for the two concerns but the Transport and General Workers Union objected and no further action was taken.

Whereas the parcels companies which NFC inherited were contracting, the general and special haulage business that it took over had been expanding. Between 1963 and 1968 the capacity tonne mileage appears to have increased by 47%, although the bulk of the increase in turnover was due to the acquisition of Tayforth, Harold Wood and other companies from the private sector. There appears to have been a substantial increase in productivity but receipts per capacity tonne mile seem to have declined and profitability fell. During 1963, which was not an especially favourable year, the general and special traffic companies had a net profit of about £10 million (after depreciation at historic cost) which was equivalent to over 5% of revenue. In 1968 the surplus was no higher and the net margin had fallen, and during the following year the original undertakings had a net profit of £7 million, and a margin of only 3%.[1] It is apparent from a survey by the Department of the Environment that the nationalised companies were less profitable than the industry as a whole, whose profit margin was 12–15% during 1965 as against 7½% for the Holding Company's general and special haulage companies.[2]

Freightliners had only commenced operations in 1965. By 1968 traffic had built up to 2½ million tonnes. This was a far cry from the 30 million tonnes which the Beeching Report had envisaged.[3] The programme for introducing Freightliners had fallen behind schedule and, what was more important, the original plans were wildly unrealistic. Half of the traffic which had been projected was to be carried less than 150 miles although only for heavy products and maritime containers were Freightliners competitive with road over distances of this length.[4] During 1969 Freightliners sustained a loss of £7 million, which was equivalent to 22% of its revenue. Some loss was probably inevitable until traffic had built up and capacity was more fully utilised. But when the NFC took over and an effort was made to identify the financial results of each route, it was found that even those that were well established and had good loadings were often unprofitable because rates had been pitched at an unduly low level.

So long as British Rail was in charge the principal concern was not viability but volume. BR continued to believe that it would secure 40 million tonnes of work and its more go-ahead managers were saying that the aim should be at least 100 million. By the end of 1969 twenty-eight terminals had been brought into operation, but BR was planning by 1970 to expand the system to around fifty.[5] However the Corporation, which found it impossible to make some of the secondary depots pay, vetoed the construction of further terminals because there was little prospect that they would attract any great volume of traffic. The transfer of Freightliners to the NFC, which was motivated by the belief that BR was under-charging and over-optimistic, was therefore amply justified.[6]

OUTPUT AND MARKET SHARE

Initially there was a rise in the output of the NFC companies, but it fell away during the recession of the early 1970s and failed to recover in the boom. It can be seen from Table 7.1 that by 1973 the volume of work was already somewhat less than in 1968. During the period of economic contraction after 1973 the Corporation's output fell sharply and during 1978 it appears to have been 22% lower than it had been in 1968. The reduction in work has been particularly large in the parcels field (45% between 1969 and 1978) with huge declines at both Roadline and National Carriers. The rest of the freight transport business fared much better but even here there was a significant fall in output (of perhaps 12% between 1969 and 1978) and in real receipts (−9%).

Although the National Freight Corporation is by far the largest road haulage undertaking it accounts for only about 17% of the

TABLE 7.1 National Freight Corporation: Output, Productivity and Finances

	Ton miles carried by all hire and reward operators (1968=100)	NFC output (1968=100)	Employment[a] (000)	Average weekly hours worked[b] (000)	Output per equivalent worker[c]	Real unit operating costs (1968=100)	Real unit staff costs (1968=100)	Real staff costs per employee (1968=100)	Real revenue per unit (1968=100)	Revenue (£m, 1978 prices)	Gross surplus (£m, 1978 prices)	Gross surplus as % of revenue (%)	Net surplus (£m, 1978 prices)
1963[d]	..	76.6	34.7	..	83.4[e]	101.8	108.4	88.9	102.8	242	33	13.7	..
			38.3[d]							313[d]	38[d]	12.0[d]	..
1968	100.0	100.0	64.9	55.6	100.0	100.0	100.0	100.0	100.0	447	−16	−3.6	−56
1969[f]	104.8[f]	103.0[g]	65.5	55.6	102.0[g]	101.9	100.3	103.3	105.4	489	−1	−0.2	−41
1970	106.9	103.9	64.5	54.4	105.2	103.9	108.0	112.1	112.9	514	18	3.5	−22
1971	106.1	100.0	59.4	53.3	110.5	98.5	105.3	113.0	112.3	488	39	8.0	−1
1972	109.6	98.0	53.5	53.8	119.8	97.2	101.5	118.3	111.1	470	37	7.8	−3
1973	122.0	96.8	51.1	54.5	123.5	98.8	100.8	122.4	113.3	473	35	7.5	−5
1974	120.5	92.6	50.0	54.2	121.1	100.9	97.6	120.2	113.1	469	26	5.5	−14
1975	126.8	85.3[h]	47.0[h]	51.8	120.3[h]	100.7	105.2	124.6	109.2	413	12	3.0	−28
1976	126.0	86.6[h]	43.0[h]	52.1	132.9[h]	93.6	95.6	124.8	104.4	401	25	6.3	−15
1977	136.1	81.5[h]	40.8[h]	52.7	131.6[h]	98.6	93.4	119.4	112.5	407	34	8.4	−6
1978[i]	127.3	78.3[h]	39.4[h]	52.3	131.1[h]	102.4	97.8	122.3	118.2	415	42	10.0	2

Note The output index for 1968–75 comprises eight weighted indicators: parcels volume, vehicles provided for BR, containers and capacity tonne miles (mileage multiplied by average capacity per vehicle). Allowance was made for the transfer of NCL's trunk haulage work from rail to its own vehicles (by subtracting payments to BR from NCL revenue and deflating this with a price index for NCL estimated with its indicators). The indicators were combined with 1969 net output weights except that those used for NCL were spliced with revenue weights. My output index does not appear to be distorted by the switch from general haulage to contract hire because the net output per capacity tonne mile was approximately the same for both activities. For 1975–78 output was measured as previously except that 1976 weights were used and that the indicator for the BRS Group, where the original method gave misleading results, was its receipts deflated by a price index derived from Freightliners' revenue per container and the Special Traffic Group's receipts per capacity ton mile. The per unit series were estimated using gross output at 1963, 1969 and 1976 prices.

[a] Average of beginning and end year. [b] Drivers and manual maintenance workers covered by BRS negotiating machinery. [c] Only allows for change in average hours worked by drivers and maintenance workers covered by BRS negotiating machinery. [d] THC road haulage subsidiaries. [e] OMY. [f] Tartan Arrow included from 1969. [g] Affected by industrial dispute. [h] Excludes Tempco. [i] Includes Freightliners for the whole of 1978.

employment in road haulage contracting. Over the period 1969–78 there was an increase of 21% in the tonne mileage of hire and reward traffic and it seems, both from this and other evidence, that there has been a substantial fall in the NFC's share of the general haulage market. In parcels the only firm figures are for those carriers which are in public ownership, viz. the Post Office, British Rail and, of course, the NFC carriers. The latter have been losing business at a particularly rapid rate. Between 1968 and 1978 their share of all public sector parcels traffic, at constant prices, fell from 42% to 35% and there was an overall decline of 38% in the amount of parcels work undertaken within the sector. While the state carriers have been contracting private firms appear to have expanded. In 1969 they accounted for only a small part of the market and there was only one firm — Atlas Express — which possessed a network of depots and provided an extensive service. There are now six: Atlas, United Carriers, Wilkinsons, Inter-County, Carryfast and Securicor. During 1978 these undertakings had a joint turnover of some £105 million as against the £125 million which was earned by the NFC companies from their own parcels work. Although private carriers have grown mightily (and the other state carriers, much of whose work is household delivery, have lost business because the mail order houses have started to distribute for themselves), parcels has not been a very buoyant market.

The bulk of the traffic that parcel carriers receive is carried on behalf of firms who want their products distributed from their factories or warehouses to destinations all over the country. Parcels are collected and taken to the operator's local depot where they are sorted and dispatched on a trunk haulage vehicle to an intermediate depot or straight to the outward depot. When a parcel arrives there it is re-sorted and placed on the appropriate local delivery vehicle. This method of distribution is relatively expensive because of the labour that has to be devoted to sorting and to loading and unloading individual packages. Moreover it is not particularly reliable because, as parcels move in stages, they may be held up at depots if, for instance, these become temporarily congested.

Over the years production has been concentrated in the hands of fewer firms, output per factory has increased and the number of outlets has diminished due to the emergence of supermarkets and the cash and carry type of distribution. As a result of these changes, and due to the introduction of the fork lift truck and other forms of mechanical handling, it has become possible for manufacturers to move goods in bulk to strategically placed warehouses and thence to their final destination. The consequent reduction in the volume of work available for the nationalised parcel carriers, together with the loss of business to the private carriers, has faced them with the problem of cutting their costs and preventing their efficiency from falling. Their response has been less than satisfactory and there has been a rapid rise in their rates which has, in turn, led to a further fall in traffic. Between 1968 and 1978 Roadline's revenue per parcel increased by 35%.

More traffic would have been retained if greater efforts had been made to meet customers' changing needs. There has been scope for Roadline and NCL to move goods from factories to warehouses, undertake local distribution, or even supply warehouse facilities and provide firms with a total distribution service. That there were possibilities of this type was recognised by NFC in the early 1970s and National Carriers has since 1974 established specialised services for carrying china and glassware and fashion clothing for Marks and Spencer and other concerns.[7] However the parcels companies do not appear to have made the most of their opportunities; and it is BRS which has seized the chance to provide a distribution service where goods are collected and then distributed from its depots in the quantities, and at the times, that the manufacturer specifies.

Although the disappearance of traditional parcels work constitutes the main reason why traffic has declined, the loss of business to private carriers has been a contributory factor. The private carriers provide a faster and more reliable service. During the latter part of the 1970s United Carriers' average delivery time was about 2.8 days and Wilkinson's has claimed that it averaged only 2.4 days with 99% of all consignments arriving within 5 days. Roadline had an average transit time of 3.5 days and 12% of parcels took more than 5 days. At National Carriers the average was also about 3.5 days, but used to be longer. The main reason why the private carriers have shorter and more dependable delivery times is that their networks are smaller. The great majority of their depots are linked by direct trunk services and they are able to maintain recording systems which show the whereabouts of any parcel they have received.

The decline in NFC's non-parcel work is explained by the contraction of its general haulage business. In 1969 the general haulage side of British Road Services accounted for 40% of the Corporation's turnover, excluding parcels, but produced little or no profit after depreciation.[1] There is no convincing evidence that general haulage has been a particularly unprofitable section of the industry, although there is some reason to believe that it is one in which large firms, with their higher overheads, find it difficult to compete.[8] However what seems to have been the problem was that BRS was to a considerable extent engaged in spot hire work as opposed to carrying on a regular basis for particular customers. Moreover its network of trunk services had been undercut by Freightliners. BRS therefore decided to eliminate its unprofitable activities and reduce the size of the general haulage business. Between the end of 1969 and the end of 1972 the aggregate carrying capacity of the BRS general haulage fleet was slashed by almost 30% and there was a further large reduction during 1973. Although BRS had some success in obtaining new contract hire work a considerable number of depots had to be closed and this led to the loss of some business that it would have liked to retain. This obviously provokes the question of whether the process of disengagement should not have begun earlier and been less precipitate. Since 1973 BRS has been building up its tailor-made distribution services, has successfully entered the truck rental market (1975) and has launched a vehicle recovery service (1977). By the end of 1978 about 100,000 vehicles had been signed on and the truck rental fleet comprised about 1,200 lorries and vans. There has however been a continued and offsetting reduction in general haulage work which, despite the contraction of the early 1970s, has remained an important source of revenue.

Although the contraction of the non-parcels side of NFC has been wholly attributable to the BRS Group, this does not necessarily mean that the specialised companies have made the most of their opportunities. The number of containers carried by Freightliners increased two and a half times between 1968 and 1978. The system was only in its infancy at the beginning of the period, but the Company does appear to have been reasonably successful in promoting and developing its services, though it has worked under two considerable handicaps. Its reputation for reliability has suffered because of the cancellation of trains by BR and congestion at some depots. A large throughput is required in order for a depot to pay its way and the attempt to utilise a high proportion of the available capacity has sometimes resulted in delays and difficulties. The Company's other main weakness is that its 30-foot containers have a capacity of only 1650 cubic feet whereas a large lorry can be loaded with up to 2840 cubic feet of goods provided they are sufficiently light. As a result Freightliners tend to be more expensive than road haulage for bulky commodities.[4] The obvious response was to introduce 40-foot containers, which have a volume of 2300 feet, but Freightliners has very few for hire, although there is a considerable demand.

Pickfords and the other special traffic companies have expanded since 1968 but the growth in their business does not appear to have been very large. A massive expansion into Europe was launched but had to be abandoned. This ill-conceived project absorbed a large amount of energy and capital. However the Corporation has successfully moved into the movement and disposal of waste products; and also into cold storage and the importation of wine, although these non-haulage activities are not reflected in my output figures.

PRODUCTIVITY

In 1968 the NFC companies employed about 65,000 workers, but by 1978 the number had been reduced to 40,000 which was a cutback of almost 40%. Between 1968 and 1973 output per equivalent worker rose by something like 23%. The subsequent slump in output led to some decline but productivity seems to have shot up in 1976 when the Corporation, which was trying to improve its financial position, sharply reduced its employment. During 1978 OEW appears to have been around 30% higher than it had been a decade earlier. When National Carriers is excluded the Corporation's productivity appears to have risen somewhat less between 1968 and 1973 (16%) than that of the Holding Company's road haulage concerns over the period 1963–68 (20%). Because road haulage is so competitive it seems unlikely that there can have been any great divergence between the rate at which the industry's productivity has been growing and that of the Corporation's non-parcel companies. Any marked tendency for their productivity to grow more slowly must be expected to show up not in the figures for output per worker but in those for NFC's market share. It is interesting to observe that those BRS depots where the drivers refuse to have the lorries scheduled at more than 23 mph were shut down.

However, in parcels price competition is muted and productivity is less closely constrained; Roadline has, as the only profitable state-owned parcels carrier, tended to act as a price leader; and in 1968 National Carriers was making large losses and obviously had scope to raise its productivity. It appears that between 1969 and 1978 there was a rise of about 30% in OMY at National Carriers. This is only a very rough figure but there is no doubt that there has been a marked rise in efficiency. The depot system has been rationalised and over the period 1969–77 the proportion of salaried workers has been reduced from 22% to 17%, the tonnage per handling worker has been increased by some 13%, the number of vehicle miles per fitter has risen 55% and the number of miles per driver has shot up 65%, though this has been partly due to the growth in road trunking. In 1968 trunk haulage absorbed half of National Carriers' revenue because of the expense of using BR. The switch to road has led to a great reduction in costs and to an improvement in the quality of service. By 1978 net output per worker was as high at National Carriers as at Roadline.

Productivity has been falling at Roadline. During 1978 the number of parcels handled per employee was 22% lower than the 1964 peak and 16% smaller than in 1958. Roadline is badly in need of reshaping. For instance between 1958 and 1968 there was a reduction of 46% in parcels but only 14% in vehicle miles. One problem, which is now being tackled, is that the trunking system has many illogical features, that can only be explained by history. Because of this and the decline in traffic many runs are very lightly loaded. Both Roadline and National Carriers could raise their productivity by adopting more efficient handling methods at depots. Goods are often still pushed around in barrows, and the power trolleys used by National Carriers require drivers. However United Carriers has developed a system by which trucks are magnetically guided along rails from the trunk vehicle to the appropriate local delivery van. This may help to explain why during 1978 its revenue per worker was 27% higher than Roadline's although the main reason is probably that it has succeeded in attracting traffic that can be handled more economically.

COSTS, PRICES AND PROFITS

Between 1968 and 1978 the Corporation's unit costs were more or less stable but its prices rose by something like 18% due, in the main, to the large increase for parcels. As a result there was a sharp improvement in profitability. In 1968 NFC had a gross margin of −3½% and a net loss of something like £55 million. By 1978 this had been replaced by a positive margin of 10% and a net profit of £2 million. However progress was not steady. During the Corporation's early years there was a substantial improvement in its financial position, largely due to the swift reduction in National Carriers' losses. By 1971, when the economy was in recession, NFC's net loss had been almost eliminated. However National Carriers still had a loss of £20 million and the Corporation's other concerns were less profitable than private hauliers. Those with fleets of over fifty vehicles had a net margin, after historic cost depreciation, of 14% whereas the figure was only 5% for NFC, excluding the ex-BR concerns.[9]

After 1971 the Corporation's profitability steadily deteriorated until during 1975 there was a net loss of £28 million of which some £18 million was incurred at National Carriers. It was, of course, a very difficult year. Private hauliers with fleets of over 100 vehicles had a net margin of only 4.8%, after depreciation at historic cost, but the figure for NFC was a mere 2.2%, even ignoring National Carriers and Freightliners.[8] Moreover what this (and the net deficit of £28 million) ignores is that a substantial loss was incurred on the French firms which had recently been acquired. Their loss and the amount set aside to cover the costs of their closure amounted to £11 million.

The Corporation's continental venture was from the beginning over-ambitious. It was planned that within five years NFC would be earning half its turnover in Europe, although at the time the proportion was very small. A number of foreign firms were hurriedly purchased at an extremely high price. When they had been taken over it became apparent that the French companies were highly unprofitable and were riddled by corruption and abuse. The acquisition of these firms was the most flagrant but not the only example of bad management within NFC. At that time its subsidiaries were run as personal fiefs by managing directors whose stewardship could not be seriously questioned so long as they retained the confidence of the Corporation's chairman. In addition some very poor appointments were made. The drive to eliminate National Carriers' deficit lost momentum and at Roadline serious mistakes were made. For instance during 1975 it deliberately held its prices at a lower level than those of the Post Office, although the latter was known to be losing money on its parcels traffic. Roadline, which had long ago been chided by the Prices and Incomes Board for not relating its tariffs to its costs, had failed to recognise that small parcels tended to be unprofitable under a changing system in which the rate per parcel rose sharply with weight but the cost per parcel increased far more gradually.[10] One of the secrets of the private carriers' success is that they have recognised this and only accept customers whose traffic contains a sufficient proportion of large parcels. During 1976 Roadline, once highly profitable, had a net loss of around £3 million, although parcels was the type of work where private hauliers were most profitable.[8]

Since NFC's financial crisis in the mid-1970s there has been a sharp recovery in its profitability. The loss-making foreign operations have been terminated, its subsidiaries have been subjected to financial discipline and those who have been placed in charge have been coming to grips with their concerns' problems. During 1977, which at least for the larger firms in the industry was a somewhat better year than 1975, private undertakings with over 100 vehicles (and with fewer) appear to have only just managed to cover their depreciation at replacement cost.[11] When their results are combined the same was true of the BRS Group, Roadline and the Special Traffics Group. But it would perhaps be premature to conclude that NFC, even excluding National Carriers and Freightliners, is as profitable as the larger private firms in the industry. The Transport Development Group's UK road transport undertakings constitute the largest general and special haulage group and United Carriers is one of the biggest private parcels undertakings. When their results are combined these road transport concerns had a net margin, after historic cost depreciation, of 9.7% in 1979, as against 4.8% for the NFC companies, which obtain about the same proportion of their revenue from parcels. However it should be borne in mind that during 1977 United Carriers and TDG had a net margin that was above the average for firms with over 100 vehicles, viz. 9.2% as against 6.8%. Regardless of the precise comparative status of BRS, Roadline and Special Traffics it is clear that NFC as a whole barely managed to meet its replacement cost depreciation during 1978 because although the BRS Group and the special traffic companies were in a fairly healthy financial position, National Carriers, Freightliners and Roadline were not.

The Corporation's record has been mixed. On the one hand it deserves credit for having almost turned National Carriers into a viable concern and for having improved the position of the companies in the BRS Group at a time when the industry's financial position was deteriorating. On the other hand it is open to criticism for having failed for so long to tackle Roadline's problems and for squandering so much treasure on its European escapade. Moreover a question mark must inevitably be placed against an undertaking which has contracted so greatly in an industry which has not.

CHAPTER 8

British Airways

The British Airways Board (BA) came into existence in the spring of 1972 when it took over British European Airways (BEA) and British Overseas Airways (BOAC).

SCHEDULED OPERATIONS AND EFFICIENCY

It is impossible to understand BA's behaviour and performance without knowing something about the market within which it operates. Competition from other scheduled airlines has been restricted on both international and domestic routes, though the latter are relatively unimportant because they only account for 9% of BA's revenue. After the war governments made bilateral agreements under which their aircraft were permitted to operate scheduled services between the countries involved, and in many cases agreement was also reached for airlines to pick up and set down traffic *en route*. However, it was sometimes specified that each of the parties should be represented by a single airline and even where this was not laid down it was the policy of most governments. The only exceptions have been the United States and Britain; and the British aviation authorities have made only intermittent efforts to secure dual designation. As a general rule and with the important exception of the North Atlantic, British Airways has faced competition from a small number of scheduled carriers on each of the routes over which it operates. On the great majority BA is the only British scheduled operator, although British Caledonian flies from Gatwick to some, but not all, of the principal destinations in Western Europe.

What is more important than the number of airlines on any route is the type of competition in which they engage. Until recently there

129

129

was no price competition between scheduled carriers. Price fixing was endorsed in all of the bilateral route agreements, and most made reference to the International Air Transport Association (IATA) — the body through which the airlines determine the level of air fares on each route. The result might simply have been monopoly pricing and excessively high profits. However, this did not happen partly because most international airlines are in public ownership, and have had little incentive to maximise profits, and partly because a policy of crude profit maximisation would ultimately have led to the withdrawal of the privileges and protection which governments had conferred. What happened in practice was that the flag-carrying airlines, whether in public or private ownership, came to see their role as the provision of a high quality service. In this way they were able, while avoiding price competition, to engage in rivalry; they provided themselves with a *raison d'être*; and were able to satisfy politicians and airline users that they were providing something in return for the exclusive rights which they possessed and the high prices which they charged.

In order to supply a high quality service British Airways and other carriers have done their best to provide frequent services; to maintain them throughout the year; to ensure that a seat is available when it is wanted; to fly to a large number of destinations; to avoid arriving or departing at inconvenient times; to keep seating densities low; and to employ an ample number of staff at terminals and on cabin duties. One obvious consequence (of the first four factors) is that scheduled airlines have been put to the expense of supplying a large amount of capacity which remains unfilled. Some restriction on the provision of extra capacity should have resulted from the partnership agreements which were frequently concluded between the airlines on a particular route. During the late 1960s these agreements, which provided for the sharing of capacity and some measure of revenue pooling, covered nearly all of BOAC's routes except those to the United States, and BEA earned three-fifths of its receipts within such agreements. However, in practice they do not appear to have had a restrictive effect and BEA defended them by pointing out that its passenger load factor had declined over the period since it had begun to participate.[1] Certainly BA's passenger load factor has, like that of other scheduled carriers, been very low. During the period from 1975–76 to 1977–78 it averaged about 61% on BA's international services. Even taking the month when it was

at its highest the figure was only about 68% whereas charter operators reached a peak of about 90%. They achieve such high load
factors by closely controlling their capacity. Those travelling at the
peak times of the week have to pay a supplementary charge and
when planes become full passengers are fitted into spare seats on
other flights. If bookings turn out to be low flights are cancelled and
passengers transferred to other carriers.

The scheduled carriers' policy of providing an extensive route
network has been expensive because it has been pushed to the point
where a large number of unprofitable services are maintained. Large
losses have consistently been sustained on the secondary domestic
services, on many of the routes to secondary foreign centres and on
most of the overseas services that are operated from British provincial cities. For instance British Airways reports that its revenues fall
short of its expenditure (including depreciation at historic cost) by
10% on the routes from Belfast to Newcastle and London, and by
20% on the Cardiff services.[2] And while the services from London to
North America are profitable those from provincial centres are not.

The departure of BA's services has been timed to suit the convenience of the business traveller. As a result there has been a tendency to avoid early and late starts and, in the case of Europe,
midday flights. Because of environmental restrictions night flights
are not always possible but even where they are permitted they
have, as BA concedes, been avoided. The way in which flights are
timed has obviously tended to depress the utilisation of both crew
and aircraft and in a joint study by the Civil Aviation Authority
(CAA) and BA, known as Cascade, it was assumed by the Corporation that charter operators' utilisation would be 25% higher over the
same routes. British Airways also incurs considerable expense by
providing higher standards of comfort and service than charter
operators. There are about 15% fewer seats on BA's planes than
there would be if the Corporation adopted the less generous seating
densities to which charter firms work.[3] Cabin crews are larger on
scheduled services. When BA's Tridents and Tristars are on scheduled work they have 40–50% more cabin staff than when they are
engaged on charter operations, and this despite the smaller number
of passengers. Staffing levels at stations are also higher and the cost
of free meals and drinks is greater.

Some idea of the high cost of running scheduled services can be
gained from Cascade, which was an investigation of why BA's

expenditure per passenger was so much higher than that of charter operators on three representative routes in Europe. It appears from this and other evidence that BA's costs per passenger were some 75% greater than those of the charter firms because its standards of comfort and service were higher, the utilisation of its aircraft was lower and its load factor was assumed to be 55% as against 85% for charter work. (On the other hand the seasonal variation is greater for charter traffic and this tends to make it more expensive to carry. However there is no need to allow for this because the question at issue is what additional costs BA incurs by carrying *its traffic* in the existing way instead of by charter methods.)

Another reason why BA's costs are so high is that its British built planes tend to be inefficient. As the Board has commented 'US aircraft are more economical on fuel, more productive and reliability is better'.[4] During 1978–79 Super VC 10s, BAC One-Elevens, Tridents, and Concorde accounted for nearly half of the revenue hours flown within British Airways. The Super VC 10 has higher fuel and maintenance costs than the Boeing 707, which is a similar aircraft; and the BAC One-Eleven and Trident series are expensive planes to operate. The Trident 3 is a far more economic aircraft than the Tridents 1 and 2, but its costs per seat mile (including fuel, crew and maintenance) are 6% higher than those of the Boeing 727-200. The latter was one of the aircraft which BEA had wanted to purchase back in 1966 but the Government said that it must buy British. The Corporation had also wanted to acquire Boeing 737-200s but as a result of the Government decision it had to buy BAC One-Eleven 500s and their costs per seat mile are 8% greater. More recently, British Airways would not have purchased Concorde but for the Government's assurance that it would, if necessary, provide the Board with financial assistance. During 1977–78 Concorde made a net loss of £18 million, after depreciation at historic cost, and there was an operating loss of £2 million. This was scarcely surprising as its cost per seat mile was roughly three times that of the Boeing 747. The Government has decided that BA's investment in Concorde should be written off, but as the plane continues to make an operating loss it should probably be withdrawn from service.

Although the use of high cost planes cannot be regarded as an inevitable feature of scheduled operations it is made possible under the IATA system by the absence of price competition and the high level at which fares have been maintained. It also seems possible that the protection which IATA has afforded has enabled British Airways to operate at a low level of efficiency even when allowance has been made for the type of work on which it is engaged and its somewhat inferior aircraft. However, Cascade appeared to show that, when such factors were taken into account, there was no great difference between BA's costs and those of charter operators. Only about 5% of the differential was not explained, and might be due to over-manning and similar causes.[3] Moreover, British Airways concluded, after making a detailed comparison between its European operations and an efficient US domestic airline, that only 25% of the American airline's large cost advantage was attributable to what it described as 'work-place culture'.[4] It would, however, be wrong to take these studies at their face value. In the Anglo-American comparison 'work-place culture' would have played a very much larger part but for the fact that American wage costs are so high that they offset much of the massive productivity lead which the US carriers must be presumed to have displayed. And the way in which BA's costs were adjusted in Cascade meant that it was almost inevitable that there would be no great difference between it and the charter operators. In all the main areas where the Corporation might display inefficiency (except perhaps for maintenance) it was assumed that the whole of the differential between its costs and those of charter operators (as represented by its subsidiary British Airtours) was attributable to the fact that they were not providing the same type of service.

In order to discover whether BA is as efficient as the charter carriers it is necessary to find out what it would cost them to operate scheduled services of similar standards to those which the Corporation provides. Such an investigation has now been made by a charter firm for one of the routes which was included in the original Cascade study. In the latter, BA's costs per passenger (granted a 55% load factor) were about 175% greater than those for charter services (assuming an 85% load factor). However, it appears from the new investigation that the charter firm would be able to provide a scheduled service at a cost per passenger which was only 120% greater than its cost for charter work. If so, BA's cost per passenger is some 25% greater than is necessary. This figure must obviously be treated with caution but the assumptions that were made about load factors and the use of aircraft were either the same or very similar. One important difference between the two studies was that the reduction in seating density, through the use of aircraft for scheduled work, was assumed to be greater by the charter company than by British Airways. This however tends to narrow the cost gap. It is, of course, possible that the charter concern underestimated the extra expenditure which would be required in order to provide a scheduled service, but its estimates appear to be realistic.

That British Airways does not operate at the minimum cost for the type of work on which it is engaged is confirmed by both domestic and international comparisons. According to the CAA, 'forms supplied to the Authority show that, some special cases apart, British Airways has substantially higher costs than other British airlines on domestic services . . . British Airways is consistently a higher cost operator than BMA and Dan-Air even if costs outside the airline's control and specific aircraft costs are excluded'.[5] In civil aviation as in so many other fields, the United States appears to represent the best practice. Unfortunately there is no single American concern with an extensive international network which has a distance per flight, or per passenger, similar to that of British Airways. These closely-related characteristics have a crucial effect on productivity when this is measured by load tonne miles per worker. Long haul airlines have the advantage that they are able to use larger aircraft and to fly them faster, that proportionately less time is wasted while aircraft are on the ground and that part of the work which airline staff perform is determined by the number of passengers rather than by the distance they travel.

Mr William Taussig has argued that by combining the figures for Pan-Am and Allegheny it is possible to obtain a composite concern with characteristics remarkably similar to those of British Airways.[6] During 1978 the average distance per departure was 28% lower for Pan-Am/Allegheny than for BA. Hence, other things equal, British Airways operates under more favourable conditions. Despite this Pan-Am/Allegheny's labour productivity was 114% greater than that of BA. Although there are no other American operators that, like Pan-Am and British Airways, possess a world wide network, there are a number of US carriers that have stage lengths similar to or shorter than that of BA. All of these have a very much higher productivity. The most interesting cases are TWA, which has a considerable overseas network, and Braniff. When they are combined they have an almost identical distance per departure to BA. During 1978 their productivity was 75% greater than that of British Airways.

When manning is examined area by area the Americans turn out to have lower levels in every field. For instance the productivity of cabin attendants (in terms of passenger miles per employee) is 55% greater for Pan-Am/Allegheny and that of ticketing and sales staff (as measured by passengers per worker) is 71% higher. The most striking difference is for maintenance and overhaul personnel where the number of aircraft miles per employee is over 250% greater at Pan-Am/Allegheny, and this despite the fact that British Airways Engine Overhaul has not been treated as part of BA, although less than a third of its work is for other operators. The exclusion of this concern should, incidentally, guard against the danger that comparisons with Pan-Am/Allegheny would be unfair if the latter engaged in sub-contracting to a greater extent.

According to the Chairman of BA, 'The blunt fact is that British Airways, in comparison with its major competitors . . . is in certain areas . . . overstaffed by any form of measurement that we can introduce'. And, after making an efficiency audit, BA has revised its estimates of its manpower requirements down by 9,400.[7] British Airways attributes its low productivity to restrictive practices and the fact that it operates too many different types of aircraft. Moreover much of BA's fleet is composed of British planes which are expensive to maintain, and American operators have relatively small numbers of overhead staff by European standards, partly because of their greater use of computers. Although British Airways' performance leaves much to be desired the Corporation has now recognised that its efficiency needs to be improved, and its productivity has been increasing at about the average rate for major international airlines, which means that the position has been stable and not deteriorating. Between 1968 and 1978 (weighted) traffic per worker increased by around 165% at Air France; 145% at Qantas and Japanese Airlines; 135% at Swissair; 115% at British Airways and KLM; 90–95% at SAS, Lufthansa and Pan-Am and by 40% for Alitalia.

CHARTER COMPETITION AND MARKET SHARE

Although competition between the scheduled carriers has been restricted to quality of service, they have been subjected to some genuine price competition from charter firms. Some countries maintain tight restrictions on charter operators and to this day they carry little or no passenger traffic between the UK and Southern Ireland, the Netherlands, Belgium, South Africa, India and Australia. However in many countries it gradually became established that they could provide a variety of services, of which the most important were inclusive tours and affinity group charters.

Some organisation or affinity, which was not supposed to have travel as its primary purpose, would charter an aircraft and sell seats to its members. Bogus organisations were established and during 1973 affinity group charters were replaced by advanced booking charters (ABCs) on the routes from Britain over the North Atlantic. These services were open to anyone who purchased a ticket more than a minimum period in advance. The rules governing ABCs have been progressively relaxed and in 1977, after years of argument with licensing authorities and Government Departments on both sides of the Atlantic, Laker Airways was permitted to launch Skytrain. One of its features was that seats could not be booked in advance, although this has now been modified.

With the exception of the West Indies and Ghana advance booking charters are restricted to the North Atlantic. However charter operations to most of the European and Mediterranean lands have flourished in the form of inclusive tours, viz. holiday trips for which there is a comprehensive price covering both accommodation and travel. They are largely organised by promoting firms like Thompson Holidays and Inghams, which in the main hire aircraft from operators such as Britannia and Dan-Air, who specialise in this type of work. Originally the price of the package holiday was not allowed to be less than the lowest fare on a scheduled service over the route being flown. But this requirement was subsequently relaxed and in 1972 it was abolished by the CAA. During the mid-1970s charter operators started to provide 'throw-away' inclusive tours, where the accommodation is primitive, and the customer is, in reality, purchasing pure transport. Certain foreign governments, including Spain and Greece, permit charters of this type but others dislike the practice and have prevented it by establishing a minimum charge.

Despite charter competition there has over the past decade been a massive increase in BA's traffic. Between 1968 and 1973 the Board's output increased by over 80%, as Table 8.1 shows. During 1974 and 1975 there was a pause but by 1978 it was 30% greater than in 1973

TABLE 8.1 *British Airways Airline Activities: Output, Productivity and Finances*

	Output	Employment	Average weekly hours worked by manual workers, October week^a	Output per equivalent worker^b	Quantity of capital	Output per unit of labour and capital	Real unit operating costs^bc	Real unit staff costs^bc	Real staff costs per employee^bc	Relative weekly earnings of manual men, October week^a	Real cost of fuel per unit^bc	Real revenue per unit^c	Revenue^c	Gross surplus^c	Gross surplus as % of revenue^c
	(1968 = 100)	(000)		(1968 = 100)	(1968 = 100)	(1968 = 100)	(1968–69 = 100)	(1968–69 = 100)	(1968 = 100)	(1968 = 100)	(1968–69 = 100)	(1968–69 = 100)	(£m, 1978 prices)	(£m, 1978 prices)	(%)
1963^d	62.3	37.5	45.8	68.4	..	..	118.4	117.0	83.8	102.3	130.5	114.3	605	124	20.6
		43.3^d											833^d		21.1^d
1968	100.0	44.7	44.2	100.0	100.0	100.0	100.0	100.0	100.0	100.0	100.0	100.0	858	176	20.5
1969	112.6	46.8	45.3	102.7	100.0	106.4	95.5	99.3	105.4	100.0	91.4	95.3	947	212	22.4
1970	119.3	50.2	44.1	102.4	100.8	108.0	100.9	111.8	113.2	107.2	87.6	88.9	910	110	12.0
1971	131.8	52.6	43.3	108.9	109.0	113.3	92.6	105.0	115.9	111.2	84.2	81.4	942	111	11.8
1972	160.8	53.1	44.0	130.6	118.9	132.5	77.7	87.3	120.4	105.9	72.1	73.0	1,057	186	17.6
1973	182.2	53.2	46.0	145.3	123.0	146.6	75.9	82.7	125.5	106.3	97.0	72.7	1,160	222	19.1
1974	180.4	53.3	45.6	144.1	127.0	143.4	86.7	84.9	122.8	93.3	163.9	73.6	1,124	98	8.7
1975	188.2	52.7	45.0	152.7	131.1	149.3	79.5	79.7	126.2	101.7	143.8	66.5	1,092	80	7.3
1976	202.9	52.7	44.7	165.1	137.7	158.1	80.0	71.7	121.9	94.8	148.1	72.3	1,283	182	14.2
1977	209.4	53.6	45.4	166.6	148.4	156.1	79.0	70.5	119.8	95.2	134.8	68.3	1,235	127	10.3
1978	237.4	54.3	45.5	186.1	157.4	171.2	74.9	65.8	129.7	100.3	113.2	64.9	1,376	146	10.6

Note Output and employment figures were derived from financial year data. The output index comprises sub-indices for long haul and short haul work combined with 1968 (and 1963) net output weights. The sub-indices contained eleven indicators (passenger and freight tonne kilometres for different regions) combined with revenue weights. The unit series were estimated using gross output at 1968–69 (and 1963–64) prices. The quantity of capital is the CSO's estimate for BA's aircraft but includes, during latter years, an allowance for those leased. A capital weight of 36.5% was used.

^a Air transport industry. Manual workers account for a relatively small proportion of BA's employment.

^b Allowance made for the effect of industrial dispute during base year.

^c Financial year (April–March) beginning during year shown.

^d Excludes British Air Services and BEA Airtours.

and 137% greater than in 1968. Nevertheless there has been a considerable reduction in BA's market share. The market in which BA is involved can be roughly measured by taking the number of passengers carried on British aircraft and the number travelling to or from the UK on foreign planes. The Board's share of this traffic declined from 45½% in 1968 to 40% in 1973, and then to 36½% in 1978. During the first part of the period, charter business grew at a spectacular rate and its proportion increased from 18% in 1968 to 27% in 1973 (including foreign non-scheduled operations but excluding BA's charter work). However during the second half of the period there was little growth in non-scheduled work and the charter share fell back. During 1978 it was only 25%, even though Skytrain, which is technically a scheduled service, has been included. The reduction in BA's relative importance after 1973 was not due to charter operations, or to the private scheduled sector, but to the large increase in traffic on foreign scheduled services whose share of the market shot up from 25% in 1973 to 30% in 1978. This rise was partly due to a shift effect: the largest increase in traffic took place on scheduled international routes which is, of course, the place where the scheduled services of foreign airlines are to be found. However, even if attention is confined to scheduled international routes it remains the case that there has, *taking the period as a whole*, been a considerable increase in the role of foreign airlines. Their share of passengers increased from 45½% in 1968 to 51% in 1978. Meanwhile British Airways' stake declined from 47% to 41½%.

This review of the way in which market shares have changed provokes two questions: how have foreign airlines managed to increase their proportion of scheduled traffic, and why have the charter operators not been able to capture more business from British Airways? The increase in foreign operators' share of international scheduled traffic appears to be explained mainly by the fact that passengers usually prefer to travel on their national airline and that the number of foreigners making trips to Britain has increased more rapidly than the number of UK residents making trips abroad. Excluding those on inclusive tours, there was a rise of around 140% in the number of foreigners making trips to Britain compared with an increase of 112% in the number of UK residents going abroad.[8] The reasons why the charter airlines have not succeeded in increasing their traffic more rapidly, despite their very low costs, are more complex and more interesting.

The most obvious explanation is that the openings available to them have been restricted. As we have seen they have been largely confined to inclusive tour work within Europe and the Mediterranean area and to the provision of ABCs and Skytrain services across the Atlantic. Moreover they have been subjected to considerable competition from British Airways which has made selective price reductions in order to stem the loss of traffic. The first pricing response took place as long ago as 1955 when the charter operators were just beginning to provide inclusive tours. BEA started to provide discounts where passengers were travelling on inclusive tours arranged by travel agents. This concession, known as ITX, only secured a relatively small amount of business and did not prevent the growth of charter operations because the agents could not match the prices of the package tour promoters. The latter were able to charge very low prices by taking hotels for the whole of the season and filling up virtually every room.[9] By adjusting their charges and slotting passengers into vacant places they could also utilise nearly all of the seats on the planes which they hired. BEA was not able to do this and it is interesting to observe that during the late 1960s the load factors on its Spanish routes, where holiday traffic bulked large, were only fractionally higher than they were on the Scandinavian services, where it was much less important.[10] This suggests that the discounts which BEA provided on an increasing scale were not based on its operating costs, and that it was practising price discrimination.

From around 1970 BOAC and BEA responded to the continued rise of charter traffic by selling part of their capacity on a wholesale basis. In contrast to ITX, where a discount was given on individual seats, they started to sell off blocks of seats to those organising package tours under a number of fare arrangements such as SGIT (Special Group Inclusive Tour). It was hoped that in this way it would be possible to reduce reservation and marketing costs and to avoid the empty seats that were entailed by the sale of individual seats to the airways' traditional customers. It therefore seems possible that, in contrast to ITX, part charters represent a legitimate commercial response to competition. A joint investigation by BA and the CAA throws some light on the relationship between prices and costs. In this study BA's expenditure, using 1976–77 budget data, was distributed between fare types for six representative routes in Europe. Where there was no evidence of any variation between fare types expenditure per passenger was deemed to be the same. This was, for instance, the treatment accorded to reservation and marketing costs except for part charter traffic where they are negligible and were disregarded. Expenditure which was obviously being incurred in respect of a particular passenger category was assigned to that category, e.g., the cost of meals and cabin service for first class passengers. In the case of other expenditure — including aircraft operating, maintenance and replacement costs — it was assumed that the cost per seat mile would, after allowing for the lower first class seating density, be uniform but that the cost per passenger would vary in line with occupancy rates. The budgeted load factor was used for the first class cabins and an occupancy rate of 85% was adopted for part charter work for inclusive tour operators (SGIT and TOP), where reservations are controlled in order to obtain a high load factor. The occupancy rate in the rest of the plane and hence for other types of traffic (apart from IPEX) was then estimated using the overall passenger load factor which it was hoped to achieve.[11] In this way allowance was made for the fact that BA is put to considerable expense in providing a large amount of capacity which remains unfilled in order that intending normal economy passengers will be able to obtain a seat on the flight of their choice.

In the interests of convenience BA also maintains a frequent service and this means that on some routes it is uneconomic to use large, low cost aircraft. It was therefore decided to estimate what BA's costs would have been if it had cut out flights and consolidated traffic into large planes or if, alternatively, it had maintained its existing frequency but catered only for first class, normal economy and other traffic for which a frequent service was being provided. This would have involved the use of small high-cost aircraft, and the difference between their cost and that of large aircraft was regarded as the price of providing a convenient service and was ascribed to 'on demand' traffic. This almost certainly gives an exaggerated impression of the costs of convenience because what was relevant was the additional expense of having, as at present, to operate a medium size, medium cost plane as opposed to a large low cost aircraft. It is also questionable whether BA needed to provide such a frequent service in order to satisfy the requirements of first and normal economy passengers. On one of the routes, which was cited as an example, fifty-three return services were being operated per week in summer and forty-six in winter. Even BA's own studies suggested that it was providing about 10% more flights than were necessary.[12]

TABLE 8.2   *British Airways' Revenue by Fare Type as a Percentage of its Operating Costs on European Routes*

Route	First Class	Normal Economy	Youth and Spouse	Excursion	ITX	SGIT	IPEX[a]
			Before allowing for schedule convenience				
1	63	111	94	71	61	—	314
2	62	157	106	110	85	73	—
3	93	117	91	72	65	—	329
4	50	117	86	84	61	—	—
5	115	183	136	136	114	75	—
6	—	145	126	107	93	83	—
			After allowing for schedule convenience				
1	60	105	88	79	66	—	314
2	49	130	83	135	107	97	—
3	91	117	88	79	69	—	329
4	47	110	82	97	71	—	—
5	103	167	126	156	131	90	—

[a] Instant purchase excursion.

Table 8.2 summarises the results of the BA/CAA investigation. In the top section no adjustment has been made in respect of frequency and the figures for first class, normal economy and youth and spouse traffic may give a somewhat exaggerated impression of their profitability. The bottom part shows the position after attributing the (over-estimated) cost of convenience to these fare categories and must show them in an unfavourable light, especially in the case of route two, where on first class, normal economy and youth and spouse tickets it would have been necessary to use Trident 2s, which have very high costs. The Table shows that there was a marked variation in the profitability of different types of traffic. Apart from IPEX, which is a special case, the most lucrative traffic was passengers who pay the standard fare and buy what are described as normal economy tickets. (Although there was a marked variation within this category — and certain others — due to pro-rating, which occurs when passengers on a multi-stage journey are charged the tapered and therefore relatively low through fare between the terminal points instead of the sum of the fares for the separate hops.) In contrast first class traffic tended to be very unprofitable and only on the route which was most profitable did revenue exceed costs.

Inclusive tour work, in the form of ITX and SGIT traffic, was also very unprofitable. The only cases in which a positive margin was shown were ITX traffic on the best route and ITX work on route two after an excessive amount of expenditure had been attributed to other categories. Traffic travelling on excursion and youth and spouse tickets occupied an intermediate position. On three of the services excursion work appeared to be unremunerative. However, on two of these (routes three and four) the tickets were for weekend excursions which were conceivably making use of otherwise unproductive capacity.

Normal economy traffic, which was the one really profitable type of work, consists in the main of those travelling on business. The price elasticity for this type of traffic is known to be very low and a regression study made within the Department of Trade found no relationship between fares and the volume of business travel to Western Europe.[13] The BA/CAA investigation therefore provokes the suspicion that British Airways overcharges those travelling on normal economy tickets, in order to generate profits out of which to meet the losses that it incurs where traffic is highly elastic, because it is in competition with charter operators. It seems significant that, as the CAA observes, 'The charter-competitive fares generally did not cover costs'.[14] This was also true of first class traffic where there is no charter competition. But here cross-subsidisation is explained by BA's desire to provide a high quality service and the fact that first class fares would, if they were based on costs, be prohibitive.

That BA has been engaging in predatory pricing has been confirmed by the subsequent investigations that have been conducted by the CAA and British Airways. About ten more routes have so far been investigated and, unlike the first batch, they are not all confined to Europe. No results have been published but it is known that the same pattern has emerged: BA overcharges its normal economy passengers and tends to make a loss on its discount fares. In some cases normal fares are greatly in excess of costs. According to the CAA, 'Studies conducted by the Authority in conjunction with British Airways show that, in relation to fare-type costs, the normal economy class fares to Scandinavia are exceptionally profitable. There would appear to be much substance in the view that British Airways and SAS [the Scandinavian operator] have been consistently exploiting full-fare passengers on the routes between the United Kingdom and Scandinavia'.[15] There appears to be some tendency for normal economy fares to be particularly high on routes like those to Scandinavia where charter traffic is or was relatively unimportant. In a study of sixteen European routes Messrs Cooper and Maynard found a 0.7 correlation between the fare per mile in 1970 and the proportion of charter traffic on the route.[10] However subsequent investigations by the CAA, using a larger and more representative sample of routes, produced a much lower figure and showed that a high concentration of charter traffic appeared to have the effect of encouraging airlines to introduce a much wider range of fares.

One development which has taken place in Europe since the original BA/CAA inquiry into fares has been the introduction of advance purchase excursion fares (APEX). They were first introduced under the name 'Early Bird' by BOAC in 1970. The distinctive feature of APEX was not advance purchase or the minimum stay requirement but the fact that control could be exercised over bookings in order to ensure that a high occupancy rate was obtained for the seats that were set aside for passengers travelling on this type of ticket. Until 1975 APEX was only available on a few routes (viz. to the Caribbean, Hong Kong and Johannesburg) but during that year it was introduced on the North Atlantic and in 1977 APEX fares made their appearance on BA's European routes and were also introduced to Australia. During the following year there was a further widening of their availability. The introduction of APEX on the North Atlantic meant that the gap between excursion fares and the ABC fare was cut in half and in Europe the saving was even more dramatic. This provokes the question of whether APEX fares are based on costs or whether they constitute the latest form of predatory pricing.

The investigations which BA and the CAA have carried out show that on the North Atlantic, where the Board's efficiency is at its highest, APEX fares just about cover costs. However this is not the case in Europe, where BA is less efficient, and where APEX was introduced in order to ward off competition from the charter airlines. Moreover it seems likely that the costs of carrying APEX traffic have been understated. It is assumed that BA will be able to obtain a load factor of around 85% for this type of work because this is what charter operators achieve. But they only do so by providing far less capacity during the winter months, and 85% is therefore a misleading figure to use when analysing costs.

COSTS, PRICES AND PROFITS

The increase in the availability of concessionary fares and in the size of the discounts has been accompanied by a substantial reduction in BA's revenue per unit of output, though the latter development is not an inevitable consequence of the former. Between 1968–69 and 1978–79 the Board's unit revenue declined by 35%. However, as can be seen from Table 8.1, most of the reduction took place during the first part of the period and since 1975 prices have been more or less stable. The fall in prices could not have taken place without there being a large reduction in unit costs. By 1978–79 they were a quarter lower than they had been in 1968–69. This was due to the massive increase in output per worker which, because there was only a moderate increase in staff costs per employee, led to a fall of nearly 35% in unit staff costs. This fall would have had a greater impact on the overall level of costs but for an increase in unit fuel costs due to the rise in petroleum prices. During the second half of the period higher fuel costs offset lower staff costs and BA's unit costs were much the same in 1978–79 as they had been in 1973–74.

Because, over the course of the decade, the reduction in unit revenue has exceeded the fall in costs, profitability has fallen. In 1968–69 British Airways had a gross margin of just over 20% and but for the pilots' strike at BOAC the figure would have been significantly higher. During 1978–79 the gross margin was little more than 10%, although this was slightly better than in 1975-76 when the figure was as low as 7%. In 1968–69 there was a net profit of something like £75 million but a decade later the figure was only around £20 million, which was a return of about 2% on net assets. There is a marked variation in the profitability of the different divisions into which BA is now organised. In 1978–79 virtually all of the surplus after historic cost depreciation was earned on the routes to Asia and Australia, to Africa and Central America, and to North and East Europe. These are the regions in which there is relatively little competition from charter operators and prices are still fixed in the old way through IATA. However for BA's other services — across the North Atlantic, to Benelux and the Mediterranean region, from provincial centres to the continent and within the UK —

almost no surplus was shown and there must, after depreciation at replacement cost, have been a substantial loss. These are the foreign routes where British Airways faces the heaviest competition from charter operators and where, as in the case of the North Atlantic, price fixing by the scheduled operators has to some extent broken down.

This has been a highly critical chapter, though not so much of British Airways as of the oligopolistic market within which it operates. However it would be churlish not to acknowledge that BA is aware of the weaknesses of the scheduled system, of its low productivity and of the need to provide cheap travel; and it has ambitious plans to reshape its operations.

CHAPTER 9

Postal Services

The mail services that are operated by the Post Office (PO) will be regarded as a separate industry. They are now being split off from telecommunications and are to become a separate corporation. The postal business includes not only the letter post, where the Post Office has a monopoly, but also the parcel service where it does not. The postal services (PS) also include non-mail work which is undertaken at post office and sub-post office counters on behalf of government departments and the Giro, which will be regarded as forming part of posts.

PROBLEMS AND PLANS

By 1968 it was evident that the postal services were getting into difficulties. Up to the mid-1960s output had been growing at a moderate rate, but during 1968 production was no higher than it had been five years earlier and was significantly lower than in 1966. Employment was slowly rising and OEW was no greater in 1968 than it had been in 1963, and was somewhat lower than in 1966. The postal services are highly labour intensive and the Post Office increased charges by 18% over the period from 1963–64 to 1968–69. Postal prices had previously been more or less stable and the rise in charges helps to explain why output had stopped growing. A vicious circle was developing in which falling output led to a reduction in productivity and this, in turn, resulted in higher prices and lower output.

Despite these discouraging developments the postal authorities remained optimistic. At the beginning of 1968 it was forecast that during the next five years the volume of business would grow by

10%, the number of staff would rise by only 1% and productivity would consequently increase by something under 2% p.a.[1] These forecasts were unrealistic. The PO was in the process of making a large increase in postal charges and it was assumed that parcels traffic would increase, although there had been a substantial decline both in the PO and elsewhere in the public sector. Moreover, it was (rightly) expected that the mail services would face increased competition from telecommunications. The PO was expecting that trunk calls would, during coming years, increase by 13% p.a.[1] In the previous quinquennium there had been a rise of only 7½% p.a. The forecast that postal business would increase turned out to be very wide of the mark. As we shall see it fell.

It is, of course, easy to be wise after the event and the Prices and Incomes Board, which examined the PO's projections, did not recognise that they were over-optimistic.[2] Nevertheless the PO is open to criticism for having gone on forecasting that postal output would increase. As late as 1970 it still believed that the volume of business would grow by 2% p.a. although some of its officials were sceptical.[3] Because it did not see what was happening to PS production the Post Office did not realise how gloomy productivity prospects had become. However an increase in traffic was not the only possible source of productivity growth and what we must now try to discover is whether the PO was making any moves which would reduce costs.

During the autumn of 1968 the Post Office recast its mail services and introduced the first and second class post. One of the most important features of the letter services is that the volume of work varies sharply during the course of the day. There is one peak of activity around breakfast time when postmen are making the first delivery. The second peak occurs during the late afternoon and evening when about 70% of letter mail is posted. Those items which are accorded priority and will be delivered the next morning have to be sorted in time for their overnight dispatch. In order to secure the prompt delivery of letters and to reduce the volume of work during the evening peak it was the practice to defer the sorting of a major part of all printed papers, which used to be carried at a cheap rate. In 1966 it was decided to change to the present system of first and second class mail because the new sorting machines could not handle unsealed items and, due to the growth in traffic, it was becoming difficult to sort all letters in time for their overnight dispatch. Moreover the Post Office regarded the distinction between letters and printed papers as anomalous and believed that all mail users should have the choice between a fast service at a premium price or a slower service at a reduced rate.

This would only be of benefit to customers if the fall in evening sorting work led to a reduction in costs, which would enable the Post Office to bring down the average price for carrying letters. However, the Post Office believed there would be little if any saving — although it never made any detailed costing investigations — because it had been found that the productivity of workers engaged on sorting was considerably higher during the evening peak period than at off peak times. Other things being equal, the transfer of work and workers away from the peak would therefore depress output per worker, and the fall would be even larger if the PO did not manage to maintain the previous rate of working during the peak or decided, as it seemed to be planning, to reduce the pressure of work with the object of ensuring that first class mail was sorted on time.[4] It was expected that when the new postal arrangements were introduced it would be necessary to employ less labour at premium rates in order to cope with mail which had to be sorted during the evening. However unless postmen were willing to accept a reduction in earnings this saving would not materialise, and the new system would simply lead to a fall in productivity and an increase in costs.

At the same time as the introduction of the first and second class posts was being mooted the Post Office was drawing up a programme by which the sorting of both letters and parcels would be mechanised. This activity was almost entirely performed by hand and was a particularly time consuming activity because each item was, on average, sorted about three times. However the PO had managed to develop machines which would greatly improve the productivity of those engaged on sorting. The key machine for letters enables the operator to type the postal code on the envelope in the form of chemical dots. These can then be read by subsequent machines and put into the appropriate destination box in the inward sorting office and then, after dispatch, at the outward office. Because sorting machines are expensive but highly productive, mechanisation is only worth while where there is a large throughput and it was thus necessary to concentrate traffic on a limited number of sorting offices. In the case of the letter post it was planned that by 1976 about seventy-five mechanised offices would be in operation and

TABLE 9.1 Postal Services: Output, Productivity and Finances

	Output	Employment[a]	Average weekly hours worked by full time postmen	Output per equivalent worker	Real unit operating costs[bc]	Real unit staff costs[bc]	Real staff costs per employee[abc]	Real revenue per unit[b]	Revenue[b]	Gross surplus[bc]	Gross surplus as % of revenue[bc]	Net surplus[bc]
	(1968 = 100)	(000)		(1968 = 100)	(1968–69 = 100)				(£m, 1978 prices)		(%)	(£m, 1978 prices)
1963[d]	100.8	190.2	51.5	101.0	85.1	82.7	87.3	84.7	945	22	2.3	11
1966[d]	104.1	192.8	50.5	104.2	..	..	..	..	..	..	..	..
1968[d]	100.0	195.5	49.4	100.0	100.0	100.0	100.0	100.0	1,112	41	3.7	24
1969[d]	99.4	197.2	50.3	97.5	105.0	105.4	104.9	101.4	1,127	−1	−0.1	−23
1970	94.0	198.9	50.2	91.5	112.4	114.7	104.6	97.9	1,010	−106	−10.5	−130
1971[e]	93.3	199.7	50.3	90.2	120.6	125.6	117.0	120.4	1,270	45	3.5	17
1972	95.2	199.1	50.3	92.4	121.7	127.2	121.5	117.7	1,276	14	1.1	−21
1973	96.8	197.3	51.7	93.2	121.4	128.3	126.2	117.5	1,301	17	1.3	−11
1974	96.7	197.4	52.3	92.5	130.6	141.5	137.3	118.9	1,318	−62	−4.7	−91
1975	89.3	202.1	49.5	86.2	143.0	156.3	135.9	150.8	1,506	140	9.3	111
1976	84.6	198.1	49.8	83.1	139.9	151.8	130.7	150.0	1,460	161	11.1	131
1977	84.8	194.8	50.8	83.7	134.3	144.6	129.0	145.3	1,442	171	11.9	142 / 131[f]
1978	88.5	193.7	50.9	87.7	137.4	147.6	137.4	139.6	1,456	95	6.5	54

Note Output and employment figures were derived from financial year data. The output index comprises twenty-one indicators (number of items and counter transactions handled) combined with 1968–69 (and 1963–64) revenue weights, except that payments for conveyance were excluded. The per unit series were estimated using gross output at 1968–69 (and 1963–64) prices.

[a] Part time staff are counted as half. Includes sub-postmasters.
[b] Financial year (April–March) beginning during year shown.
[c] Before provision for pension deficiency contributions.
[d] Excludes savings department.
[e] There was a serious industrial dispute during early 1971.
[f] Includes supplementary depreciation on buildings, hitherto ignored.

that they would handle about 75% of all traffic.[5] For parcels it was intended that there would be around thirty concentration points and that the new system would be complete by the late 1970s. The mechanisation of sorting would, it was hoped, eliminate over 9,000 jobs.[6]

Although this was significant it was only equivalent to 5% of the total labour force and there was not going to be much benefit until the programme was in an advanced stage. Moreover part of the saving would be offset by the capital charges on the capital expenditure that would be necessary, though it was estimated that there would be a handsome return in dcf terms. It was therefore apparent, as the Prices and Incomes Board commented, that there was a pressing need to make savings by other means.[6] One possibility was to reduce the loss which was being incurred on collection and delivery in rural areas. Although the PO charged a uniform rate it was estimated that rural services cost an extra £50 million to provide. However, both the Government and the PO regarded the cross-subsidisation between urban and rural services as being desirable for reasons which were too obvious to require explanation.[7]

OUTPUT

Between 1968 and 1978 output fell by 12%, as Table 9.1 indicates. The amount of non-mail work performed at counters and by Giro increased but the volume of letters and parcels declined by 15%. It is natural to suppose that this was the inevitable consequence of the spectacular growth in the ownership of telephones and of the extension of subscriber trunk dialling. However the UK appears to be the only major developed country in the world, apart from Australia and perhaps Italy, in which letter traffic was lower in 1977 than it had been in 1968, despite the fact that not a few have also had very large increases in phone ownership. The volume of mail would not have declined so rapidly, and might even have increased, but for the huge rise in postal rates and the reduction in the quality of service. Between 1968 and 1978 there was an increase of 35% in the cost of using the letter and parcel post. Even if the price elasticity is only 0.2, as the PO seems to believe, this rise would have led to a reduction of about 5% in total PS output.[8] Due to the increase in charges there has been a large reduction in the volume of Christmas cards, postcards and pools traffic, although the postal strike also had an adverse effect on work for the pools.

At first sight the quality of the first class post appears to have remained about the same, with 89% of letters arriving on the working day after posting in 1978–79 as against 91½% in 1968–69. However delivery periods are measured from the time at which the letter arrives at the sorting office. Hence if a letter misses the last collection between Monday and Friday it is treated as having been posted the next day and if it is posted on Sunday it is now dated Monday. During 1975 the PO withdrew the Sunday collection and the restricted collections which used to be made between 7 and 8 p.m. It was estimated that, unless letters were posted earlier, at least 9% of first class (and 6% of second class) letters would be delayed.[9] The proportion of second class mail delivered on the second working day after postage has declined from about 90% in 1968–69 to 66% in 1977–78.[10] In 1978 the PO tried to reinstate Sunday collections but the Union of Post Office Workers (UPW) refused, although its leadership was in favour.

The volume of mail would have declined slightly less rapidly if the PS had made the most of its opportunities to gain and retain business. That it has not done so is shown by the relatively small amount of advertising material which it carries. The PO only handles about 40 million unaddressed items, although the market amounts to about 800 million items per year, which is equivalent to 8% of the letter traffic which the PO handles. Such material can obviously be delivered cheaply because no sorting is necessary but in 1966 UPW imposed an embargo on the ground that postmen would be demeaned by handling it. This ban has at long last been withdrawn but due to continued opposition in some parts of the country the PO's marketing efforts have been severely restricted. Direct mail advertising — unsolicited items bearing an address — forms a relatively low proportion of UK mail (8%) and in Japan and the USA the percentage is two or three times as great. The Post Office believes that it has considerable opportunities to increase the volume of direct mail through better marketing.[11]

The PO has of late been making greater promotional efforts and since the early 1960s it has offered discounts of up to 30% to those posting large quantities or pre-sorted mail, if they are prepared for its delivery to be delayed. However only 5% of all mail is carried at a concessionary rate and there are various types of mail where the

PO's costs are below average but for which there is no rebate or it is insufficient, e.g., bulk postings of mail that will be delivered locally and direct mail addressed to business premises, where the cost of household delivery is avoided. It is, however, important not to get carried away, like the Carter Committee, and advocate that discounts be granted where they have no economic justification. The Committee proposed that the PO should make selective price cuts in order to secure traffic which would involve very little extra cost because it could be sorted during slack periods and delivered when postmen make their second rounds.[12] What this ignores is that if the labour force is properly adjusted to the volume of work there will be no slack periods at sorting offices and that the amount of time required for letter delivery is by no means independent of the volume handled. Moreover, as we shall see, there is no need for a comprehensive second letter delivery. However, some mail can be delivered at little or no extra cost on the days when traffic is light — for instance, on Tuesdays.[13]

EMPLOYMENT AND PRODUCTIVITY

Between 1968 and 1975 the postal labour force increased from 195,000 to 202,000 but by 1978 it had dropped back to 194,000. The combination of rising employment and declining output led, over the period 1968–75 to a substantial reduction in productivity. During 1978 OEW was a little higher than it had been in 1976–77 but was still 12% lower than in 1968. It may be maintained that there is nothing remarkable or discreditable about this fall: (a) because there is little scope for making productivity gains in posts; and (b) because a large part of the labour involved in carrying mail is a fixed cost. The Post Office has argued that only 35% of the labour time used on the mail services relates to sorting and other operations where the number of staff hours bears a fairly direct relationship to the amount of traffic.[14]

It may appear self-evident that the amount of time spent on delivery (33% for postmen) will be unaffected by volume but, as anybody who has ever engaged in household delivery can testify, this takes far longer than it does to simply walk along the street. An investigation by the Post Office led to the conclusion that for every 10% by which traffic falls it should ultimately be possible to make a saving of 7.5% in the delivery time for parcels and 4% for letters.[15]

This figure appears surprisingly low. In urban areas the second delivery accounts for about 16% as many letters as the first and takes about 40% as long.[16] This suggests that for every 10% by which volume falls the PO should be able to cut delivery time by 7%, or by a greater amount if allowance is made for the second delivery being a more leisurely affair than the first. None of these figures take any account of preparation, which is the time that postmen spend arranging their mail in the order in which it is to be delivered. Preparation accounts for about a third of the time spent on delivery and its length should vary directly with the quantity of mail. If it is assumed that for every 10% by which traffic declines there will be a reduction of only 5% in delivery time, excluding preparation, a fall of 10% in postal output will cause postmen's productivity to decline by a mere 1¼% providing, of course, that time devoted to other activities is adjusted in line with traffic.

The other elements in postal employment which appear at first sight to be fixed are collection and the movement of letters and parcels to and from stations and between sorting offices. These are much less important than delivery (at only 10%) and might well, on closer examination, turn out to vary partly with volume. Moreover the Post Office has managed to make significant savings in the amount of time devoted to collection and station and inter-office transport. Between 1968–69 and 1978–79 there was a reduction of around 15% for each of these activities, despite a partial switch from rail to road for the trunk movement of parcels. However there was only a fractional fall (about 2%) in the aggregate time spent on delivery and sorting, although sorting is clearly a variable cost. Between 1968–69 and 1978–79 there was a decline of 10% in the volume of mail per sorting hour. This was partly due to the introduction of the two tier postal system. 'As was foreseen', the Post Office commented, 'productivity during the evening sorting period has declined because the pressure to get through excessive peaks of work in the brief periods available between the main evening collections and the first evening despatches has been reduced'.[17] Another reason for the decline in efficiency was the progressive concentration of work into large sorting offices, which were more difficult to manage, where productivity tended to be low, workers were less cooperative and the UPW was more powerful.

Having dealt with the contention that there is relatively little scope to reduce postal employment when traffic declines, let us turn to the supposition that the postal services have little opportunity to make productivity gains. This is implausible because OMY is much higher in some foreign countries and, although productivity appears to have been stagnant in most foreign countries, there has been a significant improvement in the United States. Between 1968–69 and 1977–78 there was an increase of 29% in the number of items carried per equivalent employee, though this may give a slightly exaggerated impression of the progress that was made.[18] Comparisons of productivity levels are fraught with difficulty because of differences in the number of deliveries per day, the composition of traffic, the extent to which post offices are provided and the amount of work that they undertake. However, it is possible to make some rough adjustments. For instance, where a foreign administration did not provide a second delivery the British postal labour force was reduced by the number of workers that could be dispensed with if it made only one. According to my estimates the number of weighted items per equivalent worker was, during 1978, around 135% greater in the US than in the UK, and in the mid 1970s it appears to have been 30% larger in Holland, 25% higher in Sweden and 15% larger in Australia. On the other hand productivity seems to have been 10–15% lower in Germany, France and Belgium. However as postal administrations tend everywhere to be inefficient no comfort can be drawn from the fact that Britain compares favourably with some foreign countries. What is significant is that OMY is so much higher in the United States and also in Japan and Switzerland.[19]

International comparisons are by no means the only reason for believing that there is considerable scope for higher productivity in the British postal service. Postmen tend to work very long hours. During 1978 they averaged about fifty-one hours per week compared with the general average of forty-three and a half for manual men in manufacturing. Long overtime and low basic rates are usually associated with an inefficient use of labour and the postal services are no exception.[20] The Post Office discovered during the latter part of the 1960s that substantial savings in labour could be made by using work study and introducing better working methods. In 1965 McKinsey & Co., the management consultants, were called in to advise on the way in which the efficiency of the postal services could be improved. A number of investigations were launched of which the most important was an examination by study teams of more than sixty of the larger sorting offices. It was discovered that a substantial proportion of postmen's time was being spent unproductively and that it should be possible to make significant savings. In addition to this gain, which was the fruit of conventional work study techniques, a research group set up in 1966 had devised a new method by which the number of staff engaged on sorting could be adjusted to the volume of work. Remarkable as it may appear the Post Office did not (and still does not) have reliable information on the volume of traffic being handled at each sorting office. A detailed count is made over one week each October and there is continuous and accurate information for those letters which go through stamp cancelling machines. But there is no continuous information for 40% of all letters or for the average number of sortings required. The group thought out a procedure by which traffic could be counted at no extra cost. It would then be possible, by applying standard times established through work study, to discover how many men were required on each operation. Experiments at nine places during 1969–70 suggested that it would be possible to cut staff costs in letter sorting offices by 15%.[21]

It had also been found that productivity could be raised by improving the design of traditional sorting equipment. A new type of table had been devised for those engaged on positioning letters for cancellation, which led to a reduction in arm movements. An experiment at the Ipswich office showed that when it was used workers could outpace the automatic letter facer — one of the new pieces of equipment by which sorting is being mechanised. The bank of pigeon-holes into which letters are sorted has only forty-eight compartments which means that re-sorting is often necessary. If wings were fitted, postmen engaged on preparation could sort into a much larger number, thereby saving a substantial amount of time.

When study teams visited local offices it was discovered that delivery rounds were often badly routed and that it was possible, by making common sense changes, to secure a saving of something like 15%. The Post Office believed that further gains could be made by using work study techniques; and the Secretary of UPW was impressed, when he visited Sweden, at the speed with which their postmen moved and concluded that significant gains in productivity could be made through the use of incentive payments. It had also been discovered, as a result of the McKinsey investigations, that it was possible to cut the cost of operating post offices. For instance some of the Corporation's counters could be replaced by sub-offices.

The PO estimates that the cost per minute of productive time is 33–50% greater for its own post offices than for sub-offices.[22]

Another way in which the Post Office could raise efficiency would be to cut out the second letter delivery. At about the same time that McKinseys were called in the PO began to give serious consideration to its discontinuation. In urban areas the first delivery occupies the period from 7 a.m. to about 9.45 a.m. and the second delivery usually takes place between 11 a.m. and 12.36 p.m., the intervening period being spent on sorting and preparing the letters and on a meal break. Because on the second delivery postmen have to cover a greater distance for each letter that is delivered their productivity is relatively low. Only about half as many letters are delivered per hour of preparation and walking time as during the first delivery.[16] The PO estimates that if it eliminated the second delivery and extended the first delivery into the afternoon it would be able to reduce its employment by around 10,000.[23]

The objection to doing this is, of course, that many letters would arrive later and that some would not be delivered until the next day. During 1976, 8.7% of all first class mail arrived by the second delivery. If this were discontinued, about a quarter of the post would be delivered during the latter part of the extended first delivery, and it would be possible to include letters which arrived too late for the present first delivery. Hence 6.5% of mail would arrive the next day, viz. 75% of 8.7%.[24] However it might well be possible to cut this figure. A second delivery could be made to a limited number of large business concerns that would, together with most other firms, have received their mail during the first wave of deliveries. In 1975–76 nearly 45% of all letters were received by 175,000 large recipients who accounted for about four-fifths of all mail delivered to non-residential addresses. It should also be possible to improve the PO's transport arrangements so that more letters arrived in time for the initial round of deliveries. At present no letter posted in Newcastle after 4.30 p.m. will reach anywhere south of Yorkshire — save for some places in Lincolnshire — in time for the first delivery.[25] It should not be beyond the wit of man to do better than this. Although the withdrawal of the second delivery should only result in a small proportion of mail arriving a day later, residential areas would not receive their letters so early. Market research carried out when the withdrawal of the second delivery was first being mooted showed that, though most householders would be opposed to an extended first delivery, two-thirds of town workers would not be unduly concerned if there were only one delivery during the late morning, and that 30% of all letters arrive after the recipients have left home.[26]

At the end of 1971 the Post Office made an important declaration of policy entitled *Reshaping Britain's Postal Service*. It stated that, if the programme which it put forward were carried out, postal employment would drop by about 25,000 by 1978. Mechanisation was expected to account for a staff saving of 5,000, the elimination of the second delivery and other minor service cuts would lead to a reduction of around 7,500, and the remaining 12,500 would be contributed by the use of work study and the adoption of better working methods.[27] This was a surprisingly small number in view of the large opportunities for economy which the PO had already identified. One reason was that the Post Office believed that, because of house building and the growth in the number of addresses, about 500 more postmen were needed each year. If so, around 3,000 additional jobs would have been created by 1978.

Had the reshaping proposals been carried out PS employment would have fallen to 175,000 in 1978. But at that time there were still 194,000 workers and this despite the fact that output was over 10% lower than it had been during the early 1970s. If the Post Office had managed both to make the saving planned and to reduce its labour force in line with production, employment would have dropped to about 155,000, which is 20% less than the number actually engaged.

Unfortunately the Corporation decided to put off the withdrawal of the second letter delivery when the Post Office Users' National Council (POUNC) objected to its discontinuance, and the PO's hope that the Carter Review Committee would recommend its termination was disappointed. Some of the savings which withdrawal would have conferred, together with some additional economies, could have been obtained through the use of more part-time staff. This was proposed, not for the first time, in the reshaping document. However UPW was adamantly opposed, although part-timers are widely employed on the Continent. The Union also blocked the introduction of continuous traffic measurement and of work study to determine manning levels on sorting. In December 1971 the Union conference rejected the Executive's advice and turned down the idea of a productivity deal incorporating these proposals. This decision was not reversed although the Executive tried on a number of occasions to persuade the conference to adopt a more progressive policy.[28] The improved equipment for use in the facing and sorting of letters fell foul of UPW's decision in 1972 not to cooperate with mechanisation or other new developments. By 1975, when this ban was lifted, management had lost its enthusiasm and wing fittings for sorting frames have only been introduced in a few places. The restrictive attitudes of postal workers, together with the lengthy investigations which have under existing arrangements to be undertaken, also explain why so little has been done to adjust the number of staff to the fall in traffic.[29] If the PO had been more determined it could, after a decent interval, and on the occasion of a major price increase (mid-1974), have rejected POUNC's advice and withdrawn the second letter delivery. It could have disregarded UPW and introduced traffic measurement and work study. The Union would have been most reluctant to call a national strike after the defeat that it had suffered during 1971, and it is difficult for unions to prevent local productivity deals and a gradual crumbling of resistance.

The ineptitude of PO management and the intransigence of postal workers also help to explain why so little progress has been made with the mechanisation of sorting. As we have seen it was originally intended that the mechanisation programme for letters would be completed by 1976. However progress was from the beginning far slower than had been intended. According to Mr Michael Corby, who witnessed what happened from within the PO, 'Although the Postal Mechanisation Department was nominally responsible for projects it had little formal power . . . and details of planning were scattered among headquarters, regional and head post office levels. This system provided ample scope for alibis and excuses for delays and mistakes. Coupled with bureaucratic inertia it resulted in the planning process becoming drawn out. Planning meetings often contained far too many people to accomplish anything beyond demands for further studies, and senior people tended to become enmeshed in problems about mail bag seals, labels, railway time tables, loading bay platform heights and the like'.[30] There were also doubts about whether mechanisation was worth while and these came to the surface after the postal strike when traffic slumped. As a result the PO embarked on a series of studies to decide whether and how mechanisation should take place. In mid-1972 UPW decided not to cooperate with mechanisation until a comprehensive agreement had been reached about its scope and timing. It was not until October 1973 that a joint working party recommended that mechanisation should go forward but that instead of 120 mechanised sorting offices — the number which had been adopted in a previous review — there should only be 80, viz. the original figure, though not the original plan. At long last in mid-1975, after the PO had agreed to make a special payment in respect of postal mechanisation, UPW lifted its ban.[31] The mechanisation programme has slipped badly since 1975 due to union objections and other difficulties, and it will not be completed until 1983 or after.[32]

Although twenty-three mechanised offices were in use by the spring of 1979 there has so far been little, if any, saving in manpower because not until a very late stage will it be worth doing a mechanised sort at the receiving end. The PO now estimates that there will only be a staff saving of 6,000, which is considerably less than was originally hoped.[33] Moreover the level of productivity which is being achieved by those who encode letters is at present about 15% below the target level. The reason is that the PO has conceded that Postmen Higher Grade should be employed although special staff, who would probably be largely female, are required. Moreover the Monopolies Commission reports that 'the United Kingdom has fallen behind other countries, both in the development of [new] mechanisation techniques, and in their implementation'.[34]

Costs, Prices and Profits

Between 1968–69 and 1978–79 unit costs rose by 37%. This was due to the fall in productivity and the increase of 48% in staff costs per unit of output. During the period up to 1975–76, when the increase in costs took place, there was a relatively large rise in staff costs per employee. Since then unit costs have fallen back slightly as there has been some recovery in productivity and staff costs per employee were only a little higher in 1978–79 than they had been in 1975–76.

Up to 1974–75 postal charges lagged behind costs and profitability deteriorated to the point where a large gross loss was being sustained. However during 1975–76, after price restraint had come to an end, there was a spectacular increase in charges and the PS earned a substantial net surplus. By 1978–79 prices were 40% greater than they had been in 1968–69, although they were somewhat lower than in 1975–76. Because the rise in prices was even larger than the growth in costs the gross margin rose from about

3½% in 1968–69 to 6½% in 1978–79 and the net profit increased from £25 million to £55 million. However, it was considerably smaller than at any time since 1975–76 and there is a large variation in the profitability of the different postal services. First class letters show a large surplus because the PO charges a high price, although the cost per item is only slightly greater than for second class mail. During 1978–79 the first class post appears to have had a net profit of around £50 million, which was equivalent to 14% of its turnover.[35] In contrast the second class post had a net deficit of something like £30 million, or 7% on revenue, and the inland parcels service did little more than break even. This, however, represented a great improvement as a few years previously there had been a large loss.

Within each of the postal services the level of costs varies widely according to the type of customer and the nature of the area. It seems likely that the costs of collection and, what is far more important, delivery are substantially above average in rural districts. On the other hand costs will be relatively low for items that are addressed to business and other large recipients because the average number that arrive is far greater than the average number received at each dwelling. Nearly 100 times as many items arrive at each of the 176,000 big delivery points that have their own postal codes as at the average dwelling or small business. The PO gives discounts to those posting large quantities of pre-sorted items and is starting to make special contracts with large customers who provide a big volume of mail which can, for some other reason, be handled particularly cheaply. However, neither its general tariffs nor its negotiated rates reflect the fact that items that do not involve household delivery can be carried at a low cost and those that are sent to houses in rural areas will be exceptionally expensive.

It would almost certainly be undesirable for the Post Office to introduce a complex pricing system in which allowance was made for all of the factors which help to determine the cost of carrying each particular item. However, it seems unlikely that it would be very expensive to differentiate between mail for delivery to those large recipients who possess their own postal codes and to other places. It would probably be somewhat more of a problem to distinguish between mail for delivery in urban and in rural areas. However, this might be accomplished by including an additional symbol in the postcode to indicate that the letter was being sent to a rural district.

MONOPOLY OR COMPETITION?

The postal services are grossly inefficient. Prices do not reflect costs, and costs are excessively large because far too many workers are employed. Management has been inert and inept and the labour force has been intransigent. These weaknesses are scarcely surprising. Due to the PO's legal monopoly the letter post has not had to face direct competition and, because the elasticity of demand is low, it has been able to jack up charges in order to cover its escalating costs. What therefore needs to be considered is whether the law should be changed to permit independent postal services to be established.

There are two main arguments in favour of preserving the PO's monopoly. The first is that private operators would cream off the profitable work. Second, if two or more postal concerns operated over the same ground the costs of delivery would inevitably be raised. These arguments are to some extent inconsistent because the low cost work which private firms would be most anxious to secure would, apart from unaddressed mail, be traffic which involves little or no household delivery. This is what they have captured from the public sector carriers in the parcels field and it is the most profitable type of postal business. Now, if independent operators do not engage to any great extent in door-to-door delivery it is difficult to see why the ending of the PO's monopoly would make it significantly more expensive.

Let us, however, assume that the private postal concerns do become involved in delivery to dwellings. There is no reason to suppose that unit costs would rise because the Post Office would be forced, as a result of the competition, to do away with its second delivery. Instead of a first and second delivery both operated by the PO there would then be one by the Post Office and another by a private operator. It seems unlikely that there would be more than one private postal undertaking engaged on local delivery as there would be a great incentive for firms to merge in order to provide a comprehensive service. Even if the worst came to the worst and there were several rival concerns operating over the same ground it is doubtful whether delivery costs would be very much inflated. As we have seen, a fall in the volume of traffic ought to be largely matched by a reduction in expenditure. Any tendency for unit delivery costs to rise should be more than offset by the general improvement in postal efficiency as a result of competition.

It is of course true that private operators would seek to capture low cost business and that, as a result, the PO would not be able to practise cross-subsidisation on such an extensive scale. However, this would have beneficial, and not adverse, consequences. Charges would be raised for those postal activities where the price, viz. the value which marginal customers place on the service, is lower than the cost of provision. On the other hand, charges would fall where the price is now higher than the value of the resources being used. On balance prices would therefore remain the same but the community would be better off because low value but high cost traffic would, for instance, be discouraged. It may be suggested that some particularly deserving group, such as domestic users, might be left worse off. However, it is difficult to see why this should be the case as the PO's market research indicates that business and other mail users dispatch the same proportion of their mail to private addresses, viz. 48%. Moreover, if the PO were compelled, either by competition or by some other means, to relate its charges more closely to its costs and reduce the differential between the first and second class post this would benefit the ordinary consumer. During 1975–76 private individuals used the first class post for 47% of their mail whereas the figure for all postings was only 32%.

The Government has now reviewed the postal monopoly and the Monopolies Commission has recently examined the operation of the postal service in London where there has been a marked deterioration in standards of service and where, as it discovered, the reduction in productivity has taken place. The Commission's report was the most critical that it has ever produced and it went so far as to declare that, 'management is in danger of losing its will to take management decisions, and forgetting that it has a duty to do so'. Nevertheless the Commission rejected the idea that the Post Office's monopoly should be ended in a single dismissive sentence.[36] Moreover the Government has decided to restrict private carriers to express letter work, although the Minister is to be given the power to sanction full private postal services if this should appear desirable. Under the threat of competition UPW, or rather the Union of Communication Workers as it is now known, has just agreed to a

system of productivity payments in which local branches can participate if they so desire, although the PO has had to pay a very heavy
price. Perhaps the threat of competition will be sufficient to secure
the necessary reforms in the postal service but it seems doubtful.

CHAPTER 10

Telecommunications

In 1968 the Post Office's telephone, telex and other telecommunication services (TS) appeared to have no problems except for those brought about by their own success. During the preceding five years the size of the system had increased by more than 35% and TS output — which embraces the provision of apparatus, traffic and work of a capital nature — shot up by well over 50%. Expansion was accompanied by a relatively modest increase in employment (17%). This was due, among other reasons, to better use of workers engaged on maintenance and installation, and also to the replacement of manual exchanges and the spread of subscriber trunk dialling. By 1968 manual exchanges had been all but eliminated and two-thirds of all trunk calls were being dialled direct. As a result there was some reduction in the number of telephonists, despite a marked improvement in the quality of service they provided. Although there was a substantial increase in the quantity of capital in use (31%), total factor productivity rose by 28%. Because of the gains in efficiency which were taking place the industry's prices declined by 13% over the period 1963–64 to 1968–69, without there being any reduction in the size of its profit margin.

ELECTRONIC SWITCHING

The telecommunications services experienced certain growing pains. The number of would-be subscribers who had to be placed on the waiting list for telephones because there was insufficient equipment increased by over three times and averaged around 120,000 during 1968. However the real problem the industry faced, and the one which showed that it was not as successful as it appeared, was

164

its failure to develop satisfactory electronic exchange equipment to take the place of electro-mechanical systems. The earliest type of automatic switching equipment was invented by an American named Strowger as long ago as 1889, and first made its appearance in Britain in 1912. During the mid-1920s the Post Office decided to adopt this step-by-step system which was robust and, even allowing for heavier capital charges, much cheaper than manual arrangements. The disadvantage of strowger is that maintenance costs are high because the switching mechanism has to perform fast jerky movements that result in heavy wear and tear. Crossbar, which is the other main electro-mechanical system, requires much less maintenance because the switches only have to make very small on–off movements. However the other costs are more or less the same as for strowger and the total annual cost per connection is only around 7% lower.[1] Moreover the two systems are not directly compatible and some of this cost advantage might be lost if crossbar were introduced into a strowger network due to the need to provide bridging equipment. Nevertheless most foreign telephone administrations moved over to crossbar, which in its present form dates from 1938.

The Post Office, in contrast, decided around 1950 to continue using strowger. It may have been afraid that if it adopted crossbar there would be a large loss in the number of maintenance jobs and it was certainly hoping to be able to develop an electronic exchange in the reasonably near future. What it wanted to do was to move directly from strowger to electronic switching and avoid the intermediate stage of crossbar. The Post Office engineers decided to develop an advanced electronic system based on the idea of time division in which a large number of conversations would be carried on the same speech path, each conversation being sampled at very short intervals and the sound sustained during the intervening period.[2] This may sound far sighted — a quarter of a century later this principle was put into practice on the American telephone network — but it was at that time foolhardy. It was necessary to employ valves and neon tubes and, as engineers working for the American Telephone and Telegraph Company (AT and T) had discovered back in the 1930s, the valve was unsuitable. According to the official history of the Bell Laboratories it was found that the electron tube, 'could not possibly be used to any great extent [in switching], for it consumed far too much power, produced far too much heat, and in any case could not be made in quantity with the reliability required, at anything like a reasonable cost'.[3] Attention was therefore turned to the use of semiconductors, which were already known to have remarkable properties, and not long after the war physicists at the Bell Laboratories discovered the transistor: a semiconductor device which is able not only to detect, amplify and rectify currents but also to switch them on and off. Early in 1952 Bell Laboratories gave a comprehensive account of what they had discovered, but the Post Office was committed to employing valves. Moreover the head of switching research was determined to make everything electronic and banks of valves were therefore used instead of simple non-electronic solutions. These mistakes were compounded by poor organisation and lack of proper coordination between the twelve different research teams that worked at different places. The original plan was to construct an electronic exchange at Highgate Wood by 1958, but it was not completed until 1962.[4] It was a fiasco.

By this time AT and T was already well on the way towards developing an electronic exchange. This project had been started around 1954 and in 1959 Bell's first electronic exchange, at Morris in Illinois, was given a field trial. However the difficulties were far greater than had been anticipated and a huge amount of time and effort had to be expended before they were overcome. The Post Office commented disparagingly that the Bell Laboratories' approach had been to 'take the problem and trample it to death'.[5] However this was the way to get results and in 1965 AT and T opened its first commercial electronic exchange at Succasunna, New Jersey. This was a central exchange of the type known as No. 1 ESS (Electronic Switching System), but it was followed up by units for use in suburban and rural areas (Nos 2 and 3 ESS). In these exchanges switching was controlled by means of a special computer and performed by a new device known as a reed-relay, which was a small and simple electro-magnetic switch.

The principal advantage of No. 1 ESS and its sister exchanges is that they are very cheap to maintain. This is partly because there is little physical wear on the reed-relays and they are easy to replace, and partly because rearrangements at exchanges, such as the connection and disconnection of customers, are made by reprogramming the computer rather than by rewiring. However the principal reason is that computerised error detecting and correcting facilities have been built in. These deal automatically with the most frequent and easily handled faults. The surveillance of a number of exchanges takes place at Switching Control Centres from which the more difficult maintenance tasks are undertaken. By the mid-1970s the maintenance costs for AT and T's semi-electronic exchanges were little more than half those of crossbar; and crossbar's maintenance costs are, in turn, some two-thirds of those of strowger. In addition, the electronic units have the advantage of occupying relatively little space and being readily able to provide subscribers with a range of new services, such as letting those who are using their phones know that there is a call waiting.[6] It appears that the total annual cost of service to the customer, including capital charges calculated with a 5% rate of interest, is 20–25% lower for a semi-electronic exchange than for a strowger unit, and 15–20% less than for a crossbar exchange. Moreover, because electro-mechanical equipment can often be re-used and therefore has some value, the (net) capital cost of buying new electronic equipment in order to replace strowger plant is much lower than it appears. AT and T usually finds, at least at its larger step-by-step offices, that immediate replacement with No. 1 ESS is economically justified.[6]

Just over a decade after its first semi-electronic exchange went into service AT and T opened, in Chicago, the first major exchange that was wholly electronic. In this unit, known as No. 4 ESS, the switching components are electronic as well as the controlling computer. The switching elements use time division which means that the waves of voice frequency that are received from customers' phones have to be converted into pulses before switching takes place. Although this involves some cost it was found to be worth while because No. 4 ESS is a trunk exchange and feeds messages into a trunk network in which pulse transmission is used. When both transmission and switching function digitally, by means of pulses, the interface is relatively simple and very cheap. No. 4 ESS has enabled AT and T to make large capital and operating savings where, because of its huge capacity, one of these units is used instead of having to rely on a number of crossbar exchanges. Moreover it costs only a third as much to maintain as the most advanced electro-mechanical toll switching machines.[7]

Although the Bell System has hitherto led the world in the development and application of electronic switching, considerable progress is now being made by other organisations. Ericssons of Sweden have produced a local exchange that is wholly electronic (the AXE 10) and ITT's System 12 provides for the digital transmission of calls right through to the end telephone. It is almost certain that by using fully electronic switching equipment telephone administrations will ultimately be able to make large economies. Estimates by Messrs Cripps and Godley, which do not pretend to be more than rough approximations, suggest that the total annual cost of service to the customer will be around 40% lower for a digital electronic system than for one where the switching is electro-mechanical. Moreover costs would be even lower for business users who are transmitting data which can readily be conveyed because, unlike conversations, it does not have to be decomposed into exceedingly long strings of digits.[8]

Having briefly examined the developments in switching that have been taking place abroad we must now assess, in their light, what progress the Post Office has made. The failure of Highgate Wood and the development of the reed-relay led to a change of course. The potential advantage of time division was that, because speech paths were shared, it was unnecessary to have so many switching points. However, now that reed-relays were available these points did not have to be controlled by expensive valves and time division (temporarily) lost its attraction.[9] Consequently the Post Office decided to develop reed-relay exchanges. The first of these was able to go into operation as early as 1966, at Ambergate, because a considerable amount of work had already been undertaken by the manufacturer before the PO became interested. It contained electronic components and was called TXE-2, which stands for Telephone Exchange Electronic Type 2. However it was not computer controlled like No. 1 ESS and was only suitable for use in small exchanges. Work was also undertaken on a large reed-relay exchange which became known as TXE-3, but when, at long last, the design work had been completed it was found that it would be far more expensive than strowger. A cost reduction exercise was then undertaken by one of the manufacturers and in 1972 the PO decided to adopt this system, which was now called TXE-4. It was still very expensive but the PO hoped that the capital cost would decline as experience was gained and that it would be relatively cheap to maintain. The first TXE-4 exchange — Rectory in Birmingham — was not opened until 1976. Although the TXE-4 appeared more than a decade after the No. 1 ESS it was a greatly inferior product. It has some computer control but the way in which it functions is still determined by the form of its circuitry and not by its programming; and this is still largely true of the improved version known as TXE-4A. Moreover because of the delay in developing the large TXE exchange the Post Office decided very late in the day to use crossbar as a stop-gap, although its whole strategy had been based on avoiding this system.

Not until mid-1980 when the first System X exchange came into operation did the Post Office begin to use fully electronic switching. Why has the Post Office made such slow progress? There was, to begin with, a delay of some years before its engineers saw the full significance of No. 1 ESS and grasped the importance of controlling switching by computer. This may have been partly due to the fact that previous British research had concentrated on the process of switching rather than on the means by which it was controlled.[10] It also seems likely that after the débâcle at Highgate Wood the PO engineers had decided to play safe and avoid advanced technology. This however makes it even more surprising that, once the Post Office had woken up to the American lead, it did not make a comprehensive licensing agreement with AT and T in order to learn from American experience. This was one of the steps that was taken by the Nippon Telegraph and Telephone Corporation which in 1964, after No. 1 ESS had been announced, launched a ten-year plan to develop computer controlled switching. Such an agreement would not have prevented the British telecommunications manufacturers from exporting because although AT and T owned Western Electric it only supplied the Bell system.

It was not until the late 1960s that the importance of computer-controlled switching was fully recognised. Staff were recruited and plans laid but at this point the head of switching research became seriously ill. He was out of action for about two years and during this period the project was leaderless, morale declined and little progress was made. After his return at the end of 1970 the manufacturers were persuaded to come together in a joint committee with the Post Office. This Advisory Group on Systems Definition (AGSD) was meant to draw up plans for future switching systems. However the PO had no real idea what it wanted and the firms engaged in unconstructive argument. In 1969 the Post Office had terminated the market sharing agreement for the supply of exchange equipment and the manufacturers, who were now in competition, jealously guarded their plans and data. Moreover a bitter conflict was in progress as to whether the Post Office should order TXE-4, which had been developed by STC, or whether it should opt for further development of crossbar (including computer control), which was the policy favoured by GEC and Plessey. 'By 1973', writes an observer, 'things were clearly not going well, AGSD had produced mountains of paper covered with grand ideas, but not a single practical design or design approach. The switching project in Research Department had lost all direction and fragmented into many little projects of little practical value. The manufacturers had played around with a few private venture projects but had no real products to sell to anyone.'

The Post Office Board decided that action was necessary and in the spring of 1974 a new Telecommunication Systems Strategy Department was established. It was headed by the man who had, with such unhappy results, previously presided over switching research and AGSD. An excessively large organisation was created and staff were housed at different places. However the crucial weakness was that no clear or coherent view emerged as to the form that System X should take. It was first decided to commission the manufacturers to write a series of papers and then to sign up development contracts. However, about two years were wasted arguing about their small print and meanwhile very little progress was made. Not until the summer of 1977 were the bulk of the development contracts awarded. The late arrival of System X has not therefore been due to the inherent difficulty of introducing electronic switching but to the way in which the Post Office frittered away the decade which followed the introduction of No. 1 ESS.

The failure to develop satisfactory switching equipment has had serious consequences. Due to the rapid growth in the size of the system the Post Office has been forced to install a huge amount of obsolete strowger plant. Between March 1969 and March 1979 exchange capacity, as measured by the number of exchange connections, more than doubled and strowger accounted for 57% of the increase at automatic exchanges. Not until 1973–74 did strowger cease to be the staple element in Post Office orders for new exchange equipment and it was only in 1977 that step-by-step sunk to insignificance.[11] Twenty-eight per cent of the growth in capacity took the form of obsolescent crossbar plant. Its integration into the network at such a late stage has involved some difficulty and, according to the Post Office, 'Elimination of the many defects and deficiencies has involved considerable delay and continuing expenditure'.[12] In practice crossbar has not been very much cheaper to maintain than strowger, although there ought to have been considerable savings. The remaining 15% of exchange equipment has been so-called electronic equipment, i.e. TXE-2 and TXE-4. These have certainly been no cheaper than strowger, in terms of initial capital cost per unit of capacity, and TXE-4 still appears to be more expensive.[13] Moreover they have not produced the large savings in maintenance costs that were planned and by which they were justified. To begin with TXE-2 plant involved more maintenance than strowger due to the extensive failure of reed-relays and although it is now slightly less costly, TXE-4 may not yet show any saving. However the Post Office expects that large reductions in maintenance expenditure will eventually be made.[14]

The Post Office would not have had to introduce so much obsolete and defective plant if it had adjusted its capacity more closely to its traffic. The measurement of peak traffic flows is a time-consuming process at electro-mechanical exchanges and only a limited amount of information was collected. However it was ultimately decided to assemble much fuller data, and better methods for measuring the utilisation of plant were devised. As a result it was found, during 1976, that there was 20% of excess capacity in the exchange system and it was this which led to the virtual termination of orders for strowger.[15]

There is no doubt that Britain has fallen badly behind the United States in the introduction of electronic switching. By the end of 1978, 30% of AT and T's customers were being served by electronic exchanges and it is planned that by the beginning of 1982 the proportion will have risen to well over half. No other major telephone administrations, apart from Canada and Japan, had introduced electronic switching on any appreciable scale by 1978.[16] However, a considerable number are now making very rapid progress not only with computer controlled switching but also with digital equipment. Indeed Sweden and Germany have decided to stop producing non-digital plant in 1980–81, Canada will probably stop during 1982–83 and France is planning to cease production in 1985. Some of these countries and others, including the United States, will continue to put in switching which is electronic but not digital.[17] However the installation of electro-mechanical equipment either has or is being discontinued.

The Post Office introduced its first System X exchange —

TABLE 10.1 *Telecommunications: Output, Productivity and Finances*

	Output	Employment[a]	Output per equivalent worker	Capital stock	Output per unit of labour and capital	Real unit operating costs[bc]	Real unit staff costs[bc]	Real staff costs per employee[abc]	Real revenue per unit[b]	Revenue[b]	Gross surplus[bc]	Gross surplus as % of revenue[bc]	Net surplus[bc]
	(1968 = 100)	(000)	(1968 = 100)	(1968 = 100)	(1968 = 100)	(1968–69=100)	(1968–69=100)	(1968–69=100)	(1968–69=100)	(£m, 1978 prices)	(£m, 1978 prices)	(%)	(£m, 1978 prices)
1963	65.4	193.0	72.3	76.5	78.3	114.4	119.6	88.4	114.3	1,279	583	45.6	334
1968	100.0	225.2	100.0	100.0	100.0	100.0	100.0	100.0	100.0	1,721	780	45.3	441
										1,744	772	44.3	434
1969	108.7	228.0	106.8	107.4	104.1	95.2	93.4	102.4	99.3	1,898	873	46.0	493
1970	121.8	231.9	117.5	115.2	111.7	90.2	85.6	104.3	99.1	2,093	1,018	48.6	596
1971	133.8	236.7	126.4	123.8	117.0	89.2	85.6	114.0	91.7	2,165	984	45.5	516
1972	146.9	239.5	136.5	132.4	123.1	87.6	83.7	124.6	86.3	2,280	984	43.1	410
1973	160.8	244.7	145.3	141.5	128.4	83.3	76.9	121.6	81.4	2,373	1,016	42.8	423
1974	171.0	247.6	155.5	150.8	132.3	76.9	78.9	130.7	74.5	2,264	896	39.6	267
1975	179.6	249.2	163.4	159.1	134.9	79.7	74.4	131.7	89.0	2,952	1,452	49.2	792
1976	187.2	239.3	177.7	165.9	139.8	72.7	68.4	132.3	88.7	3,174[d]	1,697[d]	53.5[d]	1,007[d]
						75.0[c]					1,650[c]	52.0[c]	960[c]
1977	204.9	230.9	197.4	171.0	151.1	67.8	58.8	132.1	77.7	3,116	1,576	50.6	814
													793[f]
1978	229.2	229.6	219.9	175.3	166.3	62.3	55.1	139.1	70.3	3,174	1,582	49.8	821

Note Output and employment figures were derived from financial year data. The output index comprises seventeen indicators: traffic, items of equipment rented and capital work (expenditure on materials deflated). Revenue weights for 1968–69 (and 1963–64) were used, except that payments to other administrations were excluded, and that capital work and total revenue output were combined with net output weights. The per unit series were estimated using gross output, apart from capital work, at 1968–69 (and 1963–64) prices. The CSO's gross capital stock estimates for postal, telephone and radio communications were used for the quantity of capital and a capital weight of 47.3% was employed.

a Part time staff are counted as half. b Financial year (April–March) beginning during year shown. c Before provision for pension deficiency contributions. d Before provision for refund to eliminate profit above Price Code reference level. e Boundary between revenue and capital expenditure changed. f Includes supplementary depreciation on buildings hitherto ignored.

Baynard House — in mid-1980 but according to its projections digital exchanges will only account for 15% of connections as late as 1988–89 and production of TXE equipment will not end until 1990–92.[18] It seems inevitable that for some years relatively few System X units will be introduced because although, after a very late start, rapid progress has been made in developing the hardware, the Post Office may well have considerable difficulty in perfecting the software. This is an area where several telephone administrations have run into difficulties and the PO has no real experience of computer controlled switching on which to build. It is also questionable whether the quality of System X will be as high as the Post Office believes. The small local exchange, which will ultimately replace the TXE-2, is likely to prove fairly satisfactory but may be somewhat inferior to foreign manufacturers' second generation systems. It is the trunk exchange which is the real cause for concern. The computer control system, which was selected back in 1973, has been strongly criticised on the ground that it is large, slow and, despite its size, has a relatively low switching capacity. On the other hand it is pointed out that great improvements in performance have already been made and that the exchange's capacity may be further enhanced before it goes into production. Another question mark with respect to System X is how expensive it will turn out to be. The Post Office if paying out very large sums to the manufacturers in order to finance its development and is now suggesting that customers who are linked to System X exchanges will have to pay a supplementary charge.

Although switching has a crucial role in a telephone system it would be wrong to give the impression that nothing else is important or that the PO's record in other fields, such as transmission, has been correspondingly poor. Elsewhere the Post Office appears to have been far more successful.

OUTPUT, EMPLOYMENT AND PRODUCTIVITY

During the past decade the industry has been expanding at an enormous rate. Between 1968 and 1978 the size of the system grew by 115% and traffic increased by 170%. As can be seen from Table 10.1 the overall increase in the industry's output, including work of a capital nature undertaken by Post Office employees, was 130%.

Although output rose slightly less rapidly during the second half of the period, there was nevertheless an increase of 42%.

Why has there been such a huge growth in TS output? Prices have declined and by 1978–79 were 30% lower than they had been ten years previously. The Post Office's studies suggest that the price elasticity for both calls and phones is very low, at around 0.1. There is some doubt about the reliability of these figures but although the reduction in prices has obviously played some part it seems doubtful whether it has been a major influence. Another possible explanation is that increasing affluence has had some direct impact on traffic. The Post Office's investigations show an income elasticity of only 0.1 for local calls but of 1.5 for trunk calls.[19] The rise in real incomes must also have contributed to the increase in the proportion of households that possess a telephone from 30% in 1968 to 62% in 1978. However it seems likely that there has been a powerful snow-ball effect since it becomes more and more desirable both to have and to use the telephone with the growth in the number of people that can be called. Although there does not appear to have been much increase in the number of calls per subscriber, this is misleading as the calling rate is very much lower for domestic than for business users and it is households which have been largely responsible for the huge growth in the size of the telephone network. Telephone traffic has been stimulated by the improvement in the quality of service. Trunk dialling has now been extended to the whole of the UK and the proportion of overseas calls that can be dialled has increased to the point where only 10% go through the operator. Moreover the proportion of dialled trunk calls which failed to connect due to some fault in the system fell from 8½% in 1968–69 to 3½% in 1978–79, though this may not have had much effect on traffic.

The rise in TS output was accompanied by only a tiny rise in employment. Between 1968 and 1975 the labour force increased from 225,000 to nearly 250,000, but by 1978 it had fallen back to 230,000. As a result there was an almost breathtaking increase in labour productivity, with output per equivalent worker rising by 120% over the period 1968–78. And although there was a substantial rise in the quantity of capital in use it appears to have been smaller than the growth in output. There seems therefore to have been an increase in output per unit of capital which is an infrequent occurrence. According to my estimates, output per unit of labour and capital grew by two-thirds, which is a spectacular rise and compares favourably with the increase of 52% at AT and T.

Early in 1968 the Post Office told the Prices and Incomes Board that, although the size of the telephone system was expected to increase by 50% between 1967 and 1972, no growth in employment was anticipated. This ambitious objective was not quite realised because the TS labour force rose by 8%. However what is perhaps of greater interest is that the Post Office was anticipating that it would be able to make a staff saving of only something over 70,000 through the extension of trunk dialling and the introduction of computers and improved methods of working.[20] As TS employment would have risen by around 110,000 if it had increased in line with the size of the system, this suggests that growth in telecommunications does not lead to a corresponding rise in the amount of labour required. There are a number of reasons why this is the case. (1) Expansion has resulted in an increase in the size but not in the number of exchanges and this is a place where there are considerable economies of scale. (2) Once the local distribution network has been established it is relatively easy to connect additional customers. (3) Work of a capital nature does not appear to have changed very greatly over the period 1968–78. It is highly labour intensive and accounted for 25% of TS employment in 1968 compared with only 14% of net output. The fact that there has been little or no change in capital work has therefore tended to raise output per worker and to mean that employment increased more slowly than production. (4) The final reason for this tendency is that telecommunications traffic has been rising at an exceptionally rapid rate. Between 1968 and 1978 telephone, telex and telegraph traffic (as measured by the weighted number of calls and other message units) has increased over 25% more than the size of the system (as measured by weighted connections, phones and private circuits). As the maintenance requirements for some plant and equipment do not increase in proportion to its usage this will have tended to raise productivity. For instance the need to test and repair telephone lines and cables does not increase in step with the amount of traffic that they carry. This and some other types of maintenance work are almost wholly a time cost. Moreover a large part of the clerical work load is related to the number of customers rather than to the volume of traffic. This will in particular be true for the billing of subscribers and the preparation of directories. (It should be noted that the greater expansion in traffic than in the size of the network helps to explain why output has increased more rapidly than employment but not, of course, why the labour force has lagged behind the growth of the network.)

Technological progress has made a large contribution to the increase in TS productivity. The most important advance has been the completion of domestic trunk dialling and the great extension of international dialling. This largely explains why, instead of rising, the number of telephone operators fell by over 20,000 between 1968 and 1978. The decline in the number of calls via the operator has also led to a reduction in accounting work. Another important development has been computerisation and this has been a major reason why there has been comparatively little increase in the number of clerical workers. However technical progress has not been confined to a few developments, which have resulted in huge savings, but has occurred over a broad front. For instance, the need for operators has been reduced by providing them with push button dialling; new types of cables have been introduced which are less prone to water damage and can be laid in longer lengths; the jointing of cables has been mechanised; and the use of electronic components at exchanges has reduced the maintenance workload because of the ease with which they can be replaced and the fact that there is no need for preventive maintenance to counteract the effects of wear.[21]

Telecommunications employment would have increased more rapidly, and productivity more slowly, but for the adoption of more efficient working methods. The Post Office's thinking on productivity was originally dominated by the concept of work measurement and it was believed that labour could be saved by undertaking a given operation more efficiently. This approach had the disadvantage that each work study investigation was time consuming and only covered one particular job. However the major drawback was that a large amount of unnecessary work was being performed and that working arrangements were often defective. It was found that productivity was higher in the United States, not necessarily because less labour was required for a given task, but because unproductive work was avoided and jobs were better organised. One small example which illustrates the difference is that lightning protectors were installed in Britain although this was usually unnecessary, as the Americans had recognised.

During the 1960s the Post Office started to address itself to the problem of how tasks could be simplified and unproductive labour avoided. One important step was the construction of productivity indices for different activities in order to measure the growth in useful output per man hour devoted to its production. During 1970–71 a considerable degree of responsibility was devolved from headquarters on to the new Regional Directors and the Post Office began to use its productivity measures for the purpose of setting their targets and monitoring their performance. Annual targets, which do not exclusively relate to productivity, are now agreed between headquarters and the Regional Directors after the latter have established what progress each of their General Managers should be able to make within his area. Another important move was the conclusion in 1965 of an agreement with the Post Office Engineering Union (POEU) by which its members received a proportion of any savings that were obtained through higher productivity. In this way the Post Office secured a considerable measure of cooperation from the Union in making changes in working arrangements, although this would not have been provided so readily but for the POEU's belief that its members long-term interests would best be served if the TS were efficient and profitable. Similar productivity agreements were made later for clerical staff (1969) and telephonists (1971).

During the past decade alterations in work methods have taken place in every sphere of telecommunications activity. For instance when extra capacity is required new cables are now often laid over the existing network rather than being married in with it; a scheme for making appointments with customers who require installation work has been fully implemented; the reduction in the size of installation parties has continued; and simplified operating procedures have been introduced at exchanges to enable telephonists to handle more calls. However it would be wrong to imagine that the Post Office has not encountered any obstruction. An office work measurement and productivity campaign had to be abandoned because of union opposition and, due to the POEU's insistence, engineering workers are employed overnight at crossbar exchanges.[21] This is not always necessary, as shown by the fact that they have been dispensed with abroad at exchanges of similar design. In 1977 the Post Office conceded national staffing standards for crossbar and TXE exchanges, although it believed that manning levels should vary according to local circumstances.[22] Moreover despite the increased emphasis on attaining targets, the Carter Committee found that the Post Office's book of regional performance statistics 'does not enjoy anything like the same status within the organisation as does its transatlantic counterpart'.[23]

How does TS productivity compare with that of foreign telephone systems? This question raises the problem of how output should be measured. The customary yardsticks are the number of telephones and exchange lines. There is much to be said for this as telephone administrations earn a large amount of revenue by renting apparatus and lines and a substantial proportion of all staff is engaged on their provision and maintenance. However the number of conversations has at least an equal claim for consideration as a large percentage of revenue is derived from calls and they account, directly or indirectly, for much of the labour that is required. For instance at strowger exchanges extra traffic means extra wear, and hence additional maintenance; while maintenance requirements at electronic exchanges will depend on the amount of plant and equipment which will, in turn, be related to the volume of (peak) traffic. Despite the fact that productivity can be measured in different ways, and that the available statistics are crude, they show some foreign countries to be so far ahead of the British telephone system that there is little doubt that their OMY is substantially greater. During 1978 the Bell System's productivity was nearly 60% higher in terms of telephones per worker and 175% greater as measured by conversations per employee.[24] The corresponding figures for Switzerland were (after rounding) 150% and 100% and for Holland 115% and 95%. There is no data on calls for Sweden and Japan but the number of stations per worker is 45% greater than in Britain and in terms of connections they are even further ahead. However in the case of France, Belgium and Germany the margin is much smaller and it has been shown by Mr Christopher Lorenz that the German lead is a statistical illusion.[25] This is because some administration and installation work that is undertaken within the British TS is performed in Germany by private firms. In Australia productivity appears to be about 30% lower than in Britain whichever measure is used.

These international comparisons may be questioned on the ground that those countries where telephone penetration (and usage) is high enjoy an advantage. The number of telephones per 100 population is greater in the UK (at 42) than in France and

Belgium (around 32) and about the same as in Holland, Japan and Australia. In Switzerland (66), Sweden (72) and the USA (74) penetration is considerably higher.[16] However their productivity is so much larger that it seems doubtful whether greater penetration accounts for all of their lead. The Post Office points out that, as measured by phones per employee, productivity was no higher in Sweden and the US than in Britain when their level of penetration was similar to our own. But what this overlooks is the technical progress which has taken place during the period that has elapsed since the time when American and Swedish penetration was at the current British level. One factor which needs to be taken into account in making productivity comparisons in telecommunications is that in some foreign countries the telephone systems have not been operated along commercial lines. There is, for instance, little comfort to be drawn from the fact that productivity in the UK appears to be only slightly lower than in France since the French telephone system is notoriously inefficient.

COSTS, PRICES AND PROFITS

Between 1968–69 and 1978–79 the industry's unit costs fell by about 40% due to the huge rise in productivity and the consequent reduction in staff costs per unit of output. This occurred despite the fact that the increase in staff costs per employee (39%) was considerably greater than in industry as a whole, as represented by manufacturing (about 29%). Although prices fell by 30%, this was substantially less than the reduction in costs and as a result the gross margin improved from 44% in 1968–69 to 50% in 1978–79. However between 1971–72 and 1974–75, when price restraint was in operation, prices fell more rapidly than costs and the gross margin declined until it was only 40%. During 1975 large price increases took place and the profitability of the TS was more than restored.

The net surplus, after depreciation at replacement cost, appears to have grown from £435 million in 1968–69 to £820 million in 1978–79. There has, of course, been a large increase in business and in the quantity of capital employed but, after allowing for accounting changes, the net margin increased from 25% at the beginning of the period to 28% at the end. During 1978-79 the TS appear to have earned a net return of 7% on net assets, at replacement cost, but there is a substantial variation in the profitability of different TS regions and services. Large losses are incurred in Northern Ireland and substantial losses in Scotland, though whether this is before or after interest is not clear. Costs are relatively high in these areas but the Post Office does not charge higher prices.

The Post Office identifies those costs that arise from the provision and maintenance of the apparatus that its customers use and the lines and exchange equipment by which subscribers are connected to the common switching units at exchanges. This expenditure should be recovered by means of the rents which are charged by the TS while those capital and running costs that result from the use of common switching units, trunk lines and other trunk equipment ought to be covered through call charges. The PO incurs a net loss or makes an inadequate profit everywhere except for subscribers' calls and for its external services, where it earned a net return of 28% during 1978–79. Moreover the bulk of its profit from calls is almost certainly being made on trunk traffic where, since the net return on subscribers' calls averaged 11%, charges must be vastly in excess of costs. The TS costing system is based on average rather than marginal costs but the Post Office does not believe that the use of marginal costs would yield significantly different results.[26] The Post Office is therefore open to serious criticism for maintaining a pricing structure which is likely to result in the misallocation of resources.

It is interesting to observe that exactly the same pattern of cross-subsidisation between local and trunk calls is to be found in the United States, but is now having to be abandoned because the telephone utilities are being subjected to some competitive pressure.[27] Are there lessons here for Britain?

PART 3

Manufacturing

CHAPTER 11

British Steel

In the middle of 1967 the British Steel Corporation (BSC) took charge of thirteen companies which were together responsible for two-thirds of the steel industry's (net) output. These firms were already in a difficult and deteriorating position as their financial performance shows. In 1957–58 they had earned a net profit of over £400 million; by 1962–63 this had fallen to around £200 million and during 1967–68, which was the Corporation's first year, the figure was less than £60 million. This represented a return of only ½% on net assets at replacement cost. Although some parts of the industry were still financially healthy losses were being incurred at four works where the companies had concentrated a large part of their investment, including Llanwern in South Wales and Ravenscraig in Scotland. Another even more important reason why profits had declined was that the price of steel fell by 20% between 1958 and 1968. The reduction was due initially to the Iron and Steel Board's system of price control, and the pressure which the Government exerted on the Board, but prices continued to be depressed because there was a world steel recession and cheap imports were available. During 1967–68 demand recovered and prices could have been raised, but BSC was engaged in a major price review. This meant that its financial position was slightly, but only slightly, stronger than it appeared.

The industry's productivity performance was also disappointing. It is true that output per equivalent worker rose by 42% over the period 1958–68, which was not far short of the increase in manufacturing. However, when allowance is made for the use of capital, productivity increased much less than in manufacturing, viz. by 21% as against 39%. What was also worrying was that, although labour productivity was increasing at a moderate rate by British standards, our foreign competitors were making much faster progress. Between 1955 and 1965 output per man hour grew by around 150% in Italy and Japan, by about two-thirds in France, Holland, Canada and Belgium, and by 58% in Germany. In Britain there was a rise of only 39% and the US was the sole major steel producing country whose increase was smaller, viz. 25%. The British steel industry was labouring under the handicap that its output was growing less rapidly than in any of the other countries except the United States. Nevertheless the fact remains that whereas in 1955 productivity in Britain was only slightly lower than in the Common Market, by 1965 output per man hour in the Six was about 25% higher. Moreover it appears that Poland and Czechoslovakia were level or ahead, that in Sweden and Russia output per man hour was around 50% greater and that in the US it was well over twice as great.[1]

Productivity was low in Britain because plant was over-manned and because the utilisation of equipment was poor. For instance blast furnaces, in comparison with good foreign practice, were operated at an average efficiency of only 43% partly due to the use of low grade British coking coal, much of which was produced at a high cost.[1] In addition the great bulk of our steelmaking capacity was obsolescent. During the period 1958–68 the revolutionary LD process, which had been pioneered in Austria, was adopted on an extensive scale by the major steel producers in the non-Communist world. By 1968 LD and other pure oxygen processes accounted for 43% of the crude steel produced in the other OECD countries, but in Britain the proportion was only 28%. Open hearth and other high cost processes accounted for approaching two-thirds of BSC's output. The reason for this was that relatively little new steelmaking plant was constructed because production was growing comparitively slowly.[2]

REPLANNING THE INDUSTRY

Basic oxygen steelmaking (BOS) has the great advantage that, because oxygen is blown into the furnace, it takes as little as thirty-five minutes to convert the materials — principally molten iron and scrap — into steel, whereas in the traditional open hearth furnace the process can take ten hours. As a result the operating costs for BOS are much lower and, because two or three converters can produce an immense amount of steel, it is relatively cheap to install. At a BOS plant with a capacity of something over 3 million tonnes the cost of transforming iron and other materials into steel was about £7.50 per tonne including capital charges (equivalent to 20% of the necessary investment). The conversion costs for the open hearth process were substantially higher at £12.90, ignoring capital charges.[3] Hence it was desirable that BSC should begin replacing its open hearth capacity by BOS. This was a policy which its private predecessors had already adopted, and the installation of LD at Port Talbot was already under way when nationalisation took place.

Although a considerable programme of capital expenditure was called for, there were strict limits to the amount of investment that could be justified. BOS has led to dramatic savings in both capital and operating costs, but during the previous and subsequent stages of the steelmaking process there had been no comparable technological development; and the reduction in operating costs through replacing existing blast furnaces and rolling mills was generally too small to cover the capital charges on the new plant. Hence it was not worth scrapping serviceable ironmaking and finishing plant in order to construct a huge new steelworks on a greenfield site. The Corporation was therefore right to adopt what it termed a 'heritage strategy' and to develop and modernise the best of the plants which it had inherited.

This does not necessarily mean that it was desirable to concentrate investment and production at the works that BSC selected, i.e. Llanwern, Scunthorpe, Ravenscraig outside Glasgow and Lackenby on South Teeside. There were it was true powerful arguments for development at these plants. At Scunthorpe the effective capacity of the existing blast furnaces could be stretched by means of a partial switch from lean home ore to imported ore, which has a high ferrous content and therefore produces far more iron per tonne. United Steel was planning to bring this latent capacity into use, through its Anchor project, by constructing an LD shop, together with some extra finishing plant. On South Teeside a large amount of finishing capacity was available, but could not be properly employed because there was insufficient steelmaking plant. Hence it was planned to construct a BOS shop and a scheme was submitted to the Iron and Steel Board just before nationalisation. There was also spare strip mill capacity at Llanwern and Ravenscraig, because of the Government's decision in 1958 on political grounds that two mills should be built. As a result only a limited amount of steelmaking capacity was installed and at Llanwern another blast furnace was needed. However there were other works which had powerful claims to consideration such as Shotton, which had an excellent record and Consett where development would have taken place but for nationalisation. These works were, of course, situated inland but so were Scunthorpe, Llanwern and Ravenscraig, which was much further from the major markets than Shotton. The concentration of production at the big four — or, when Port Talbot is included, the big five — may nonetheless have been correct. I do not want to assert the contrary but merely point out that it is an open question. Unfortunately it was treated at the time as if it were closed because of the belief, which I shared, that the future lay with giant works and that economies of scale were all important. However, what has become evident over the past decade is that good management and a co-operative labour force are even more vital, and that small works have the advantage of being more flexible and of being able to load their plant more fully. Moreover it is not even clear that the works which BSC selected for development offered all of the most profitable opportunities for investment at the steelmaking stage.

What is certain is that the Corporation's investment programme had serious weaknesses even if it is accepted that concentration at the five big works was desirable. BSC made the old mistake of leaving works out of balance. For instance at the main Scunthorpe plant there is only enough finishing plant to process about 4.5 million tonnes of crude steel. However, the BOS shop was designed to produce at least 5.3 million tonnes and, as this assumed a very long tap-to-tap time of fifty minutes, equipment was designed for a much higher rate of production. If it were worked to the best foreign standards it could produce 7 million tonnes, although BSC has never succeeded in making sufficient iron to attain even 4.5 million tonnes (and has now knocked down some of the blast furnaces). At Lackenby the Corporation put in a huge BOS plant with three vessels, despite the fact that only a limited amount of ironmaking capacity was available. The blast furnaces at Clay Lane could only provide enough iron to produce about 2.7 million tonnes of steel, and the furnaces of Cargo Fleet, which could have supported extra production, were demolished. What BSC should obviously have done, and what Dorman Long had been planning, was to put in two vessels. A third converter could then have been installed together with additional ironmaking capacity if and when demand justified further expansion. By acting prematurely the Corporation not only spent £33 million on steelmaking capacity which it could not utilise, but was also led on to construct ironmaking and other facilities at a cost of £400 million, although the extra capacity was not required.[4]

These were by no means the only weaknesses of the Corporation's development programme. Some of the schemes appear to have been badly designed and at Lackenby extensive re-engineering has been necessary.[5] A large amount has been invested in new finishing plant at works like Ebbw Vale and Shotton where the Corporation later decided that the production of crude steel should come to an end. Construction costs appear to have been excessively high. BSC's rod mill at Appleby Frodingham cost 40% more than one that GKN installed because, although the equipment was the same, the Corporation erected a cathedral-like structure to house it. Finally it should be observed that there was a considerable delay, while the Corporation was taking stock, before it began modernising the industry. The Anchor project was deferred at the request of the Organising Committee which was set up in advance of the Corporation; and it was not until July 1969, three years after the project had originally been put forward, that BSC gave the go-ahead. In 1966 the Iron and Steel Board forecast that if the steel companies carried out the projects they were considering, BOS would account for nearly 45% of all steel by 1970.[6] The proportion turned out to be only 32%, although it would probably be wrong to attribute all the shortfall to nationalisation.

Although BSC got off to a slow start it was planning to equip itself with more than enough capacity. Not long before nationalisation the Iron and Steel Federation had estimated that home steel consumption would increase from 23.4 million tonnes in 1965 to 31.4 in 1975 if the economy grew by 4% p.a.[7] (Here and henceforth the figures relate to crude steel unless otherwise stated.) In its Corporate Plan of 1969 BSC postulated 3% growth, which was reasonable, but went on to forecast that home demand would rise to 29.6 million tonnes by 1975. This was surprisingly close to the Federation's figure and implied that there would be some increase in the rate at which consumption was rising. What was even more dubious was the Corporation's prediction that net exports would shoot up from 2.6 million tonnes in 1968 to 6.1 million in 1975. This assumed that BSC would export some 4 million tonnes at prices that would be from 5%

to 20% lower than those on the home market, and it was noted that 'in the absence of any measures to restrain international price movements, export prices could on average be appreciably lower than the estimates suggest'. Such measures were highly unlikely, and the creation of extra capacity for the purpose of exporting would be justified only if the price was sufficient to cover the full costs of production, including capital charges. It was argued that for some products incremental output would be very cheap, but the proper comparison was between the export price and the cost of the Corporation's most expensive tranche of production. Thus BSC's estimate that it would need to be able to produce 33 million tonnes in 1975 was unrealistic. What almost certainly happened, both then and later, was that the Corporation based its plans on the tacit assumption that certain expansion schemes were desirable and would be carried out, in which case it made sense to use spare capacity for exporting.

In its Development Plan of February 1971 the Corporation tried to map out its long-term policy. The Corporation had replaced the semi-geographical groups, into which the old companies had been fitted, by product divisions. In the process the old steelmasters had been ousted, old loyalties had been destroyed and power had been centralised. Hitherto investment projects had been submitted by the groups who had lobbied and manoeuvred for their adoption. Under the new system headquarters took the initiative and it was in no doubt as to what it wanted to do. The Chairman of BSC and his deputy had visited Japan and had come back determined that Britain should catch up through the construction of a monster works on a greenfield site with an ultimate capacity of 15–17 million tonnes. It was also intended to construct a 'brown field' plant on South Teeside, which it was argued would be able to use the facilities and spare capacity that would be available. These new works would be producing over 15 million tonnes by 1980–81. To make way for them it was planned that by the early 1980s steelmaking, though not finishing, would have come to an end at all of BSC's integrated works outside the five main centres that were being modernised and expanded under the heritage strategy. Despite these closures it was anticipated that the Corporation's production would increase from 25 million tonnes in 1970 to 42½ million in 1980–81. This was only possible because it was assumed that there would be a massive rise in home consumption (from 24 million tonnes to 37 million) and a huge growth in net exports (from 2½ million to 10 million).

This programme was totally unrealistic and wildly expensive. The Corporation thought that it would need to invest about £11 billion; and it was assumed that home consumption would increase by 50% between 1970 and 1980, although it had risen only by 16½% between 1960 and 1970. The forecast for net exports was so high as to be incredible and no allowance was made for possible entry to the Common Market, although it was well known within the Corporation that this was likely to have an adverse effect. There was no estimate of what the return on investment would be, apart from a projection which started from the assumption that it would produce 15% on a dcf basis. Not only did this assume what it was necessary to prove, but the figure was, as the Corporation itself admitted, 'high in relation to past performance of the steel industry in Britain, to the average performance of overseas steel companies and to experience in heavy manufacturing industry generally'.

The Development Plan caused alarm and incredulity within the Department of Industry and a Joint Steering Group was set up. Although BSC fought hard for its green field works it was vetoed and after a fierce battle it was agreed that by 1980 BSC would need a capacity of something between the Department's estimate of 28½ million tonnes and BSC's figure of 36½ million. The Corporation then mounted a highly elaborate exercise to discover the profitability of ten different plant configurations which would provide outputs within the range that had been identified. The method they used was to estimate the costs and revenues associated with each option and then work out the net present value using a discount rate of 9½%. However, the results were to a considerable extent predetermined by the inclusion in every option of various developments, e.g. the new blast furnace at South Teeside, and by the exclusion in every case of open hearth plant. It was simply taken for granted that this should be scrapped, though at Shotton it was assumed in some options that it would be replaced by oxygen convertors.

Of the alternatives that were considered, the most profitable was to provide 33 million tonnes of capacity in 1980 by retaining the Corporation's smaller works, viz. Shotton, Consett, Corby and Normanby Park, and by slightly increasing potential output at Port Talbot. It was decided to re-examine this and two of the other options. One of these, which provided for 36 million tonnes of capacity, assumed that all the smaller works would be closed, but included major expansion at Port Talbot and Redcar. It was the sixth most profitable but, after various assumptions had been changed and the figures had been reworked, it became the most profitable, albeit by a very small margin, and was duly selected. It is difficult to avoid the conclusion that the scales were deliberately weighted against the less ambitious strategies. It was postulated that if BSC had a large share of the home market its domestic price would be higher than if it had a smaller share. If this ridiculous assumption had not been made, the most profitable option out of those which were finally considered would have been to provide 30 million tonnes of capacity by means of a small expansion at Port Talbot and the retention of Corby, Consett and Normanby Park, but not Shotton.

Not only did the Corporation engage in statistical legerdemain, but it assumed that it would require far more plant than it could possibly need in order to produce 36 million tonnes. Once again the Corporation was leaving works out of balance and was assuming that low standards of performance would persist. The Department was rightly sceptical about the Corporation's revised plan, although its doubts probably centred on whether BSC would be able to sell all the steel it was planning to produce. However at the crucial moment the Department of Industry was put in the hands of Mr Peter Walker, who it will be recalled treated the railways in such an open-handed manner. He was quickly convinced by the Corporation's leaders that their modernisation programme was essential for Britain's future industrial strength, and it was sanctioned at the end of 1972.

Before any action had been taken Labour, which was greatly concerned at the loss of jobs, had come to power and as a result BSC's plans were re-examined (by Lord Beswick) to discover whether the closure programme was justified. As we have seen it had simply been taken for granted that steelmaking should cease at most of the smaller works and when it came to argue the case for closure the Corporation had difficulty in establishing that *some* projected closures would lead to an overall saving in costs. For instance, Hartlepool works possessed one of the Corporation's newest blast furnaces and made its cheapest iron, and its open hearth furnaces could, like all open hearths, use a high proportion of cheap scrap.

BSC's problems were compounded by the fact that costs were, and would remain, very high at some of the steelmaking centres where output was to be concentrated. Unit costs, for instance, were virtually the same at Shotton and Port Talbot, even though the latter had LD. When presenting the case against installing the new steelmaking plant at Shotton it became apparent that if oxygen converters were installed the cost per tonne would be much lower than at Port Talbot if the output of the latter works were expanded to 3½ million tonnes, viz. £41.2 per tonne for hot rolled coil, including capital charges, as against £45.2 per tonne (at original prices). Even if Port Talbot were, as the Corporation wished, expanded to 6 million tonnes its cost per tonne would, at £40.4, be only fractionally less than the cost at Shotton. The crucial figures were deleted from the Brochure in which the Corporation set out its case.

However, it was probably BSC's inability to meet the demand for steel which convinced the Government that some closures should be postponed. Its concern was understandable since, as we shall see, BSC had considerable supply problems during 1973 and 1974 primarily because of the shortfall in production at its principal works. Nevertheless it was evident by the beginning of 1975, when it was finally announced that some of the closures would be delayed, that BSC was running into a problem of serious over capacity. The Corporation was proposing, with the Government's blessing, to accelerate its development strategy and provide 35 million tonnes of capacity in the early 1980s. This was totally unrealistic. No allowance had been made for the slow down in economic growth or for the decline in the Corporation's share of the market. I estimated at the time that BSC would only be able to sell 24 million tonnes of steel in 1981, though even this will turn out to be a wild over-estimate.[8]

The expansion of Port Talbot and the construction of the brown field works at South Teeside have now been dropped; the Corporation has managed to end the production of crude steel at all of the open hearth works; and output has, for better or worse, been largely concentrated at the five main steelmaking centres. However, the Corporation has failed to transform the industry by either building a monster green field works or undertaking large developments that were not on the stocks at the time of nationalisation. As its plans were over-ambitious and ill-conceived this is no bad thing,

TABLE 11.1 BSC Iron and Steel: Output, Productivity and Finances

	Weighted output	Crude steel production	Crude steel capacity	Percentage of capacity employed September	Employment in September	Average weekly hours equivalent worked by manual workers, Sept. week	Output per equivalent worker manual	Quantity of capital	Output per unit of labour and capital	Real unit operating costs	Real unit staff costs	Real staff costs per employee	Relative weekly earnings of manual men, autumn	Real cost of materials and fuel[a]	Real revenue per unit	Revenue	Gross surplus	Gross surplus as % of revenue	Surplus as after stock appreciation[b]
	(1968=100)	(m tonnes)	(m tonnes)	(%)	(000)					(1968=100)						(£m, 1978 prices)	(£m, 1978 prices)	(%)	(£m, 1978 prices)
1958	78.9[a]	..	23.6[a]	82.6[a]	310.2[a]	46.4[a]	70.4[a]	66.6[a]	82.9[a]	..	..	..	..	..	126.7[a]	..	586[c]	..	..
1963	86.6[a]	20.5	29.0[a]	78.8[a]	304.8[a]	44.5[a]	81.4[a]	91.1[a]	85.9[a]	..	..	..	100.7[a]	107.1	113.9[a]	..	432[c]	..	..
1968	100.0	24.0	32.0[a]	82.2[a]	286.8[a]	44.4[a]											274[c]	8.5	
			27.4	87.4	225.3	44.3	100.0	100.0	100.0	100.0	100.0	100.0	100.0	100.0	100.0	3,331	283		
1969	104.0	24.4	26.8	90.9	227.0	44.6	102.7	100.9	102.8	99.5	100.5	104.0	100.3	96.5	99.7	3,556	309	8.7	191
1970	107.1	25.2	27.8	90.5	229.9	44.6	104.5	102.6	104.5	105.8	108.1	110.6	103.0	98.3	106.1	3,785	331	8.7	213
1971	93.9	21.8	27.5	79.4	212.0	42.8	102.2	106.2	96.9	102.8	117.3	110.4	99.0	99.7	99.9	3,250	193	5.9	..
1972	99.5	22.8	27.7	82.7	203.9	43.7	111.0	110.9	102.5	97.6	114.8	118.7	104.4	95.7	96.0	3,114	215	6.9	191
1973	101.9	23.9	27.7	86.5	201.4	44.8	112.9	114.3	103.3	96.2	115.2	123.4	103.7	95.8	97.4	3,364	323	9.6	213
1974	83.4	19.2	27.4	70.4	195.9	44.6	95.4	117.3	85.2	117.3	144.8	131.1	106.7	112.2	120.0	3,512	371	10.6	174
1975	71.3	16.8	28.5	59.4	191.7	41.9	87.1	120.6	74.7	134.9	170.3	137.5	110.1	115.9	124.3	2,959	19	0.6	-129
1976	84.5	19.1	28.3	67.3	182.6	44.8	103.5	124.5	87.5	129.4	144.6	143.1	114.6	124.5	122.1	3,216	99	3.1	13
1977	74.6	17.2	28.5	60.5	182.4	44.3	92.1	128.0	76.6	139.0	161.0	144.1	113.0	125.8	122.4	3,134	-122	-3.9	-256
1978	73.6	16.7	26.9	62.1	167.6	44.6	98.4	129.9	78.2	132.1	159.0	146.9	110.1	119.6	118.4	3,006	-62	-2.1	-134

Note The output index comprises thirty one indicators (product tonnes delivered) combined with 1963 weights for factor payments and fuel. Allowance was made for the overall change in stocks. The unit series were estimated using weighted deliveries before allowance for variations in stocks. The wholesale price index for steel shows a real increase of 38% between 1968 and 1978, but if BSC's revenue is converted to constant prices using this index the reduction turns out to be unreasonably large. Financial figures were calculated from financial year data. Capacity was derived from BSC's figures for prospective capacity on completion of investment schemes, etc., and allowance was made for open hearth plant taken out of commission. The quantity of capital is the CSO's estimate for gross capital stock less capital expenditure on uncompleted schemes at South Teeside and Ravenscraig. A capital weight of 34.9% was used.

[a] Figures for the whole steel industry.

[b] Financial year (April-March) beginning during the year shown.

especially as it greatly under-estimated the amount of capital expenditure required.

BSC's plans, although they have proved abortive, are of considerable interest and importance. Their formulation, and protracted examination by the Government, absorbed the time and energy of those who were in charge of the Corporation. This was the more serious because effort was also dissipated in other ways. After the Conservatives returned to power in 1970 they started a time-consuming debate about whether any of BSC's activities should be hived off. Energy was also wasted on administrative reorganisation: the product groups which were introduced in 1970 were scrapped in 1976. These distractions help to explain why so little progress has been made towards improving BSC's performance. Moreover while the Corporation was dreaming about monster green field works it was neglecting opportunities for unspectacular but desirable investment. In particular it was not installing sufficient plant for continuous casting in order to cut costs — a mistake which the civil servants spotted — and it was undertaking too little investment at the finishing end with the aim of providing its customers with a better product. Indeed the whole balance of its investment programme was wrong.

OUTPUT AND MARKET SHARE

Between 1968 and 1970, as Table 11.1 shows, the Corporation's output increased by 7% and crude steel production rose from 24 million tonnes to over 25 million. This was an all time high, since the most that the Corporation's predecessors had produced was something under 25 million tonnes in 1965. In the recession of the early 1970s production fell away and although it recovered slightly during 1973 less than 24 million tonnes was produced and output was only 2% greater than in 1968. After this output fell sharply and in 1978 it was 26% lower than it had been in 1968. The Corporation produced only 16½ million tonnes of steel, which was appreciably less than its predecessors had manufactured in 1956. Mention should perhaps be made of the transfer of Brymbo to GKN in the autumn of 1973, although this only reduced BSC's production by about 350,000 tonnes.

Since 1971 there has been a sharp decline in the Corporation's market share. During 1968, as can be seen from Table 11.2, BSC

TABLE 11.2. *Steel Deliveries and Market Shares*

	BSC's share of UK crude steel production (%)	Deliveries of finished steel to UK home market			Total BSC deliveries of finished steel as percentage of net home disposals
		By BSC (%)	By private sector (%)	Imports (%)	
1968	91.1	66.1	24.8	9.1	105.6
1969	90.8	69.3	24.4	6.4	106.4
1970	90.6	70.4	24.1	5.5	108.0
1971	90.3	66.6	24.6	8.8	110.0
1972	90.3	63.2	24.0	12.7	103.7
1973	89.9	62.8	24.5	12.7	96.5
1974	86.0	57.0	25.2	17.7	85.2
1975	85.4	54.1	25.2	20.7	83.6
1976	85.6	53.7	25.7	20.6	85.6
1977	84.5	54.5	25.1	20.3	89.3
1978	82.1	54.1	24.8	21.0	85.8
		Product tonnes (000)			
1968	..	11,285	4,243	1,557	17,957[a]
1978	..	8,368	3,838	3,250	13,037[a]

[a] BSC's total deliveries. The 1978 figure is partly estimated.

accounted for 66% of the finished steel that was delivered to the home market, and in 1970, when imports were expensive, its share reached 70%. Thereafter it declined rapidly to 54% in 1975: a level that BSC then managed to maintain. The ground that BSC lost has been taken up by imports. In 1968 they constituted less than 10% of deliveries, but by 1978 the figure had reached 21%. The independent steel producers have maintained their share at 25%. These figures do not take any account of the steel that the private sector purchases for further manufacture. Here, too, BSC has been losing business and in consequence its share of crude steel production has fallen from 91% in 1968 to 82% in 1978. If the Corporation's total deliveries to all consumers at home and abroad are related to net domestic deliveries it is found that during 1968 BSC's sales were 6% greater. They stayed at about this point until the early 1970s, but by 1978 the Corporation's sales were 14% smaller than domestic deliveries. If BSC had maintained the position that it held at the beginning of the period, its output would only have fallen by about 9% between 1968 and 1978. This means that approximately two-thirds of the decline in the Corporation's production was due to the fact that it lost ground and became less competitive. It may be replied that imports still account for a smaller proportion of domestic consumption than in any of the other Common Market countries and that they, like us, have been flooded by cheap steel from the Far East. However, every other major steel producing nation in the Common Market had higher net exports in 1978 than in 1968. Our net exports of steel slumped from 2,125,000 product tonnes to under 550,000, largely because of a surge in imports from the Six. Imports from the Far East have played a minor part.

The reduction in Britain's net exports and the decline in the Corporation's market position have been mainly due to its inability to meet its customers' requirements. BSC has not been able to produce enough steel and the quality of its output has not been sufficiently high. Supply difficulties started to occur in 1968 and during both 1969 and 1970 the Corporation diverted 1 to 1½ million tonnes of steel from exports to the home market, and had to import about 1 million tonnes of finished and semi-finished products to supplement its own production. During 1972 BSC again started to run into supply difficulties and they reached major proportions between 1973 and 1975. Exports were severely restricted. In 1973 the Corporation's foreign sales were about 2 million tonnes lower than had been planned and during the following year an even greater amount of foreign business was sacrificed. BSC's production problems continued throughout 1975 and 1976, even though demand was now very low and production was extremely depressed. During 1976–77 foreign sales continued to be restricted and, largely in consequence, the Corporation's exports were nearly 1½ million tonnes below target.

Despite the diversion of supplies to the home market, the Corporation was, to quote its own words, 'unable to produce sufficient steel, in many instances to meet required delivery times, or make steel of the right quality'.[9] BSC's average delivery time, which even in 1971 was as long as eight weeks, increased steadily from the summer of 1972 to the summer of 1974, when it reached nearly fifteen weeks. During 1975 it was still over ten and a half weeks and, according to a survey which BSC commissioned, customers were highly critical of the Corporation's long and unreliable delivery times. Some of BSC's major customers told the Select Committee that they had begun to buy large quantities from other sources because the Corporation had failed to meet their requirements. British Leyland reported that the proportion of sheet steel obtained from BSC had fallen, as a result of supply problems, from nearly 80% between 1971 and 1973 to 63% in 1976. Despite this a third of the steel from BSC arrived more than two weeks late. Up to 1974 BSC supplied 80–85% of the cold rolled steel that Ford used but in 1975 and 1976 the figure was only 55%. This was partly because the Corporation said that it could not supply all the steel that Fords required, partly because it failed to provide what it had promised, and partly because it was unable to meet quality requirements. The standards for body panels had been raised and although the continental producers had improved their quality BSC had not. Up to 1973 GKN purchased around 87% of its steel from BSC, ignoring supplies from Brymbo. However during 1974 the Corporation was unable to meet its needs and GKN found itself in serious difficulties. It switched to alternative sources of supply and in 1975 BSC met only 73% of GKN's requirements.[10]

Due to its supply problems the Corporation has established a poor reputation. A customer survey of 1977 showed that only 6% thought that BSC's delivery performance was better than that of other producers, while 24% regarded it as worse or much worse. Those firms who dealt only with BSC were reasonably satisfied, but those who had become accustomed to superior service from abroad tended to make unfavourable comparisons. Similarly when customers were asked to rate the quality of BSC's products it was those who regularly imported from the Continent who were most critical. Although it was acknowledged that the Corporation's delivery standards had improved during 1976, customers had great doubts about its future performance.[11] BSC had to provide exceptionally good service if it was to convince customers, who had formerly dealt with a number of its constituent companies, that it was reliable, but its standards were for a number of years particularly poor. Many steel users obviously decided to permanently diversify their sources of supply, and one of the main reasons why the private steel producers have been increasing their crude steel capacity is to reduce their dependence on the Corporation.

BSC should have been able to meet its customers' needs during the immediate post-nationalisation period. It is shown in Table 11.1 as having utilised 90% of its capacity during 1970. This seems to suggest that BSC was short of capacity. However the rate of utilisation was lower than during some previous years of high demand and BSC, whose capacity figures are being used at this point, has revised the old Iron and Steel Board estimates down by 2 million tonnes; although there is no reason to believe that they were unrealistic, since most districts operated at well over 90% during some year in the mid-1960s.[12] The Corporation complained that some plant had not been properly maintained and the breakdowns which occured when it tried to work plant intensively were a major reason why, during 1970–71, its production was nearly 2 million tonnes less than had been planned. However if maintenance had been neglected it was up to the Corporation to remedy the situation, but in fact the shortfall in production was less serious at the older works than at Port Talbot's new LD shop.

BSC should not have had any difficulty in meeting its customers' requirements during the next period of high demand. Although, as we have seen, a substantial rise in output had been planned the Corporation only managed to produce about 24 million tonnes during 1973, which was 1.2 million tonnes lower than it had produced in 1970 and 850,000 tonnes less than its predecessors had achieved in 1965. In 1974 the Corporation's output slumped to 19.3 million tonnes. This was partly due to the coal strike (and the transfer of Brymbo), but only 1.75 million tonnes of production was lost during the dispute. The Corporation attributed its production problems to shortages of scrap and coal. However this does not seem a very convincing excuse because BSC dissipated its stocks of scrap during 1972 and then rebuilt them to a relatively high level in 1974. Coal did not become a problem until after the miners' strike when more could have been imported if BSC had been willing to pay the price, and brave the Government, and scrap could also have been purchased abroad. It is obvious that there were more fundamental reasons for the low level of output.

During 1973 and 1974 BSC had much less capacity than it had been planning because the Corporation, despite its plans for expansion, was slow to sanction developments at Scunthorpe, Llanwern and Ravenscraig. As a result, and because of the closure of open hearth plant, BSC's capacity appears to have been little or no higher during 1973–74 than it had been in 1970. Despite this BSC would have been able to produce sufficient steel if it had made the most of the plant that was available. During 1973 the Corporation had a potential of about 27½ million tonnes but only managed to produce 24 million, which meant that around 85% of its capacity was utilised. When the situation is examined in detail it is found that at thirteen of the Corporation's small works, where there had been no change in plant and machinery, production was 400,000 tonnes lower than in 1965. But it was at the great steelmaking centres that the shortfall in production was most serious. Port Talbot, Llanwern and Lackenby had a potential of 8 million tonnes, but they only provided 6 million tonnes, which means that no more than 75% of their capacity was utilised. At Scunthorpe the huge new BOS plant managed to produce a mere 1.1 million tonnes.

At Scunthorpe and Llanwern industrial disputes contributed to the low level of output, and at the older works capacity had not always been maintained due to the failure to replace relatively small items of plant which had worn out. However, the major reason why BSC did not secure a higher output was almost certainly its poor operating practice and the use, under Government pressure, of the NCB's low grade coking coal. During 1972–73 the steelmaking cycle at basic oxygen furnaces averaged only thirty nine minutes at thirteen works in Austria and Japan, which were the countries with the best performance; and the (weighted) average for forty plants in eleven major steel-producing countries was 48 minutes. The corresponding figure for four of BSC's works — Port Talbot, Llanwern,

Ravenscraig and Normanby Park — was 60 minutes. Even the best of our works had a tap-to-tap time only slightly shorter than the foreign average.

During recent years BSC has been suffering from excess capacity but, as we have seen, it was still unable to meet the demand that was available. For instance during 1976, when export business was being turned away, only about two-thirds of capacity was utilised, and capacity has, if anything, been understated because of the omission of those open hearth furnaces that were no longer in use. The Corporation's production problems have been due partly to labour disputes and embargoes and partly to inability to make sufficient iron of the right quality. This in turn appears to have been due to frequent changes in the mix of materials, although as the Japanese have shown uninterrupted working is necessary if blast furnaces are to produce a high output and provide iron of a consistent quality. If the quality is not quite right it is usually possible to adjust for this at the steelmaking stage, although it should be added that due to the use of high quality materials very little correction is necessary in Japan.

The Corporation's failure to provide sufficient steel led to heavy steel imports which imposed a considerable strain on the balance of payments. During 1968–70 the UK's exports of steel exceeded its imports by about £375 million and in 1971, when exports were no longer restricted, the figure increased to £475 million. Thereafter net exports fell away sharply, at first because of the availability of cheap imports, but subsequently due to the Corporation's inability to satisfy demand. By 1973 our net exports had fallen to £140 million and during the following year the figure was −£250 million. The UK remained an importing nation until 1976 and during 1978 exports only exceeded imports by a paltry £40 million. During 1973 and 1974 steel was in such short supply that the output of the consuming industries was held back. In mid-1973 a third of the firms covered by the CBI's survey of industrial trends reported that shortage of materials and components was the factor most likely to restrict their output during the coming months. According to the Director-General of the CBI, it was lack of steel which mainly explained why the proportion mentioning materials was much higher than ever before.[13] It is clear that the shortage of steel did have a serious effect on output in industries such as construction, because of a dearth of reinforcing rods, and in firms like GKN, where production was restricted.

EMPLOYMENT AND PRODUCTIVITY

In 1968 about 225,000 BSC workers were engaged on the production of iron and steel (to which all succeeding figures relate unless otherwise indicated). During 1970 employment reached 230,000 but in the following year output fell sharply and the labour force was cut back. It has been falling ever since and by 1978 had been reduced to 168,000, which was 25% less than in 1968.

Between 1968 and 1973 output per effective worker rose fairly steadily apart from a dip in 1971 when output slumped; and by 1973 it was 13% greater than in 1968. Since 1974 output has been very depressed, and although the labour force has been reduced it has not fallen to the same extent. During 1978 OEW was slightly lower than it had been ten years previously. Because steel is so capital intensive output per worker is a relatively poor measure of productivity, and the heavy investment which the Corporation has undertaken appears to have led to a significant rise in the quantity of capital in use. As a result my estimates show total factor productivity (TFP) as having increased by only 3% over the period 1968–73, although this may be rather misleading because of the growth in the amount of capital expenditure tied up in uncompleted projects from which BSC had had no benefit. Since 1973 there has been a substantial fall in TFP and during 1978 it appears to have been 22% lower than in 1968 (and this despite the exclusion from the Corporation's capital stock of expenditure on the two largest schemes that were still under construction). In view of the reduction in the proportion of capacity being utilised, it is hardly surprising that TFP has fallen. However, even if the rate of utilisation had remained at the 1968 level there would, allowing for a little extra labour, have been very little increase over the course of the decade. (If the statistics were to be extended to 1979 BSC's record would appear slightly better, at least for labour productivity. However, this was largely due to higher output which was, in turn, partly due to heavy production for stock in anticipation of closures.)

The Corporation's productivity has been growing more slowly than that of foreign steel producers. Between 1964 and 1978 output per man hour rose by 210% in Japan, almost 110% in Germany, over 90% in France, and 33% in the US. However in the UK there was an increase of only 18%, though most of the foreign producers had the advantage that their output increased by an amount which the British steel industry could not hope to match. Because their productivity has been growing faster the other major steel producing nations have in general increased their lead over the UK. By 1978 output per man hour was greater by about 165% in Japan, 125% in the United States, 100% in Germany and about 65% in France.[14]

It is also instructive to compare the Corporation's performance with the targets that were set out in the report of the Benson Committee which examined the industry shortly before nationalisation. The Committee concluded that by 1975, 'the Industry should be able to produce about a third more steel with about a third less men'.[15] This means that productivity should have risen by about 80% between 1968 and 1975. In 1973 when, as we have seen, productivity was at a peak, BSC produced only 12% more crude steel per worker than it had in 1968. Since the Benson Committee's forecasts of demand and output were much too high it is scarcely surprising that the Corporation did not manage to obtain an increase of 80%. It is significant however that the Corporation, despite the low level of its output, has only managed to reduce its labour force to the level that was necessary if the Benson target was to be achieved. If BSC had reduced its employment in line with the reduction that the Committee postulated for the industry it would, by 1975, only have had about 160,000 steel workers. However, BSC was still employing this number in September 1978 despite the fact that it produced little more than half as much steel as the Benson forecasts imply. Perhaps the Committee, which was set up to ward off nationalisation, was over-optimistic. But the Corporation was itself planning to reduce its total employment by 50,000 to around 200,000 in 1975. By the autumn of 1978 the labour force had been reduced to 190,000, but by then extensive closures had taken place and these were not allowed for in the Corporation's original plans.

BSC's employment would have fallen faster but for the very small decline in salaried staff and in the number of workers in maintenance and service jobs. Here employment only fell from 140,000 in 1969 to 122,000 in 1978, which was a decline of no more than 13%. In contrast the number of production workers was almost cut in half, falling from 87,000 to 46,000. This was due mainly to the replacement of open hearth furnaces by BOS and to the scrapping of old labour intensive plant. It might have been expected that this would also have led to a substantial reduction in maintenance since LD converters require much less servicing than an equivalent amount of open hearth capacity. Moreover the fall in production and the fact that equipment was being used less intensively should have contributed to lower maintenance requirements. Although pressure from customers for higher quality steel has had an opposite effect, it is nevertheless surprising that the number of maintenance workers has declined so little. It is even more astonishing that there has been virtually no reduction in service jobs and that the decline in salaried staff has not been greater, if only because a large number are engaged on employment-related activities such as the payment of wages and catering.

During 1977 technical, administrative and clerical staff accounted for 30% of BSC's employment as against 24% in nine of the principal steel producing countries in OECD. Moreover, a study that BSC made at Llanwern and the Sidmar works in Belgium showed that the latter had one white collar employee for every 3.6 manual workers, whereas at Llanwern it was one per 2.1. The contrast was even sharper than it appears because Sidmar is a separate company employing staff who in BSC work at headquarters and other places away from the works. The study also showed that far more workers were employed on the maintenance of plant and equipment at Llanwern and Ravenscraig. At Llanwern there was one maintenance worker for every 1.15 operatives directly engaged on production whereas at Sidmar there was one per 1.7. This difference was largely explained by the more flexible use of labour at Sidmar, by the presence of craftmen's mates at Llanwern, and by the fact that the maintenance service operates round the clock at Llanwern but is only on a two-shift basis at Sidmar, although its maintenance standards are excellent. The level of manning did not appear to be very different in the production departments at Sidmar and Llanwern and the Corporation does not appear to be greatly over manned in this area. That BSC is over manned on the maintenance side but not in production has been confirmed by subsequent comparisons between the main BOS shop at Scunthorpe and Hoogovens in Holland, and between plate mills at Clydebridge and in Sweden.[16]

However there is no doubt that elsewhere BSC uses labour inefficiently. It was recognised at the time of nationalisation that there was considerable scope to make economies through work study, job evaluation and productivity bargaining. The Corporation hoped that it would in this way be able to slim down its labour force by 20,000. Although agreements were concluded with the unions it seems very doubtful whether any real progress was made. The reduction in BSC's employment appears to have been very largely accounted for by rationalisation and the replacement of old plant. It was not until 1975 when BSC was in serious financial difficulties that any general attempt was made to revise manning standards and improve the efficiency with which labour was being used. At the beginning of 1976 an agreement was concluded with the unions in which they recognised the need to raise productivity and reduce employment over the next two years by altering working practices and using labour more flexibly. However, the Secretary of the leading steel union was sceptical about whether the agreement would lead to any great or immediate saving in labour, and little progress was made in establishing the local joint teams which were supposed to work out the ways in which manpower could be cut.[17] As a result there was only a minute reduction in employment between April 1976 and September 1977.

But productivity is also low because BSC is 'over equipped'. The comparison between the matched melting shops in Britain and Holland showed that although the overall level of manning was similar productivity was higher at Hoogovens because of Scunthorpe's restricted output.[16] In 1978 BSC produced 11 million tonnes at its LD converters but they could have provided 33 million tonnes if they had been operated at a little below the best foreign standards, viz. 13,000 heats per annum and a tap-to-tap time of 40 minutes. The Corporation also possessed an ironmaking and finishing capacity that was greatly in excess of its production That BSC has so much plant in relation to its output was obviously partly due to the depressed state of demand and the fall in its market share. However there were other reasons. First, some of the Corporation's works are, like Scunthorpe, out of balance, which means that its effective capacity is lower than the potential production of the equipment used at each stage in the steelmaking process. Second, operating practice is very poor and BSC fails to make the best use of the capacity that is available. Although it would require a lengthy inquiry to discover how BSC's performance differs from that of the most efficient foreign producers the underlying reason is almost certainly that its managers and workers have low expectations and lack commitment. During 1978–79 absence from work averaged twenty-six days per manual employee and in Scotland the figure was thirty.[18] The same *malaise* affects much of British industry, whether in public or private ownership, but the situation is not immutable as shown by the excellent results which are now being achieved at Sheerness and some other works in the independent steelmaking sector.

COSTS, PRICES AND PROFITS

Between 1968 and 1973 BSC's operating costs per unit of output varied from year to year, but did not display any tendency to increase. Although unit staff costs rose, this was offset by a reduction in the price of fuel and materials. The latter form a larger proportion of BSC's costs than labour, which accounted for only a quarter of its operating expenditure in 1968. After 1973 unit costs shot up and during 1975 they were about a third higher than in 1968. Unit staff costs rocketed and there was a jump in the price of coking coal and iron ore. Although unit costs were lower in 1978 than they had been during the previous year they remained around a third greater than in 1968. Unit staff costs had increased to a point 60% above their 1968 level, due partly to the absence of any increase in productivity and partly to a rise in relative earnings. Between 1968 and 1978 steel workers' relative earnings increased by 10% and staff costs per employee increased by 45% compared with 29% for manufacturing.

During the period between 1968 and 1973 the Corporation's prices, like its unit costs, appear to have been more or less stable. As a result the gross profit margin stayed about the same at around 9%, except that it dipped down in 1971 and 1972 when demand was weak. During 1974, when the Corporation's costs began their rapid climb, prices increased even faster and there was a temporary rise in the profit margin. Since then prices have been on a plateau about 20% above the 1968 level and, with unit cost around a third greater, the gross margin has been severely squeezed. After allowing for stock appreciation the Corporation has, with one exception, made a gross loss every year since 1975–76. In 1977–78, when unit costs were particularly high, there was a gross loss of around £250 million, and in 1978–79 the figure amounted to £135 million which was a negative margin of 4½%. If allowance were also to be made for replacement cost depreciation, at around £300 million, BSC's deficit would become horrendous but as the Corporation has an enormous amount of surplus capacity it would be wrong to expect BSC to meet its capital charges in full.

However, BSC should have at least covered its replacement cost depreciation during the period before excess capacity emerged. It did not achieve this at any time from 1971–72 to 1973–74. The Corporation claims that it would have earned a large amount of extra revenue if it had been allowed to raise its prices. Its estimates of the revenue forgone — a total of nearly £1,800 million between 1967–68 and 1974–75 — were based on the level of prices as published by the steel companies in France and Germany.[19] However, during the early 1970s when there was an international steel recession, secret rebates were available on the Continent and it was necessary for BSC prices to be somewhat lower because the quality of its products tended to be inferior. If BSC had raised its prices imports would have risen even faster than they did. During 1969 and 1970 prices could have been increased without any loss of business, and the same was true in 1973 and 1974 when the private steel producers were for a considerable time charging more than the Corporation. But BSC's estimates imply that if it had had a free hand its prices would, during 1973–74, have been 18% higher!

BSC Now

During the autumn of 1977 BSC which had previously been waiting for demand to recover became alarmed at its deteriorating financial position, the weakness of the market and its poor long term prospects. It was therefore decided, with the Government's consent, to embark on a closure programme and, with the exception of Shotton, to shut those works and steelmaking facilities which had been granted stay of execution by Lord Beswick. Between the autumn of 1977 and the middle of 1979 the Corporation wholly or partly closed eight of its smaller works. This led to a reduction in employment of about 12,000 and brought open hearth steelmaking to an end everywhere except Shotton. The Corporation's chairman, Sir Charles Villiers, also indulged in some fighting talk about the need to cut costs and raise productivity.

However, closures apart, relatively little was done to improve BSC's performance. Those in charge were well aware that action would have to be taken, but thought that there was still time in which to persuade the unions and effect the changes that were necessary. Hence although it would be unfair to say that the Corporation's leaders were doing nothing — they were busily closing works — they are open to the criticism of having done too little. That further steps were necessary should have been evident from the huge deficit that was being incurred. Nevertheless BSC remained surprisingly optimistic and declared that it would soon have eliminated its loss. When the Conservatives came to power they pressed the Corporation to undertake what it had promised.

Finally, in the latter part of 1979, the deteriorating economic situation, and the preparation of new and even more gloomy forecasts of UK steel consumption, led the Corporation to announce drastic measures. In December it was announced that the Corporation was planning to cut back production to only 15 million tonnes of liquid steel (as against 17.4 in 1978 and 18.3 in 1979) and that it would be necessary to take a large amount of capacity out of commission. Shotton and Corby were to lose their steelmaking facilities, which was already known, and Consett and two electric arc works — Cleveland and Hallside — were to be closed down. In addition plant was to be withdrawn from use at Scunthorpe, Llanwern and Port Talbot. As a result of closures and manning reductions the Corporation hoped to reduce its steelmaking employment by 52,000 which, as it stood at 153,000 during September 1979, meant that it would fall to 100,000. BSC aimed to achieve this within eighteen months in order that it should be operating profitably by 1981.[20]

If the Corporation's plans were realised OMY would shoot up from nearly 110 tonnes of liquid steel in 1978 (and 120 in 1979) to 150 tonnes. How much of this rise could be attributed to the adoption of tighter manning standards and how much to the curtailment of output and the concentration of production on the most efficient works? At first sight it appears that the more flexible and efficient use of labour would lead to a reduction of only 12,000 jobs, as this is the figure which BSC gave. However it is necessary to allow for the saving that could be made where plant was going to be demanned. The Corporation planned to take plant out of commission at Port Talbot and Llanwern and to cut their work force by 11,000, but it estimated that it could dispense with 2,550 workers at Llanwern and over 5,000 at Port Talbot just by tightening up efficiency and reducing manning. The works in South Wales were not the only ones where the Corporation was going to take plant out of use and it can be estimated that if manning were to be reduced instead about 600 jobs would be eliminated. (This is not meant to imply that it was impossible to both maintain output and de-man plant but, because I am basing my argument on the Corporation's figures, I am assuming this to be the case.) Hence BSC could make an economy of around 20,200 simply by tightening up efficiency at those works that are not being closed or truncated. To this can be added the reduction in manpower through the closures at Shotton, Corby, Consett, Cleveland and Hallside (17,600) and the reduction as a result of minor closures and other measures which were already in hand (8,000).[20] This meant that BSC could, while maintaining its output, slim its labour force down by nearly 46,000. If employment were to be so reduced and BSC produced 17.4 tonnes, as it did in 1978, its OMY would increase to 162 tonnes. Hence the cutback in output which the Corporation was planning would tend to depress its productivity.

A reduction in employment of something under 46,000 would produce a saving in labour costs of £270 million. This was by no means the only economy that could be made. The NCB increased the price of its coking coal by about 90% during 1974–75 and as a result imports of many qualities became cheaper at coastal works. In 1979 the Corporation estimated that by reducing its consumption of British coal from 9 million tonnes to zero it could reduce its expenditure by £135 million (at April 1979 prices).[21] Home produced coal was a third more expensive, its use involved considerable cost penalties and it seemed likely that foreign coal's price advantage would widen. Moreover the cost of imports would have had to rise about 50% in order to make British coking coal competitive. Also it must be remembered that much of the coal which the Corporation received from the NCB was being produced at a large loss. As the world steel industry was so depressed there would be no problem in obtaining supplies from abroad and the only obstacle to their use — apart from the miners and the Coal Board — was the handling problems that would arise at the ports if imports were increased beyond 6 million tonnes. However these difficulties ought not to have been insurmountable and very little saving was to be made by dispensing with the final 1–2 million tonnes of home produced coal. Extensive economics were therefore possible, despite the fact that BSC had already stepped up its imports from 1.8 million tonnes to a rate of 2.9 million. (The Corporation has subsequently made a further saving due to the price concession which it has negotiated with the NBC, though this will, of course, drive more of the latter's coking coal pits into deficit.)

Thus if the Corporation had decided to cut its costs but maintain its production it could have reduced its expenditure by about £325 million which would have more than eliminated its gross deficit, which as we have seen amounted to £135 million during 1978–79. However, BSC decided instead to cutback its output and reduce its foreign sales from 3 million product tonnes to only about 1½ million. The Corporation adopted this restrictionist strategy because the prices it received for its exports were very depressed and because its more profitable home market sales were declining. What this ignored was that, as my productivity calculations show, the Corporation would not be able to reduce its costs in line with output; that if costs were reduced exporting would become more attractive; that the contraction of output would make it more difficult to negotiate a reduction in manning standards and to preserve good labour relations; that British customers might become worried about the Corporation's ability to supply and turn elsewhere; and that BSC would sacrifice export business and alienate foreign buyers which are in the long term worth retaining. Moreover the Corporation was being pointed firmly in the wrong direction: towards the declining home market and away from exporting. There is, however, no denying that BSC found itself in an extremely difficult situation, and this indeed is the major point. Having done far too little for far too long the Corporation was in an almost impossible position. Nemesis had come to the British Steel Corporation as it comes to all who fail to remain competitive and become efficient.

BSC's downfall was completed by the three months steel strike at the beginning of 1980. The Corporation made the mistake of starting with a provocatively tiny offer and many steel workers were obviously boiling over with anger at the way in which the Corporation had been managed and the job losses that had just been announced. However the strike was probably inevitable: if it had not taken place over wages it would have come over jobs. The steel workers had refused to recognise that the Corporation needed to make large scale reductions in manning at its continuing works. Because of the strike the Corporation is almost bound to lose a significant part of its home market. Its customers have suffered once again for being so dependent on an unreliable source of supply and will naturally seek to diversify their buying. It has therefore become inevitable that production should be reduced and that drastic rationalisation should take place. However, it is doubtful whether the Corporation will manage to reduce its employment faster than its output and so bring about an increase in productivity.

The time has surely come to recognise that the central planning and management of steel, of which I was once a great advocate, has failed. It is often argued that closure decisions are best made centrally. But it is debatable whether rationalisation is being handled in the optimum manner. For instance it is by no means self-evident that Ravenscraig should be loaded up in preference to Llanwern and Port Talbot, and it may be wrong to close the hot mill at Shotton. And while it is almost certainly right to end steelmaking at Corby it is questionable whether it is desirable to close Consett. Although it is badly located, it is efficiently run and must be more than covering its avoidable costs. The reason why it is marked down for closure is that BSC has surplus capacity and that it has to shut something. This provokes the question of whether it is appropriate, when the decision between closing one works and another is finely balanced, to make a central decision? It might well be preferable for local initiative to be the determining factor. Plants would survive if they were well managed, possessed co-operative employees and were successful at satisfying their customers and gaining business. Such a policy, which would mean dissolving the Corporation, has the attraction that extra business might be obtained at the expense of imports. Because the successor companies would be independent firms it would be possible for buyers to diversify their sources of supply without transferring work abroad and some of the business which the Corporation lost during the period 1971–75 might even be won back. How successful independent firms would be at regaining business it is impossible to tell but the fact that the private producers have retained their share of the home market provides ground for hope.

CHAPTER 12

British Leyland

British Leyland, or BL Limited as it has been rechristened, is still by far the largest motor manufacturer in Britain, and during 1978 it accounted for 45% of the cars and commercial vehicles that we produced. Cars and light commercial vehicles are responsible for some 80% of its revenue from its automative activities in the UK, trucks provide 10%, buses provide 6%, and tractors earn 3%. About 40% of BL's turnover is derived from exports which consist of complete vehicles and of kits that are assembled by the Company's foreign subsidiaries. The latter will however be largely ignored and so too will Prestcold and other peripheral concerns.

British Leyland came into existence in May 1968 through the merger of British Motor Holdings (BMH) and the Leyland Motor Corporation (LMC). BMH controlled Austin, Morris, Pressed Steel (acquired 1965), and Jaguar (1966); while LMC not only manufactured trucks and buses but also owned Standard-Triumph (1961) and Rover (1967). In effect LMC took over BMH though its turnover was more than 50% greater. BMH was in difficulties and the merger was partly prompted by the Government and the Industrial Reorganisation Corporation, although Lord Stokes — LMC's Chairman — did not require much encouragement.

BL's INHERITANCE AND RESPONSE

Between 1963 and 1968 the output of 'British Leyland' increased from 965,000 vehicles to 987,000 and weighted production rose by only 6%. BL's market share — as measured by its output expressed as a proportion of new vehicles registered in the UK — declined from 77% to 71% and its share of total UK production fell from 48% to 44%. This was entirely because of the poor performance of

210

BMH, due primarily to a large decline in the number of commercial vehicles that it sold. Ford introduced a range of new and highly successful vehicles and BMH lost ground. In cars, where there was a slight decline in production, the only volume car that BMH introduced was the 1800. It did not sell well because of its poor styling and initial difficulties with the engine.

The product line which BL inherited had serious weaknesses. It contained a substantial amount of deadwood such as the Minor which dated back to 1948 and was no longer profitable. What was far more serious was the absence of any satisfactory mass produced model in the range from 1200 cc to 2000 cc which was where sales had been growing most rapidly. The BL cars of this size and type tended to be old models, such as the A60 and Morris Oxford, which had been introduced in 1959, or commercial failures like the 1800. The only one that was produced in really large numbers was the Austin-Morris 1300. Although the 1300 and its sister car, the 1100, were not yet at the end of their lives, the model had been launched in 1962. The Mini, which was the other work horse in the BL stable, was even older. It dated back to 1959 and could not be expected to last for ever.

Because of the continued production of old and unsuccessful models and because the constituent companies each made different cars, British Leyland had far too many models. During 1968 Ford manufactured only five different types of body shell but BL was making twenty although its production was only about 50% greater. According to estimates by Mr C.F. Pratten of the cost of producing one basic model and its variants, operating expenditure per car is about 8% higher for an ouput of 100,000 than for one of 250,000.[1] Moreover costs per car are 9% higher where, although 250,000 cars are being made, there are three models instead of one. Another weakness was that BL's production was spread over too many sites. British Leyland had sixteen assembly plants for its cars and lorries whereas Ford, with two-thirds of BL's production, had three. The Ford car factories at Dagenham and Halewood were integrated plants whereas some of BL's assembly works received their bodies from other works. Body shells for the 1100–1300 were built at Swindon, partly from pressings that had come from Llanelli. They were then shipped to Cowley and to Longbridge at a cost of £15 per car. BL was also incurring over £10 million of expenditure on additional transport because of the construction of plants at

Bathgate and Speke as a result of the Government's policy of creating work in areas of high unemployment.[2]

These structural weaknesses were compounded by deficiences in the design of BMH's models. The Mini and 1100–1300 were both relatively expensive to build because of their complexity and because they had not been planned to have the lowest possible costs of construction. When Ford designed the Cortina it began by stripping down its competitors' models and costing each part. A cost target was then set for each item which its designers were not allowed to exceed unless there was some compensating advantage, and to which the technical cost estimators, who worked side by side with the designers, ensured that they adhered. The same approach was subsequently adopted by Vauxhall. The result was that the Cortina, the Viva and later the Escort could be built very cheaply though their design appeared somewhat unadventurous. The Mini and the 1100–1300 were in contrast the creations of a virtuoso designer — Sir Alec Issigonis — who, although he believed that cars should be functional and made some remarkable engineering advances, did not provide BMH with models that were inexpensive to produce. The Mini was said to carry an engineering cost penalty of about £100 per car, and its price was established at too low a level.

Between 1963 and 1968 output per man appears to have been stagnant within BL; and during 1967 Ford's productivity — as measured by the number of vehicles per worker — was over 25% greater than that of Austin-Morris (including related employment at Pressed Steel Fisher).[3] After Leyland had taken charge Mr John Barber, the new director of Finance, made a broad brush comparison between British Leyland and other motor manufacturers, including Ford and Volkswagen. Although he allowed for the greater average age of BL's equipment it appeared that the Company was employing 30,000 more workers than it required. This represented 16% of its labour force.

BMH had been largely run by production men who had worked their way up from the shop floor. The top management did not believe in detailed financial analysis and control, in market research or in forward planning. They placed their faith in their own experience, judgement and intuition. In practice they were insular and inward looking and were not even properly informed about their competitors' products. Barber later discovered that BMH management was not very interested in testing out other manufacturers' cars and even Issigonis declared that he tried hard 'not to be influenced by anything that comes out of Europe or America'.[4] Ford were always comparing their performance and products with those of their rivals; they had developed cost control and analysis to a fine art, had built up a cadre of managerial personnel and tried, with the assistance of market research, to provide their customers with what they wanted as opposed to what they ought to want.

The weakness of BMH's approach was shown not only by its deteriorating performance but also by the failure to develop any satisfactory new models. The only volume car which had by 1968 reached an advantage stage of development was the Maxi and this was found to have serious shortcomings. The interior was austere and the exterior was ugly because, due to Issigonis's zeal for minimum parking length, the bonnet was too short. These were the types of weakness that would have been avoided through the use of market research. In addition the gearbox was badly designed, the 1500 cc engine did not provide sufficient power, the car was expensive to build and when it was finally launched early in 1969 it had to be sold at a high price. Hence, although it had been possible to improve its appearance and performance, it was clear that the Maxi would not make any real contribution to the solution of BMH's difficulties.

That they were serious had already been recognised by Mr Joe Edwards who became Managing Director in mid-1966. The labour force was cut by 14,000 and although this was occasioned by the downturn in sales it was intended that employment should be held at a lower level. Edwards intended to make a further reduction of 8,000 by closing down unnecessary factories, he was planning to discontinue some of BMH's old cars and wanted to greatly simplify the model range. When he was in charge of Pressed Steel he had become convinced that it was desirable to abolish piecework, which gave rise to endless disputes, and to switch over to the day wage system that was employed by Ford and Vauxhall. Edwards was also concerned about the quality of BMH's management and began to recruit key men from Ford.[5]

Whether he would have succeeded in rescuing BMH it is impossible to tell. But Leyland was certainly ill qualified to act as saviour and the creation of British Leyland was a mistake. Leyland's takeover of BMH caused resentment within the larger company, and during the earlier years time and energy were wasted in pursuing sectional interests. Old rivalries persisted within BMH and the establishment of British Leyland gave rise to new divisions and fresh disputes. It also made labour relations more difficult because it widened the area within which invidious comparisons could be made and extended the scope for leap-frogging. Wages, for instance, were much lower at the truck and bus plant at Leyland than in BL's car factories in the Midlands and this was one reason for the serious strike which took place in 1969.

The Leyland Motor Corporation did not possess the managerial resources and expertise to sort out the difficulties of BMH. The Corporation was seriously short of competent executives and had not developed the skills necessary to run a large and integrated concern. Lord Stokes was the chairman of each of the companies in the group and, until a short time before the merger, made decisions without the assistance and advice of any central finance or planning departments. The subsidiaries obviously possessed a certain amount of expertise but the Triumph men who were put in charge of Austin-Morris had no experience of managing a giant concern and felt at first like fish out of water. At first Stokes tried to run BL in the same personal way that he had managed LMC. This was impossible because the new group was so much larger and he was not familiar with its problems and personnel. There was a frustrating period of inaction because Stokes blocked the moves which Edwards had been planning and insisted that even the simplest decisions had to be referred to the top. Instead of spurring on the plant managers and formulating a proper long term strategy, Stokes and his colleagues became immersed in the problems of day-to-day management and in trying to sort out local labour disputes.[6] Important decisions were either not taken or the wrong path was chosen.

One of Stokes' earliest decisions was that BL's labour force should not be cut and that no factories were to be closed. Stokes made a declaration to this effect after it had been reported that BL was planning to make 30,000 workers redundant. Stokes did not have to commit himself in this way and it is clear that he only did so because he had already decided that employment was to be maintained at around the existing level. According to Mr Graham Turner, it was Stokes':

> particular ambition to carry through the merger with only a modest number of redundancies, something which Weinstock had been unable to do in taking over AEI: Stokes had no intention of arousing a storm like that provoked by the closure of the plant at Woolwich. In

one way, this aspiration sprang from his own nature — he is essentially a soft-hearted man who finds it difficult to fire people; in another, it expressed a desire to be remembered as an industrialist who was able to combine benevolence with bigness. He was conscious of the bitterness which persisted from the mass sackings of the past and he wanted to bring to the Midlands that mixture of paternalism and efficiency which had characterised the Leyland of his youth.[7]

Stokes was hoping that BL would be able to raise its output to such an extent that it would not need to shed labour. What seemed to be holding production back was not the absence of customers but the Company's inability to produce as a result of continual strikes. Stokes had held talks with the unions and believed that they would cooperate in reducing disputes provided that redundancies were avoided. However labour relations were so embittered and the causes for contention so plentiful that it was hopeless to expect that there would be any improvement unless remedial measures were adopted, and then only in the long run. No such measures had even been put to the unions.

One possible step was to get rid of piecework since the negotiation of rates and the anomalies to which it gave rise were a prime cause of strife. A half-hearted attempt was made to introduce day work on the Maxi but it came to nothing. No further action was taken until the appointment of Mr Pat Lowry as Industrial Relations Director in the spring of 1970. It was then decided to begin eliminating piecework, but two valuable years had been lost and the attempt to introduce measured day work in a hurry was to cost British Leyland dear.

One place where some quick decisions had to be taken was model policy. It was obvious that if BL was to survive it needed some new cars as early as possible. The most pressing requirement was for a medium sized model of 1200–1600 cc that would compete with the Cortina, Escort and Viva. It was therefore decided to produce a car of conventional design which would be cheap to make. This was a sensible strategy because BL could not afford to run any risks and produce a distinctive car which might turn out to have only a limited appeal. Nor did it have the time to make any technical innovations. The outcome was the Marina which was introduced in 1971. It did not have any glaring faults except that the boot leaked. It was designed with a large boot in order to appeal to fleet buyers, since one of the weaknesses of the 1100–1300 was that it had very little luggage space and hitherto Ford's fleet sales had been twice as large as those of Austin-Morris. The Marina had a pleasant appearance, but was somewhat too slavish a copy of the Escort and Viva. In a field where there was now strong competition it lacked individuality and its styling should have been more sophisticated. The Marina's performance was acceptable, but was not of an exceptionally high standard because the powertrain — engine, transmission and axles — was largely built up from items taken from previous models. All manufacturers do this but here there was too much borrowing and better results would have been achieved if somewhat more money had been spent.

Nevertheless the Marina was a reasonably satisfactory car. What was far more questionable was the wisdom of making the Allegro which was introduced in 1973. British Leyland's top priority was not another medium-sized saloon but the production of a smaller car, which would take the place of the Mini, and/or a larger model to replace the ugly 1800 which did not sell well. Not until 1975 was the latter metamorphosed into the stylish Princess. Although there was still a substantial demand for the Mini it was obvious that it should be taken out of production as soon as possible if only because it was a financial liability. BL made a profit from the manufacture of replacement parts but only during exceptional years did the car itself cover its full costs. Avoidable costs may appear to be all that is relevent, but continuing expenditure on tooling is necessary in order to keep a car in production and some of the facilities that are employed will have an alternative use.

It was by no means clear whether or how the Mini should be replaced. One possibility was to introduce a new Mini along the same lines as the old but cheaper to produce. Unfortunately small models never seemed to make much money unless produced in extremely high volumes. Moreover cars of 1000 cc and under had already declined from 24% of new registrations in 1963 to 13% in 1969 and a further fall was to be expected as buyers became more affluent. On the other hand, there would continue to be a substantial demand for smallish cars, BL would face relatively little domestic competition now that Ford had stopped making them, and there were substantial export opportunities in the growing European market, where the Mini sold reasonably well and formed the mainstay of BL's dealer network.

Probably the most sensible decision would have been to introduce a car that was larger than the old Mini but smaller than the

1100–1300. Instead BL decided to replace the latter model by the Allegro. Although this had slightly smaller dimensions than the Marina it was very much in the same class. BL therefore compounded its error of not producing a car that would take the place of the Mini by making one that would to a substantial degree compete with the Marina. The decision to produce the Allegro was explained partly by the way in which BL had decided to reshape its dealer system. The number of cars sold per dealer was much lower than the number handled by the average Ford agent and many BL dealers were too small to finance an efficient sales and service organisation. However, one party within BL argued that in order to maximize the Corporation's market share it was necessary to maintain different networks for Austin and Morris, each of which would handle a different range of models. Morris cars would be conventional while Austin would be *avant-garde*. It was forecast that in this way Austin-Morris, which then possessed about 30% of the home market, would be able to capture around half. The other party took a more cautious and somewhat more realistic view of BL's prospects and urged that the production of different Austin and Morris ranges would lead to a dissipation of energy and resources. It was Triumph's role to produce advanced and adventurous cars and BL did not require two ranges of *avant-garde* models. However Stokes decided that Austin and Morris franchises should remain separate, although both sets of dealers would handle the Mini.[8] Hence the Marina came out under the Morris marque and BL was led into producing another medium-sized car in order to sustain the Austin dealers, although in practice many of them also handled Morris.

In order to produce the Allegro at the minimum possible cost the powertrain was largely taken over from the 1100-1300. This meant that the new car was not only very close in size to the Marina but also that, like the Marina, its performance and reliability were not particularly high.

BL's First Five Years

Having examined the problems which British Leyland faced and analysed management's initial response, the next step is to discover how it performed between 1968 and 1973 when trading conditions were favourable and Lord Stokes and his colleagues had the opportunity to make BL a commercial success. As Tables 12.1 and 12.2

TABLE 12.1 *BL Vehicles: Output, Productivity and Finances*

Calendar year	Output, UK[a] (1968 = 100)	Employment UK[a] (000)	Output per worker, UK[a] (1968 = 100)	Real unit operating costs (1967–68 = 100)	Real unit staff costs UK[b] (1967–68 = 100)	Real staff costs per employee UK[b] (1968 = 100)	Real cost of vehicle industry's fuel and materials (1968 = 100)	Real revenue per unit (1967–68 = 100)	Revenue[a] (£m, 1978 prices)	Gross surplus[a] (£m, 1978 prices)	Gross surplus as % of revenue[a] (%)	Net deficit[a][c] (£m, 1978 prices)	Financial year[d]
1963	94.7	..	101.3[e]	..	..	..	..	..	..	..	..	..	..
1965	103.3	..	101.0[e]	..	..	..	..	..	..	..	..	..	..
1968	100.0	159	100.0	100.0	100.0	100.0	100.0	100.0	2,724	247	9.1	..	1967–68
1969	103.4	165	99.8	95.2	103.0	102.9	99.9	94.9	2,716	239	8.8	..	1968–69
1970	102.5	165	99.0	104.7	107.7	106.7	103.4	100.6	2,686	145	5.4	..	1969–70
1971	111.0	160	110.7	101.9	102.1	113.0	104.5	100.4	2,866	223	7.8	..	1970–71
1972	108.6	158	109.6	100.6	108.3	118.7	102.0	97.8	2,919	187	6.4	..	1971–72
1973	107.8	164	104.7	107.7	117.6	123.6	101.2	104.7	3,288	210	6.4	21	1972–73
1974	95.3	163	93.2	106.1	125.5	117.2	112.3	100.0	2,863	104	3.6	−234	1973–74
1975	85.6	152	89.4	119.9	130.3	114.6	112.7	109.1	2,707	6	0.2	−311	1974–75
1976	89.2	154	92.2	124.6	122.5	114.3	118.8	121.0	2,764	178	6.4	−104	1975–76
1977	84.3	161	83.2	127.8	129.4	107.7	122.4	121.3	2,682	115	4.3	−156	1977
1978	82.6	158	83.2	132.8	137.1	114.1	122.7	126.8	2,913	143	4.9	−94	1978

Note Those columns which are not labelled UK include foreign operations. The output index comprises twenty nine indicators (number of vehicles produced) combined with 1973 list price weights. The per unit series were estimated using an index for vehicles sold derived from the number and the average value per vehicle at 1973 list prices, viz. the total value of UK output, at 1973 prices, divided by the number of vehicles produced.

[a] Includes companies now owned by British Motor Holdings.

[b] Before refund of selective employment tax.

[c] After £129m of replacement cost depreciation, as estimated from National Enterprise Board Report.

[d] October to September except for 1975–76 (October–December; expressed at annual rate) and 1977 and 1978 (calendar year). All financial figures are for the financial year except those relating to staff and materials.

[e] Rough estimate.

show vehicle production increased from 987,000 in 1968 to 1,062,000 in 1971, and weighted output rose by 11%. However by 1973 production had dropped to 1,013,000 vehicles, and weighted output was only 8% higher than it had been in 1968. BL's market share — as measured by production as a proportion of new registrations — fell from 71% in 1968 to 51% in 1973. BL's share of domestic sales dropped sharply because of greater competition from imports, and the Corporations's exports declined. The other British manufacturers fared no better. Indeed BL's share of UK vehicle production rose from 44½% in 1968 to 47% in 1973. Over this period the import duty on cars and vans was cut from 22% to 11%, and although our competitors also reduced their tariffs they were in most cases relatively low to begin with. However, imports would not have risen so fast, and exports would have been more buoyant if BL, and the other British manufacturers, had been able to supply more cars and if the cars had had fewer faults and been more reliable. Quality surveys showed that our cars compared unfavourably with those produced by our major competitors, and one reason for this was that management was preoccupied with the problem of producing as many cars as possible.[9]

BL's failure to produce more vehicles was not due to any overall lack of capacity, although there was a capacity constraint for Land Rovers. British Leyland should have been able to make 1,350,000 vehicles but during 1973 it only turned out about 75% of this number.[10] If BL had succeeded in producing more vehicles its productivity would have been higher. Between 1968 and 1971 employment remained around 160,000, output increased and OMY rose by 11%. But thereafter output fell and the labour force increased. By 1973 it had risen to 164,000 and output per man was only 5% higher than it had been during 1968. This was extremely disappointing. By 1973 a considerable amount of deadwood had been pruned from the product range and the Morris Minor, A 60/Morris Oxford, 3-litre and Triumph Herald/Vitesse had been discontinued. Although there was only a small decline in the number of body shells, the replacement of so many ageing and/or low volume models should have enabled BL to reduce its labour force and increase its productivity. The introduction of the Marina at Cowley ought to have yielded particularly large benefits because the cramped old factory buildings were replaced by modern facilities for body building and assembly. Although the new production line had

TABLE 12.2 BL and UK Vehicle Production and Registrations[a]

| | BL vehicles lost through strikes[b] (000) | BL vehicle production[c] (000) | UK vehicle production (000) | BL as % of UK (%) | Registrations of new vehicles in UK (000) | BL vehicle production as % of new registrations (%) | BL allocations for export as % of new registrations (%) | % of registrations of new cars and lorries in UK | | |
								BL (%)	Other UK manufactured (%)	Imports (%)
1963	..	965	2,012	48.0	1,249	77.3	..	..	..	..
1968	..	987	2,225	44.4	1,389	71.1	33.3	40.2	52.7	7.1
1969	..	998	2,142	46.6	1,264	78.9	37.5	39.7	51.5	8.8
1970	150	963	2,098	45.9	1,370	70.3	32.2	37.6	50.1	12.3
1971	150	1,062	2,198	48.3	1,577	67.3	29.1	..	..	..
1972	200	1,057	2,329	45.4	1,989	53.1	20.0	39.4	43.5	17.1
1973	239	1,013	2,164	46.8	1,996	50.8	20.0	31.0	43.7	25.3
1974	300	864	1,937	44.6	1,518	56.9	24.5	31.9	42.4	25.7
1975	170	739	1,648	44.8	1,429	51.7	22.1	30.8	39.4	29.8
1976	150	794	1,673	47.4	1,519	52.2	24.7	27.6	37.8	34.6
1977	252	772	1,714	45.1	1,570	49.2	22.0[d]	24.5[e]	34.5	41.0
1978	123	743	1,607	46.2	1,869	39.8	15.4[d]	23.7[e]	31.7	44.6

[a] Excluding tractors.
[b] Including suppliers.
[c] Including companies now owned by British Motor Holdings.
[d] Excludes vehicles dispatched to Belgium for assembly and subsequently sold in UK.
[e] Includes vehicles assembled in Belgium.

weaknesses, the plant became as good as any in the country and it was no longer necessary to transport bodies from Swindon since they were now manufactured across the road and brought in by conveyor. This was by no means the only rationalisation that took place as two factories in the Birmingham area, which had previously employed 5,000, were closed down.

Why then did production and productivity increase so little? One reason was the loss of output as a result of escalating industrial disputes. According to BL's estimates, which are given in Table 12.2, 240,000 more vehicles would have been produced in 1973 but for time lost as a result of strikes, both internal and external. This is an overstatement because the Corporation assumes, for instance, that production schedules would have been achieved during the disputes. Nevertheless it seems probable that the reduction in productivity between 1971 and 1973 was largely due to the increase in vehicles lost through strikes. However, sluggish output and rising employment were in part due to the switch from piecework to measured day work. The decision to get rid of piecework was not taken until October 1970 which meant that there was very little time for negotiating the use of day work on the Marina, which was due to be introduced early in 1971. But once negotiations had started BL could not turn back and have the car manufactured on piecework. Not only would this have been a retrograde step but it would have taken months to agree to the new piecework rates during which time production would have been delayed or disrupted. This had happened on previous cars and was one of the major reasons why it was belatedly decided to drop piecework. During 1969 production of the new XJ6 Jaguar had been crippled by disputes over piecework rates and output of the Mini Clubman was delayed because the unions tried to renegotiate the rates for every part, old as well as new. In order to obtain agreement for the Marina to be produced under the day work system BL was forced not only to make a large wage increase but to concede what was, in effect, a low daily stint. This was difficult to alter because management signed away its right of initiative by agreeing to what was known as 'mutuality'. The day wage agreements at Cowley set the pattern for those negotiated elsewhere. By 1973 piecework had been largely eliminated but management had had to agree to manning levels that were often excessive and mutuality had been conceded.[11] At some factories, such as Castle Bromwich and Drews Lane, the stint was fixed at so low a level that the men were able to complete their task and go home early.

There was, however, another reason why the ending of piecework had an adverse effect on production and productivity. At a piecework plant relatively little supervision and organisation is necessary. If, for instance, the supply of parts runs out the workers will soon draw attention to the fact, whereas if they are on time rates they will sit around and wait for them to be provided. If, therefore, the abolition of piecework was not to lead to a reduction in productivity, BL had to provide more and better management at the foreman level and above. But because of the existence of piecework BL did not have any reservoir of trained supervisors on which it could draw, and appears to have been slow to tackle the problem. It had originally been planned to produce over 250,000 Marinas per year but under the new day wage system BL managed to make only 160,000 in 1973. Moreover the ending of piecework did not lead to any dramatic improvement in industrial relations because important sources of contention remained. There were considerable variations in pay between works and no less than 246 bargaining units, usually with different bargaining dates.

By 1972–73 BL's unit costs were 8% greater than they had been in 1967–68 because of the small rise in productivity and the large increase in staff costs per employee. During 1973 unit staff costs were 18% higher than in 1968, but staff expenditure only accounted for about 30% of BL's operating costs and the price of materials stayed about the same. Between 1967–68 and 1972–73 BL's prices appear to have increased by 5%. Because this was slightly less than the increase in costs the gross margin fell from 9% to 6½%. Ford Motors earned 12%, though here too profits were lower, and BL's financial position was even weaker than it appeared. If allowance is made for stock appreciation and for depreciation at replacement cost, BL only had a net profit of some £20 million during 1972–73. This was a very small amount in relation to the size of the business and it was an exceptionally favourable year. It is therefore apparent that, even before economic conditions turned sour, BL was in a precarious financial position.

THE RYDER REPORT

Between 1973 and 1975 BL's production fell from 1,013,000 vehicles to 739,000 and its weighted output declined by over 20%. This was due to a contraction in the size of the market rather than to a fall in BL's share. If its production is related to total domestic registrations the figure remained about the same and BL also maintained its share of the home market. BL reacted to the drop in output by cutting its employment from 164,000 in 1973 to 152,000 in 1975, but despite this OMY fell by 14%. Unit costs rose by 11% between 1972–73 and 1974–75. The rise was due not only to the growth in unit staff costs (which, despite a fall in staff costs per employee, increased by 11% between 1973 and 1975) but also to an escalation in the price of fuel and materials (which rose by 10%). Although there was some increase in BL's prices, which by 1974–75 were 4% higher than they had been in 1972–73, there was a spectacular decline in profitability. By 1974–75 the gross profit had all but disappeared and there was a net loss of £300 million, though the picture would have looked slightly better but for the loss of £26 million at BL's Italian and Spanish subsidiaries, which it was decided to dispose of.

During the autumn of 1974 BL found that the banks were no longer prepared to provide extra cash and in December the Government announced that 'because of the company's position in the economy as a leading exporter and its importance to employment' it was to be provided with financial support.[12] A team under Lord Ryder was then appointed to assess the Corporation's prospects and advise on the strategy that should be pursued. The Ryder Report, which was presented three months later, was a curious document. It did not begin, as might have been expected, with an examination of why British Leyland had got into financial difficulties or contain any clear or coherent analysis of what was wrong. However the report was extremely critical of the way in which BL was organised and Ryder obviously believed that the new administrative structure which he prescribed was a *sine qua non* for success.[13]

At the time British Leyland was being run on a centralised basis. Mr John Barber was trying to reduce manpower and cut costs, and was planning to make a drastic reduction in the number of body shells and to push the standardisation of components as far as possible. Ryder proposed that central control should be reduced to the minimum and that cars, trucks and buses, special products, and overseas operations should become separate profit centres. In practice this would not result in any substantial decentralisation of authority because trucks and buses were already treated as a separate activity and cars, which accounted for 70% of BL's turnover, was to remain a single entity. The only change was that control over cars was to be transferred from the Corporation's central headquarters to the central headquarters of the new car division, and that overseas marketing would, along with BL's foreign factories, become a separate profit centre. These were dubious moves because the car business represented so large a part of the company and because of the lack of wisdom of separating production from marketing. When Mr Michael Edwardes took charge of BL late in 1977 he made the manufacturing divisions responsible for export marketing on the ground that they should be more directly exposed to the hard facts of international competition. He decided that BL was too centralised and split the car division into separate companies which would be responsible for Austin-Morris, specialist cars and body and component manufacture. This was more or less the organisational set-up with which BL had started life. Although Ryder set great store by his administrative proposals it was evident that, even if they had been better devised, they would not contribute very much to the solution of BL's difficulties: managerial reorganisation never does.

However, despite its preoccupation with administration, the Ryder team appears to have regarded under-investment as the main reason for the Corporation's difficulties. It was said to be 'the main reason for the low productivity of BL's work force compared with say Fiat or Volkswagen' and 'a massive programme to modernise plant and equipment' was proposed.[14] Because it did not wish to give offence to BL's workers and their shop stewards the Ryder Report did not make any productivity comparisons, but criticised the *Economist* for giving figures which might possibly show BL in too unfavourable a light. There is, however, no doubt that by the mid-1970s the productivity, not only of BL, but of the British motor vehicle industry as a whole was considerably lower than that of major foreign manufacturers. In 1955 the United States was the only country in which OMY was greater than in the UK, but by 1973 productivity, as measured by equivalent vehicles per worker, was at least three times greater in the US, nearly two and a half times higher in Japan, and a third greater in Germany, France and Italy.[15] Within the UK, BL's productivity was substantially lower than that of Ford as measured by the number of vehicles per employee. The Ryder Report pointed out that BL produced luxury cars and heavy trucks and buses. But it was evident from the breakdown of BL's employment which appeared in its annual report that Ford's productivity was considerably higher.

Although Ryder established that more than half of BL's machinery and equipment was over fifteen years old, no attempt was made to show that its age was the principal reason why BL's productivity was, as the Report coyly remarked, 'often less than that of its competitors'.[16] However the Expenditure Committee subsequently gave figures for fourteen British and foreign vehicle manufacturers which showed that BL had the lowest fixed assets per man, and which indicated that there was a close relationship between capital per worker and productivity, as represented by value added (or sales) per man.[17] These findings are open to the objection (a) that, as the figures were at historic cost, the value of BL's net assets would have been understated more than that of other manufacturers with newer equipment, and (b) that capital per worker may be low at British Leyland due to the employment of an unduly large number of workers. The Central Policy Review Staff (CPRS) tried to avoid the latter difficulty by relating gross fixed assets to net (and gross) output. Although BL's ratio appeared to be relatively low it did not differ greatly from those of some of the most successful continental manufacturers. Moreover Ford was in a very favourable position and its British and German works appeared to be nearly identical. Despite this the productivity of the UK concern was lower than that of Ford in Germany and of other continental vehicle manufacturers.[18]

The CPRS obtained details of the amount of time taken to assemble similar or identical cars in this country and in Europe. Allowance was then made for differences in operations, equipment and plant layout. As Table 12.3 shows, BL took about 40% longer to assemble the Marina than Ford did to assemble the Cortina. It can also be seen that BL's assembly times were far longer in relation to those on the continent that they were at Ford and Vauxhall. For instance, whereas it took 132% more man hours to assemble the Mini in Britain than it did on the continent, Ford took only 87% more to assemble the British Cortina than to assemble the Taunus in Germany. BL's productivity is low both because of over-manning and because relatively little is produced whereas at Ford over-manning is much less of a problem. One of the CPRS's most striking findings was that:

> Even where manning levels are virtually identical and the capital equipment, model involved and plant layout are the same, the output of production lines in Britain is about half that of continental plants . . . During this study, members of the CPRS team have visited six production plants in Britain and five on the continent. It is usual in the British car plants for production lines to start late, stop early, and stop between and during shifts for reasons other than materials shortages or equipment breakdowns. During visits to continental plants, the line was never seen to stop during the working day and at shift changes the relief shift was invariably waiting to take over before the time for the change, so the entire production line never stopped operating. In all cases we were assured, and have no reason to doubt, that what we saw was typical . . . All British car plants have standard procedures for transferring men between jobs to overcome sickness or absenteeism, but in every British car plant we have visited there are continual disputes over transfers, leading to loss of production on a daily basis.[19]

A subsequent study carried out by BL's management and shop stewards found that during a forty-hour week the Corporation's plants are productive for only about 45–55% of the time whereas Renault, Simca and Volkswagen achieve levels of 67–75%. Part of this difference was attributable to old plant but breakdowns do not appear to be a very serious problem.[20]

These arguments do not show, and are not intended to prove, that under-investment played no part in explaining why BL's productivity was so much lower than that of Ford and the continental manufacturers. The Mini, for instance, was built and assembled at Longbridge in old facilities and with old machinery. But even here man hours per car could have been reduced by a third just by achieving the work standards calculated on the basis of existing equipment.[21] Moreover there were substantial variations between the efficiency of different factories which had nothing to do with their age. It must therefore be concluded that the huge programme of investment which the Ryder Report contained was based on a misleading diagnosis of the *malaise* from which BL was suffering, though obviously additional capital expenditure was required on new cars.

The report recommended that the Corporation should invest £240 million per annum over the period 1974–75 to 1981–82, which represented an increase of 60% over its rate of expenditure during the preceding five years.[22] The programme of expenditure was taken

TABLE 12.3   *Direct and Indirect Man Hours for Car Assembly January – May 1975*

	Continental car = 100	Index for British car with continental car = 100
Identical Models : Continent v Britain		
Belgian Mini/British Mini	100	232
German Ford Taunus/British Ford Cortina	100	187
German Ford Escort/British Ford Escort	100	167
Comparable Models : Continent v Britain		
German Ford Taunus/Marina[a]	100	266
Italian Fiat 128/Allegro	100	201
German Opel Kadett/Vauxhall Viva[a]	100	178
	British Ford = 100	BL
Comparable Models : British Ford v BL		
UK Ford Cortina/Marina	100	142[b]

[a] Direct man hours only.
[b] Derived from the second and fourth rows.

from a submission that the Corporation had prepared at the team's request. This Concept Study had been drawn up in a hurry on the assumption, which had apparently come from Ryder, that capital would be readily available. It was intended as a basis for discussion but neither Barber nor Stokes was questioned about the figures that had been put forward and they were accepted by the Ryder Team *in toto*. Neither the Concept Study nor the Ryder inquiry provided any estimates of what the internal rate of return, or present value, would be. The detailed financial appendix which was prepared by Peat Marwick, the accountants, only contained a worthless forecast of what BL's cash flow would be during the period up to 1985. This rested on the hazardous assumption that there would be no growth in real wages and depended on an extremely optimistic view of the number of vehicles that BL would be able to sell. Even so Lord Ryder told the Expenditure Committee that 'the return on capital in

1982 . . . . is not a high one in relation to what can be obtained elsewhere . . . On purely commercial investment criteria, . . . knowing full well that in the meantime you have got to go through very lean years . . . , on a discounted cash flow basis and so forth [it] cannot commend itself to you as being the best investment'.[23]

The forecasts of BL's sales on which the Ryder recommendations rested were almost identical both in total and in detail to those which BL provided in its Concept Study. They were criticised at the time as being over-optimistic and it is instructive to compare them with those of the CPRS, which made a careful survey of market trends and of the estimates of manufacturers and independent experts. The projections for new registrations did not differ very greatly but Ryder assumed that BL would maintain its position in the UK car market. This implied that there would be no great rise in imports. However the CPRS considered that imports would rise from 28% of new cars in 1974 to around 37%, which was the mid-point of its range. It was pointed out that East Europe and Spain might well increase their exports, that Japan seemed poised to attack the German and French markets, that the American producers were planning to launch smaller cars to combat imports, that Volkswagen and Volvo might start producing in the US, and that many importing countries were building up their own production. This meant that spare capacity was likely to persist in West Europe and as a result its producers could be expected to compete vigorously in the British market and against our exports.[24]

The CPRS forecast that British car production, which had totalled 1,750,000 in 1973, would be around 1,550,000 in 1980 and about 1,800,000 in 1985.[25] It is not known what BL's output was expected to be, but if it maintained its share of 50%, it would make 780,000 cars in 1980 and 900,000 in 1985. These figures are substantially lower than the Ryder forecast that British Leyland would sell around 950,000 cars in 1980 and 1,150,000 in 1985. Because BL was unlikely to sell as many cars as Ryder was predicting it became extremely doubtful whether BL should try to provide the extensive range of models which the Team advocated. The Concept Study proposed that the number of different body shells should be reduced from fifteen to eight, of which three would be sports cars and five saloons. The first of the new saloons, of which there were to be two versions, was planned for the beginning of 1979, and would replace the Marina, the Maxi and the Dolomite. This was to be followed by

a new Mini, which would appear early in 1980, a new Jaguar/
Daimler (end 1980), a new Allegro (end 1982) and a replacement for
the Princess and Rover (end 1983). The new Mini was included at
the behest of Ryder and the only change which the Team made was
to advance this car by six months. Barber was opposed to its
production on the ground that small cars were the least profitable
part of the market and that a new Mini was not justified in view of
the total number of cars that BL was likely to be able to sell.

The strength of this argument obviously depended on the Corporation's sales prospects. Triumph and MG could hope to sell around
100,000 sports cars, which was the number that had been produced
in 1972; it was reasonable to suppose that Rover and Jaguar would
be able to find customers for a further 100,000 because, although
this was somewhat more than they had ever produced in the past,
their supply had persistently fallen short of the available demand;
and BL ought to be able to find a market for at least 50,000
Princesses. If, as the CPRS study implied, total sales only amounted
to around 800,000 BL would only produce 550,000 other cars. The
new Marina/Maxi/Dolomite and the Allegro replacement would,
provided they were successful, account for the great bulk of these,
and if it proved necessary to make three models in order to dispose of
something over half a million cars BL's costs would be excessively
great. If the Mini were replaced it might be possible to dispose of
more vehicles. But it is dangerous to adopt a figure which, although
each of its constituent parts may seem realistic, is in itself unreasonable.

The only possible justification for the Ryder Team's optimistic
plans was that BL would be able to make such a large saving in costs
that it would be able to secure extra business. It was envisaged that
by 1982 BL would be producing something like 1,250,000 vehicles
with a labour force of about the same size that it possessed at the
time of the Report, viz. around 155,000. If so, OMY would be 50%
greater than it had been in 1974. However, productivity was at a
very low ebb in 1974. The Team's targets implied that by 1982
OMY would be only 20% higher than in 1972 and that BL would
not even have caught up with exising West European productivity
levels.[26] What was worse, the Ryder Report failed to spell out how
this objective could be achieved. Because BL was losing money it
needed to make substantial gains in productivity at once and could
not afford to wait until the investment programme began to bear

fruit. Moreover unless manning standards were revised downwards and more continuous working were acheived there was a serious risk that the present would contaminate the future and the capital expenditure programme would not lead to any great rise in productivity.

What the Ryder Report ought to have recommended was that government financial support should be dependent on agreement by BL's work force and their unions to specified changes in manning, working practice and collective bargaining arrangements: an approach which appears to have been favoured by at least one of the Team's members and had support within BL. Instead it was proposed that each new tranche of Government finance should depend on evidence of a contribution both by the work force and by management to the reduction of industrial disputes and improved productivity.[27] This proposal was unlikely to mean much in the absence of firm targets and because, if projects were halted, the investment that had already been made would be endangered and BL's problems would become still more serious.

The Ryder Report was such a weak document, both in diagnosis and prescription, because of the Team's anxiety not to say anything which BL's workers might regard as provocative. Its members were impressed by the apparent desire of BL's shop stewards that the company should become a viable and successful enterprise. Moreover at that time Mr Tony Benn was Secretary of State for Industry and his policy was not one of confrontation but of cooperation and industrial democracy. Hence the Team adopted a moderate and conciliatory approach similar to that which had already been tried and found wanting under Lord Stokes. The final consequence of the Ryder Inquiry was the departure of Mr John Barber when, as the Team recommended, BL was acquired by the Government. He did not believe that the Mini should be replaced and it was found that his efforts to improve BL's performance had made him unpopular with the plant managers. It was therefore concluded that his style of management was wrong and he was dismissed (together with Lord Stokes) although at least one of the Committee's members believes that if he had been left in charge he would have succeeded in restoring BL to profitability.

AFTER THE RYDER REPORT
Although BL's production had sunk to a very low level by 1975 there

has been no recovery in output. Between 1975 and 1978 there was a fractional increase in the number of vehicles made — from 739,000 to 743,000 — but BL's weighted output fell by 3%, and was 17% smaller than it had been in 1968. Austin-Morris contracted by about the average amount (viz. by 19%); Triumph and Leyland vehicles experienced the largest falls (64% and 28% respectively); and Rover-Jaguar was the only place where output increased (by 32%).

Although BL's performance seems very bad it has not been any worse than that of the rest of the industry. The Corporation's share of total vehicle production rose slightly from 44½% in 1968 to 46% in 1978, though this was due to the nine weeks strike at Ford in 1978. There has nonetheless been a substantial reduction in BL's market share. As measured by production as a proportion of new registrations, it fell from 71% in 1968 to 52% in 1975 and then to 40% in 1978. BL has lost ground in the home market but failed to make compensating gains abroad. The Corporation's exports — as a proportion of new UK registrations — declined from a third in 1968 to 15% in 1978; and its share of domestic sales of cars and trucks fell steadily from 40% in 1968 to 24% in 1978. There was a reduction not only in cars from (41% to 23%) but also in vans (from 42% to 27%) and trucks (from 30% to 19%).

One explanation for BL's poor showing after 1975 was that the Corporation was still having to rely on the Maxi, Marina, Allegro and Triumph Dolomite, which were never first rate cars and have now lost the appeal of youth. Although the Mini continues to sell remarkably well, it is now twenty years old and has to some extent been overtaken by later models. The only new cars which BL introduced during or after 1975 were all developed in the Stokes era. There were two large saloons: the Princess and Rover 3500; and two sports cars: the TR7 and Jaguar XJS. These are all good cars. However the two coupés have inevitably had a limited appeal and the Princess and TR7, which has done much less well than had been planned, would have sold better but for mechanical problems and poor quality.[28] In trucks BL has been reaping the rewards of its failure to undertake sufficient investment during the first half of the 1970s. No new vehicles were introduced between 1973 and the beginning of 1980, although foreign manufacturers have introduced a succession of new models.

The relatively poor reliability of BL's vehicles provides another reason why its sales have been so depressed. Instead of developing new truck engines which would be able to cope with heavier loads and higher speeds it tried to squeeze more power out of existing units. This was not a success and in the case of the notorious 400 series engine it was a dismal failure.[29] Surveys of car performance by the Consumers' Association show that foreign models break down somewhat less frequently and develop substantially fewer faults than those made by the Corporation. It can be estimated from the inquiry for 1977–78 that the average number of faults reported for those British Leyland cars which were in their second year, and therefore no longer under guarantee, was about 85% greater than for imported cars of the same vintage.[30] BL's cars have a poor reputation for quality and workmanship in foreign markets. When the future Princess was shown to a sample of consumers in Amsterdam it was greeted with enthusiasm, but when they were told it was a British car they became more critical. The high incidence of faults on BL's cars seems to be partly due to the use of old equipment, and to the incorporation of too many borrowed components. However this is not the whole explanation. The Rover 3500 is an almost entirely new car from a new factory but it is, if anything, less reliable than other BL models. The CPRS found that workmanship tended to be poor at British car factories and industrial disputes and other stoppages also helped to explain why defects occurred.[31]

Despite this, somewhat more vehicles could probably have been sold if British Leyland had been able to produce them. By 1978 most of BL's models were readily available in the domestic market, though Rovers were difficult to obtain until the closing months of the year and there was still a long waiting list for Jaguars. However, the supply situation would have been less satisfactory at home but for the diversion of some vehicles from exports and a reduction in stocks, which fell by 26,000 during the course of the year. Due to industrial disputes BL was seriously short of trucks and buses and there was, as always, a lengthy waiting list for Land Rovers. This was the one place where there was a lack of capacity, though there would have been less of a problem if the Rover employees had been less reluctant to work a second shift. Although it is clear that BL's output was lower than it might have been, it does not necessarily follow that production could have been sustained at a higher level. The elimination of a waiting list will only lead to a temporary rise in output while it is being worked off. However, it seems likely that some potential customers must have decided not to wait for a vehicle from British Leyland but to buy one from another manufacturer.

Although BL's output fell between 1975 and 1978, its labour force increased from 152,000 to 158,000. As a result OMY fell by a further 8% and was, during 1978, 17% lower than it had been a decade earlier. And, to judge from what little information is available, no greater than in 1958.[32] However, BL's productivity performance may be slightly better than it appears because there has been a significant reduction in the number of hours worked in the vehicle manufacturing industry. If they have fallen to the same extent in British Leyland output per equivalent worker fell by 13% between 1968 and 1978. Total factor productivity appears to have declined by about the same amount as OMY over the decade (because BL's capacity and, presumably, quantity of capital seems, like its labour force, to have been roughly the same in 1978 as it had been in 1968). During 1978 BL's production appears to have represented only about 60% of its capacity.[33]

The new management that was installed after the Ryder Report was not, even by British standards, of a very high order. It took an optimistic view of sales prospects and promptly took on 15,000 workers, although productivity was at a very low level. Those in charge comforted themselves with the belief that changes in working arrangements were being made which, if only there were fewer interruptions, would lead to greater output and efficiency. However as these interruptions were one of the main reasons why productivity was so low the gains that were made were of no practical significance. Nor was the loss of vehicles by any means entirely due to industrial disputes which it could be argued that British Leyland was almost powerless to prevent. During 1978, when fewer vehicles were lost than in any year since 1970, production and productivity were at their nadir.

It would, however, be wrong to be too critical of BL's management. Once government assistance had been provided without any concessions from the work force there was obviously no simple solution to such problems as over-manning, late starting and restrictive mutuality clauses. Moreover the Ryder Report had a continuing negative influence. As we have seen its diagnosis was incorrect: BL's poor performance was not primarily due to inadequate investment and old equipment. What was even worse was the placatory policy which British Leyland was obliged to follow in the field of labour relations. According to the report the crucial need was to bring about 'industrial democracy' through the creation of a hierarchy of consultative committees in order 'to take advantage of the ideas, enthusiasm and energy of BL's workers'.[34] British Leyland encountered considerable local opposition to the new machinery and it has had no discernable effect on productivity.

After Lord Ryder had departed from the National Enterprise Board, to which BL had been transferred, it was recognised that a change in direction was necessary and in November 1977 Mr Michael Edwardes was put in charge of the company. He dismissed the existing top management and announced that employment at BL cars would be reduced by 12,500 during 1978. It was hoped that this together with higher production would lead to an increase of 18.5% in the number of cars produced per worker.[35] However productivity failed to increase, output declined and employment in BL cars was only cut by 7,300 during the course of the year, of which 3,800 was accounted for by the closure of the Speke factory.

The decline in British Leyland's productivity has been accompanied by an increase in its unit costs. They rose by about 10% between 1974–75 and 1978 and were, at the end of the period, a third higher than they had been in 1967–68. This rise was due not only to a large rise in unit staff costs (of around 35%) but also to a substantial jump in the price of fuel and materials (23%). The decline in productivity would have had an even greater impact on costs but for the fact that staff costs per employee fell by 8% between 1973 and 1978. BL pushed up its prices by 16% between 1974–75 and 1978. As a result of this increase, which took prices to a point 27% above the level of 1967–68, there was some recovery in profits and the gross margin rose from 0.2% in 1974–75 to 5% in 1978. However there was a net loss of £95 million and by no means all of this was accounted for by Austin-Morris. During 1978 Leyland Vehicles had a net deficit.

BL Now

BL's prospects are drear. The decline in its output and market share continues. During 1979 the number of vehicles produced was 15% lower than in 1978. A further fall seems inevitable. Although the introduction of a new range of trucks has just begun, the Corporation has failed to develop the replacement cars which are so badly needed. The new Mini, which has been christened the Metro, is to be introduced about 12 months late in the autumn of 1980. However, the replacement models for the Allegro and Marina will not appear until 1982–83, although a new medium car had originally been planned for early 1979. When BL came to implement the development programme contained in the Ryder Report it was found that it was seriously short of design staff and that recruitment was difficult because pay levels were uncompetitive.[36] Moreover, due to restrictive practices in its drawing offices and to industrial disputes, the best use was not made of those staff that were available. The new Mini was a dubious project and it was vital if BL was to survive as a major car producer that it should have a new medium car to compete in the largest and more profitable section of the market. Despite this the Mini replacement was accorded priority. When Mr Michael Edwardes became Chairman of British Leyland he seriously considered dropping it and advancing the introduction of the medium car replacement, but work on the new Mini was too far advanced. However, it had been found that its squat design was disliked by potential customers and it was decided to increase its length.[37] The Metro has been converted into a useful and perhaps even a brilliant small car. Nevertheless the need to make design changes at a late stage resulted in some delay and BL is still dependent in the vital medium car market on the Allegro and Marina, although the latter has now belatedly been given a face lift.

Edwardes' plans were based on the assumption that BL would be able to preserve its already diminished share of the market until its new models arrived. This hope has naturally been disappointed and he has been forced into more drastic rationalisation than was originally intended. In the autumn of 1979 it was announced that the total or partial closure of works would lead to a reduction of at least 25,000 in BL's work force within two years. Such rationalisation was already overdue and it is surprising that its necessity had not been recognised earlier. Even with a reduction in capacity BL's market share may by now have shrunk irremediably to a point at which the company is no longer viable. BL will not find it easy to recapture the ground that has been lost. Its dealer network was never strong abroad and has been growing weaker, and its general reputation is poor. Foreign manufacturers have built up excellent distribution systems in Britain and will not willingly be driven back in a market which has, due to BL's price increases, been very profitable and where their medium-term prospects are excellent because BL's are so dim. Although the company will belatedly equip itself with new models it is obviously doubtful whether they will be sufficiently successful to justify another generation of cars.

It is also doubtful whether BL will succeed in achieving the substantial increase in productivity that is necessary. 'By 1983', states the National Enterprise Board in its review of BL's 1979 Corporate Plan, '£1 billion of public money is planned to have been invested in the company but the improvements forecast so far for 1983 for BL cars do not match the very considerable improvements in the product range and facilities which this money will have paid for'.[38] This forecast does not allow for any benefits from the system of productivity payments which BL has now introduced. The maximum payment will be modest, and as the bonus will depend on the whole factory achieving its target, and BL's works employ up to 24,000, it is doubtful whether the scheme will provide sufficient incentive. Edwardes has now succeeded in abolishing mutuality, in establishing management's right to use labour more flexibly and in curbing the power of the shop stewards. Although he has been helped by the knowledge that BL is on the brink of dissolution and disaster, this represents a considerable personal triumph. However morale is very low and it would be unrealistic to suppose that productivity is going to improve dramatically.

The only real solution to BL's difficulties would seem to be collaboration with a foreign producer. Discussions took place with Renault who would have been willing to provide BL with a high volume medium range model to assemble, to engage in the joint development of new models and to distribute BL's quality cars on the continent, where its dealer network is notoriously weak. However BL, which did not believe that it would meet the existing demand, preferred to make an agreement with Honda for the assembly of one of its models because it feared, probably rightly, that it would be dominated by Renault which is much larger.[39] Dominance by a strong and efficient foreign producer would be a welcome development. Indeed a foreign take-over may well be the only hope for BL, providing that a purchaser can be found.

CHAPTER 13

Public Enterprise: A Survey and Evaluation

In this book eleven nationalised industries and undertakings have been examined one by one. This seemed the only possible approach but it has the disadvantage of obscuring their similarities and differences. The first half of this concluding chapter therefore contains a comparative survey and evaluation of the nationalised industries' performance. British Leyland has been included but it should be borne in mind that it was in private ownership until 1975. In the second half of the chapter I try to account for the industries' behaviour and discuss what part their ownership by the state may have played.

Part One. Production

Over the decade 1968–78 output increased by around 130% in airways and telecommunications. As Table 13.1 shows there was also a very large increase in gas and a modest rise of 23% in electricity. However, everywhere else production contracted. The postal services, BL and British Rail had falls of 10–20%; NFC and BSC sustained reductions of 20–30%; and there were declines of over 30% at the bus groups and the collieries. The year 1973 was a turning point for the nationalised industries, as it was for the economy as a whole. During the period 1973–78 all the undertakings, with the exception of coal, fared worse than they had between 1968 and 1973. The sharpest contrast occurred in BSC and BL, where there were small increases in output during the first half of the decade, but large contractions during the second half.

TABLE 13.1 Change in Output, Employment and Productivity in Public Enterprise and Manufacturing

	% Growth in output			% Growth in employment			% Growth in labour productivity[b]				% Growth in total factor productivity[b]		
	1968-73	1973-78	1968-78	1968-73	1973-78	1968-78	1963-68	1968-73	1973-78	1968-78	1963-68	1968-73	1968-78
Telecommunications	61	42	129	9	-6	2	38	45	51	120	28	28	66
British Airways airline activities[a]	76	30	129	19	2	22	46	45	28	86	..	47	71
British Gas	43	27	82	-14	-4	-18	43	67	35	126	..	..	7
British Electricity Boards	21	1	23	-20	-7	-26	31	52	10	68	4	4	7
Postal services	-3	-9	-12	1	-2	-1	-1	-7	-6	-12	..	..	..
BL: vehicles UK[b]	8	-23	-17	3	-4	-1	-1	5	-21	-17	..	..	..
British Rail	-7	-12	-18	-17	-8	-24	32	14	-6	8	..	..	..
National Freight Corporation	-3	-19	-22	-21	-23	-39	20[c]	23/16[d]	6	31	..	..	..
BSC: iron and steel	2	-28	-26	-11	-17	-26	23	13	-13	-2	16[e]	3	-22
National and Scottish Bus Groups	-15	-21	-33	-21	-9	-27	-6	10	-14	-5	..	4	-13
NCB collieries	-27	-13	-36	-23	-7	-28	19	—	-7	-7	..	-4	-13
Manufacturing, all industries	15	-5	10	-5	-7	-12	27	23	4	28	..	18	16
Manufacturing, excluding BSC (1968–78) and BL (1973–78)	16	-3	12	-5	-7	-12	..	24	5	30	..	18	18[f]

[a] Output and productivity figures allow for effects of 1968 pilots' strike.
[b] Output per equivalent worker except for BL for which OMY.
[c] Excludes National Carriers and Freightliners.
[d] Excludes National Carriers.
[e] The steel industry.
[f] Only excludes BSC.

The rise or fall in an industry's output is partly determined by factors beyond its control such as the income elasticity for its products and the price of its inputs. The Gas Corporation, for instance, has had the advantage of large supplies of very cheap gas from the North Sea and a huge increase in its sales was almost inevitable. However, where nationalised undertakings face direct competition the development of their output will depend largely on the efficiency with which they are managed and a decline in their share of the market will constitute prima facie evidence of inefficiency. BSC, the Freight Corporation and British Leyland are all subject to direct competition across the whole range of their business and all three have sustained large declines in their market shares. In 1968 BSC's sales were equivalent to 106% of home market deliveries but by 1978 the figure had fallen to 86%. The corresponding statistics for BL were 71% and 40%. But whereas BL has until recently maintained its share of UK production BSC has not. In both cases some decline in market shares was almost inevitable, but customers have been lost due to supply problems and quality considerations. Moreover BL has been seriously hampered by the undistinguished nature of its popular cars and by the lack of new models.[1] During the period 1969–78 road haulage contractors appear to have increased their traffic by around 20% whereas there was a fall of something like 10% in the work performed by NFC's general haulage and special traffic companies. During the early 1970s the Corporation rapidly relinquished and lost a large part of its general haulage traffic, much of which was unprofitable. An attempt was made to move into Europe but this came to grief because it was overambitious and badly executed. Of late vigorous efforts have been made to find new business and these have had some success.[2]

British Airways operates in a regulated market but has had to face some competition. Its share of the market — passengers carried on British aircraft and on foreign ones travelling to and from the UK — fell from 45% in 1968 to 36% in 1978. This reduction appears to have been partly due to factors that were outside BA's control but, on the other hand, there seems little doubt that the Corporation would have lost business if the charter operators had had greater freedom to compete.[3] The NCB is another nationalised undertaking which has been protected against competition and it is evident that Britain would now be importing considerable quantities of coal if the CEGB and BSC had been free to purchase abroad. The other EEC countries import a substantial tonnage of coal from outside the Community for use in power stations and for other purposes. They therefore constitute a large potential market for the NCB, but it exports very little because its marginal costs are so high.[4]

Although the other industries are the sole suppliers of their principal products there are some areas and activities where they are in direct competition. This is true in particular of parcels traffic. Between 1968 and 1978 all the public sector carriers — Roadline, National Carriers, Rail Express and the PO — experienced large declines in traffic and there was an overall reduction of 38%. This was partly due to changes in the structure of industry and the distribution system, but the state carriers have also lost business because of their own failings. During the decade (which here and henceforth refers to the period 1968-78) a number of private concerns have managed to create networks, and mail order companies and other firms have established their own distribution systems.[5]

As a result of union opposition, the PO carries very little unaddressed advertising material, although this constitutes a large potential market.[6] Between 1968 and 1978 the National and Scottish Bus Groups' share of tour and hire work, as measured by journeys, fell from 22% to 13% because, among other reasons, their costs are much higher than those of private operators.[7] Over the period 1971–79 the electricity industry's share of the total revenue that was earned by its showrooms and by privately owned radio and electrical goods shops declined from 18% to 15½%. Prices at electricity showrooms appear to be on the high side and their standards of service seem to be slightly inferior. The PO has an almost complete monopoly in telecommunications but in the private telegraph terminal market, where it faces competition, its share has fallen from about 75% to 45% because of the inadequacies of its equipment. This is by no means the only weak spot: its private branch exchanges, for instance, are out of date.[8]

Elsewhere the nationalised industries are the sole suppliers of the goods and services they provide. However, it is still possible to inquire whether they have been successful in marketing and developing their products. Over the past decade there has been some increase in the speed of BR's Inter-City services and this has stimulated traffic. However, speeds would be considerably greater but for the serious delay in the introduction of the HST and APT. The

Board appears to have devoted too much effort to raising the frequency of its express services as there is no evidence that this has generated additional traffic.[9] The National and Scottish Bus Groups have a very poor record in the area of marketing. They have neglected opportunities to introduce limited stop services and have failed to speed up services where this is possible or to adjust routes where this is necessary; although progress is now being made.[10] The quality of the postal services has declined and, although there has been some effort to obtain extra business, it has not been sufficiently vigorous.[11] There has, on the other hand, been a significant improvement in the quality of telephone services. But this was only to be expected and in America computer-controlled switching has enabled AT and T to provide a number of services which the Post Office is not able to offer.[12] In gas, marketing efforts have, paradoxically, been over strenuous. Industrial users were charged such a low price for natural gas that demand outran supply and, for a considerable period, BGC had to refuse to sign up new contracts.[13]

EMPLOYMENT AND PRODUCTIVITY

The nationalised industries can only be regarded as efficient if they employ the minimum quantity of labour and other inputs to produce the goods and services they provide. British Airways was the only nationalised undertaking in which there was a significant growth in employment during the course of the decade, and this took place during the first half of the period. In telecommunications, postal services and BL the number of staff was more or less stable, but in the other seven industries there were large falls in employment which ranged from approaching 20% in gas to nearly 40% at NFC.

What, however, has a much greater bearing on efficiency is whether the use of labour has fallen relative to output. During the decade electricity, airways, telecommunications and gas made large gains in labour productivity, which ranged from 68% to 126%. The NFC secured a moderate rise of around 30% and at BR there was an advance of 8%. The other five industries had falls of between 2% (BSC) and 17% (BL, though hours probably declined). During the first half of the period there had been a modest rise of 5–15% at British Leyland, National and Scottish, BSC and BR, but their productivity fell sharply between 1973 and 1978. Telecommunications was the only industry which had a better performance during the second half.

Labour productivity suffers from the obvious weakness that no allowance is made for the use of capital, and most of the nationalised industries are capital intensive. During the decade output per unit of labour and capital increased by about two thirds in telecommunications and airways and there must have been a large rise in gas. In the former industries the rise in total factor productivity was lower than the increase in labour productivity, but this is scarcely surprising as economic progress normally involves a growth in the quantity of capital per worker. What is significant is that electricity, which showed a large gain in labour productivity (68%), only had a small rise in TFP, viz. 7%. At the NCB, the buses and BSC, which had smallish declines in labour productivity, there appear to have been substantial falls in total factor productivity of between 13% and 22%. Even during the first half of the period, when the economy was behaving relatively normally, electricity and BSC made only small gains in TFP and the pits experienced a reduction.

Several of the industries performed less well between 1968 and 1973 than they had during the preceding five years. There was a marked reduction in the growth of labour productivity at BR, coal and steel; while the reduction in labour productivity accelerated in postal services. On the other hand both National and Scottish and BL performed better between 1968 and 1973, although in buses the gain did little more than make good the previous reduction.

The productivity performance of gas, telecommunications and the airways seems excellent while that of most of the other nationalised undertakings looks dismal. However, it might be argued that most of these undertakings have laboured under the disadvantage that the demand for their products has only been growing slowly or has been in decline. This is a handicap because, as numerous studies have shown, gains in production and productivity generally go hand in hand; and because if economic circumstances unexpectedly deteriorate, as they did after 1973, it is almost inevitable that there will be a decline in the utilisation of capacity.

This line of argument has some force. Because of the demand conditions under which they have been operating it would, for instance, be unreasonable to expect BR and postal services to have made enormous gains in productivity. And it is neither surprising nor discreditable that the nationalised industries were, at least in a statistical sense, less successful in raising their productivity or in preventing it falling between 1973 and 1978 than they had been over the period 1968–73. There are however a number of reasons why difficult and deteriorating demand conditions do not provide the also-ran industries with anything like a full defence:

1.   Low output may be the consequence of low productivity rather than its cause. If the industries in question had had a better productivity performance their prices would have risen less and they would have sold more.

2.   The postal services, nationalised buses and BR did not make the most of their opportunities to market and/or develop their products, and BSC and BL would have produced more but for the substantial decline in their market shares, due in part to inability to supply.

3.   It is by no means impossible for declining undertakings to make gains in productivity. This is shown by the large rise which BR (and the NCB) secured between 1963 and 1968, and which National Carriers achieved over the period 1968–73.

4.   Even if it is difficult to make productivity gains when output is declining there can be little excuse for failing to cut back staff. At BL and in the postal services employment was almost as high in 1978 as it had been in 1968 despite large falls in output.

5.   There is no reason to believe that the normal relationship between production and productivity holds good for coal because, other things equal, higher output means that inferior seams have to be mined.

6.   Electricity had a moderately large rise in output between 1968 and 1973 but managed to achieve only a tiny increase in TFP.

It might also be argued that the progress which BR and the NCB made between 1963 and 1968 could not be sustained because it was the result of large-scale programmes of capital expenditure which have not been repeated; because it was due to the replacement of steam engines by diesel and electric traction and the installation of cutter-loaders and power supports; because BR had tightened up its efficiency by carrying out the rationalisation measures contained in the Beeching Report; and because of the working out of the most accessible reserves and the consequent increase in underground travelling times.[14] Nevertheless both industries believed, not without reason, that they should be able to make large gains in productivity. The NCB forecast that output per manshift would increase by 75% between 1968–69 and 1975–76. Although this was unrealistic it was not unreasonable to expect a substantial increase because efficiency could be raised by introducing retreat mining, through new forms of mechanisation and by improving the performance and utilisation of existing types of equipment.[15] BR also planned to achieve a large increase in productivity but has not yet managed to reduce its labour force to the level projected for 1974, although its output is very much lower.[16] Nor can it plausibly be maintained that the other also-ran industries had no scope to improve their productivity and cut their employment. This was either planned (BSC and posts) or known to be necessary (BL) and all the undertakings had obvious opportunities to make progress.[17]

The extent to which these have been seized varies widely. In posts the second delivery, which it had been planned to drop, has been retained and the mechanisation of letter sorting is years behind schedule and very little labour has as yet been saved.[18] On the other hand, BSC has almost completed a huge modernisation programme. By 1978 it had eliminated most of its obsolete open hearth furnaces and in this and other ways has been able to make a large cutback in the number of production workers.[19] Meanwhile, the bus groups achieved a large economy by the widespread, although by no means universal, removal of conductors.[20] However, in general, the industries have had very little success in altering manning standards, tightening up efficiency or improving the utilisation of plant and equipment. On the contrary the gains that have or should have been made by the use of more productive equipment, or the adoption of new techniques, have been offset or dissipated. For instance BSC, BR and the buses have failed to make the necessary downward adjustments in the number of white collar staff; at BSC and the bus groups the productivity of maintenance workers has been allowed to deteriorate; at BR and buses the utilisation of drivers has fallen; and at BL there has been a reduction in effort and efficiency.[21] The PO has failed to reduce the use of labour in sorting and in delivery, where the time required is more closely related to volume than is often supposed.[22]

All of the also-ran industries appear to be seriously inefficient and/or have failed to adopt the best foreign practice. In the postal services OMY appears to be 135% greater in the United States, and if the British postal authorities had managed to make the economies that were announced in 1971, and reduced employment in line with output, the labour force would be 20% smaller.[23] BSC's estimates suggest that its employment could have been cut by 30% without any reduction in output, by ceasing to use unwanted plant and through greater efficiency. BSC employs too many white collar and maintenance workers by foreign standards and output per worker in Britain is only about half as high as in Germany.[24] My estimates suggest that BR's labour force could be cut by around a quarter and it is now conceded that there is scope to reduce the size of train crews, improve ticketing arrangements and rationalise the marshalling yard system.[25] Within the nationalised buses productivity could be raised by re-routing and recasting services as NBC has now recognised, by a more flexible use of labour and by reducing manning to the levels which are already to be found in some parts of National and Scottish.[26] In coal, output per man hour for underground workers is 45% greater in West Germany than in Britain, although its geological conditions are somewhat less favourable, and the cutter-loaders at the coal face are only in use for a relatively small proportion of the available time.[27] After allowing for differences in equipment, productivity at BL is considerably lower than at Ford UK because of over-manning, and much lower than at continental plants, due both to over-manning and the failure to keep production lines moving.[28]

The poor productivity performance at BL and the NCB appears to have been partly due to the abolition of piecework. The NCB mistakenly believed that the pace of work was machine determined and the ending of incentive payments seems to have led to a reduction in effort.[29] At BL payment by results had considerable disadvantages but its abolition was mishandled. The company failed to make the changes in supervision and management that were called for and, in order to secure union agreement, had to concede a low daily stint and sign away its right to initiate manning changes.[30] There has also been a reduction in effort in the postal service, although this was not due to the removal of incentive payments, but to the introduction of the second class post which, by postponing some sorting, reduced the pressure to work fast in order to get the post away on time.[31] It should however be noted that new types of productivity payment have been introduced in coal and more recently at BL. Some progress in this direction is now being made even in the postal services.

Restrictive agreements and practices, and the obstructive attitudes of unions and their members, help to explain why the also-ran industries have such a poor record. In the nationalised buses the position has not been too unsatisfactory because, although there has in some places been opposition to split shift working and single man operation, NBC is finding it possible to negotiate, depot by depot, a radical reshaping of its services.[32] At the opposite extreme are the postal workers who have managed to either delay or frustrate almost everything which the PO has tried to do, including the employment of part-time workers, mechanisation and the better adjustment of manpower to traffic in sorting.[33] In coal the NUM will only agree to collieries being closed where they are completely exhausted; at BSC there has, in general, been strong local opposition to any alterations in manning standards or work practices; and any move by British Rail to alter the agreements on train manning, which have become restrictive, would have encountered fierce opposition.[34]

Nevertheless it would be quite wrong to exonerate management and there is no doubt that the also-ran industries have been badly managed. The Railways Board has not, until recently, even tried to renegotiate restrictive manning rules and it was BL's management which botched the ending of piecework.[35] Management must also bear the blame for failing to reduce the number of white collar staff and for having made so little effort to adjust the number of maintenance workers and postmen. However the most clear-cut examples of bad management have been in planning and capital expenditure. Estimates of future sales which, even at the time, were manifestly unrealistic have been used for planning purposes by BSC, BL and British Rail.[36] Moreover capital expenditure has been misdirected and mishandled. BR has spent too much on expensive signalling and too little on getting rid of unbraked wagons.[37] BL failed to replace the unprofitable Mini but provided itself with two medium-sized models of a somewhat undistinguished nature.[38] In BSC's strategic study of 1972 it was taken for granted that smaller works should be shut and the exercise was so conducted as to yield the desired result: the largest possible amount of big plant and the closure of medium-sized works.[39]

To say that the also-ran industries have been badly managed and that their labour problems have been difficult provokes the question of why. These are second order questions which have not been my principal concern. This book has largely been restricted to the primary problems of discovering how the nationalised industries have behaved and whether the policies they have pursued have tended to increase or reduce economic welfare. To even begin to answer the secondary questions which now present themselves would require another book. However, in the second part of this chapter I shall briefly examine one of the possible reasons for bad management, namely the industries' ownership by the state and the policies which the Government has pursued. That they have played a part is certainly suggested by the way in which British Rail and BL, which had both been reducing their manpower, promptly launched recruitment drives when the Government decided to come to their rescue.[40] But before investigating the subject of Government control there is a considerable amount of ground to be covered. In particular it is necessary to look at the performance of those industries which have made large gains in productivity, namely telecommunications, British Airways, gas and, for labour but not total factor productivity, electricity.

It is scarcely surprising that these industries have made large increases and the only puzzling point is that the rise in TFP has been so small in electricity. Telecommunications, airways and electricity have been making rapid gains in efficiency the world over, and are characterised by swift technological progress. In gas the advent of supplies from the North Sea has had a similar effect. In all of these high flying industries there have been important labour and capital saving innovations, e.g. wide-bodied jets in aviation, electronic switching in telephones, big generating sets in electricity and the doubling in the capacity of BGC's distribution system because of the higher calorific value of natural gas. Moreover telecommunications, British Airways and BGC have had the advantage, partly because of the large strides in efficiency, that their output has been growing at an exceptionally rapid rate and even electricity has had a moderate increase in production. Rising output has had a beneficial effect on productivity in telecommunications, gas and electricity because the workload has not risen in step. In all three industries sales have increased more rapidly than connections and much of the work that has to be performed is customer related.[41]

Hence the productivity gains which the high flyers have made during the decade do not necessarily indicate that they have been well managed. What, however, does throw some light on the problem is whether the undertakings have made satisfactory progress by foreign standards or, in the case of British Airways, compare favourably in efficiency with private UK airlines. At first sight BA's performance appears satisfactory. Over the course of the decade its labour productivity grew at about the average rate for the major international airlines. However, comparisons with British private airlines, allowing where necessary for differences in the type of work, show that BA is somewhat less efficient; and there is no doubt that it is badly over-manned and that its labour productivity is much lower than that of the most efficient foreign operators.[42] The rise in the British Electricity Boards' labour productivity compares fairly well with the gains that have been made by foreign systems, but its total factor productivity has been growing very slowly by international standards.[43]

Although international comparisons show that the Electricity Boards and telecommunications have considerable scope to raise labour productivity, both industries deserve considerable credit for the efforts that they have made and the success that they have had in improving the efficiency with which manpower is used. The Gas Corporation has also made some progress. It may be thought that the gains have simply been due to the substitution of capital for labour and to technical progress, but this is not the case. In all three industries improvements have been made in the way in which work is organised and executed.[44] The trade unions have in general been cooperative and the question arises of why this has been the case. It is not true, save in telecommunications, that it has been possible to raise efficiency without reducing employment. BGC and electricity have both made considerable reductions in staff. However, in gas they have been confined to gas works and in electricity the agreements that have enabled manning to be reduced were concluded at a time when the industry's employment had been growing. But I suspect that other factors have been at work. It is notable that the unions in these industries — the General and Municipal, the electrical workers and the POEU — in contrast to most of the unions in the also-ran industries, have been under strong and moderate leadership and are not characterised by local militancy. However, the reason for differences in union attitudes is another second order question which has not been explored.

Unfortunately the capital expenditure programmes of telecommunications and electricity have been marred by errors and delays. In electricity there have been long and expensive delays in the construction of power stations and even when they have been completed protracted operating difficulties have been encountered. The industry has not been by any means entirely responsible for the problems that have occurred, but during the 1960s it made the mistake of choosing the wrong type of nuclear reactor, it mishandled the change from small to big generating sets and it overloaded the manufacturers with work, although their design teams were known to be inadequate.[45] In telecommunications the Post Office has installed obsolete and obsolescent switching equipment because of its failure to develop computer-controlled plant.[46] Mention should also be made of the purchase of high cost British aircraft — Tridents and BAC One-Elevens in the 1960s and Concorde in the 1970s — by British Airways, although this was a Government decision.[47]

The poor use of capital appears to be a general feature of the public enterprise sector, and also a continuing one. BL commenced a large programme of investment which (as Lord Ryder forecast) was likely to show a poor rate of return because it was, for instance, based on sales forecasts which even at the time were over-ambitious. And priority was accorded to the new Mini, though it was known that a replacement car in the medium range was likely to be more profitable.[48] Instead of constructing light water reactors the electricity industry has started to build more coal burning capacity and is beginning work on further, very expensive, AGRs.[49] Moreover the Coal Board has embarked on a massive investment programme that rests on an over-optimistic estimate of the likely demand for coal and contains a wide fringe of dubious projects.[50] That public ownership tends to be accompanied by a relaxation in control over capital expenditure and a greater willingness to invest in low yield and high risk projects seems to be borne out by the way in which nationalisation was accompanied or followed by ill-conceived programmes of investment at BL and BSC. Moreover it is notable that, although NFC is to a large extent constrained by market forces, it embarked on a European venture that was over-ambitious and badly executed.[51]

Public ownership removes the threat of bankruptcy and provides access to government funds for investment. It might be expected that departmental and Treasury scrutiny of capital expenditure would lead to ill-judged investment projects being weeded out. However, although the Treasury can be expected to oppose dubious spending, such expenditure may have the support of the Ministries, as shown by the way in which the Department of Energy has been backing the NCB's plans for expansion. Moreover, according to the

National Economic Development Office, 'Departmental scrutiny of the Post Office's investment programme is very limited, although the sums involved are immense. On the other hand, British Rail's programme is scrutinised in detail. Overall, government attempts to exercise control over investment are variable. A few departments seem to have almost given up the attempt; in some cases the department is "carried along" by the corporation, while in other cases there is lengthy skirmishing'. In the end 'investment approval is normally given after lengthy discussions with the corporations and departments rarely feel sufficiently informed to risk turning down an application'.[52] This is probably a slight exaggeration — witness the way in which BSC's plan for a monster green field works was turned down — but there is no denying that the Whitehall sieve has very large holes.[53]

Costs, Prices and Profits

There was a spectacular increase in the unit costs of most of the nationalised undertakings between 1968 and 1978. The field was led by the pits which had a rise of 80% and the buses where there was one of more than 50%. They were followed by the postal services, BL, BSC, electricity and BR which had increases that ranged from 28% to 37%. NFC held its costs stable and there were three undertakings — the airways, telecommunications and gas — where there were large falls. As can be seen from Table 13.2 these varied from about 25% to 45%. At all of the concerns, except collieries and posts, where there was a big rise in unit costs it occurred either wholly or mainly during the second half of the period, whereas the big declines in gas and airways largely took place between 1968 and 1973. In most of the nationalised industries employment costs are the most important element in operating expenditure and unit staff costs provide the principal explanation for the movement of costs per unit of output. Electricity was exceptional because, although unit staff costs fell, there was a substantial rise in total costs per unit because of the sharp rise in unit fuel costs (53%). On the other hand the gas industry had the benefit of a marked reduction (42%).

Changes in staff costs per unit have, of course, been largely due to the way in which productivity has altered in the different undertakings. Those concerns where unit staff costs have declined turn out to be the ones with big gains in OMY whereas those in which it has

TABLE 13.2 Costs, Prices and Profits in Public Enterprise and Manufacturing[a]

	% Increase in real unit costs			% Increase in real staff costs per unit	% Increase in real staff costs per worker	% Increase in relative manual earnings[b]	% Increase in real prices				Gross margin (%)			Net margin (%)[h]
	1968-73	1973-78	1968-78	1968-78	1968-78	1968-78	1963-68	1968-73	1973-78	1968-78	1963	1968	1978	1978
NCB collieries	45	24	81	80	56	23	-8	5	58	66	12.3	8.8	1.0	-8.1
National and Scottish Bus Groups	18	29	52	48	37	7[d]	7	8	24	34	13.9	10.4	-2.2	-13.1
Postal services[c]	21	13	37	48	37	..	18	17	19	40	2.3	3.7	6.5	3.7
BL: vehicles[e]	8	23	33	37	14	-13[e]	..	5	21	27	..	9.1	4.9	-3.2
BSC: iron and steel	-4	37	32	59	47	10	-12	-3	22	18	..	8.5	-2.1	-15.0
British Rail	7	20	28	21	26	1	-11	-2	14	12	-5.9	-3.8/0.1	-14.7	-43.1
British Electricity Boards	-1	30	28	-9	43	24	-1	-19	23	—	35.4	40.4	25.0	5.4
National Freight Corporation	-1	4	2	-2	22	..	-3	13	4	18	..	-3.6	10.0	0.4
British Airways airline activities[f]	-24	-1	-25	-34	30	⌠	-13	-27	-11	-35	20.6	20.5	10.6	1.6
Telecommunications[g]	-17	-28	-40	-45	39	2[g]	-13	-19	-14	-30	44.6	44.3	51.3	25.9
British Gas	-41	-8	-46	-42	63	18	-16	-39	6	-35	14.7	19.3	32.2	15.7
Manufacturing	..	..	..	11	29	—	-5	-4	9	5	..	..	..	..

[a] In some cases figures are for financial years.
[b] % increase in average weekly earnings of adult manual men relative to increase for manufacturing.
[c] Foreign subsidiaries included in figures for unit costs, prices and profits.
[d] Road passenger transport, excluding London Transport.
[e] Motor vehicles.
[f] Air transport industry.
[g] Includes posts.
[h] Stock appreciation excluded where significant.

fallen show large increases in staff costs per unit of output. However productivity has not been the only factor at work. BL experienced a large reduction in OMY (−17%) whereas at BSC there was little change. Nonetheless BL displayed a considerably smaller increase in unit staff costs than BSC (37% as against 59%). The explanation is that at BL staff costs per worker increased less than the average for manufacturing whereas they rose more rapidly at BSC. British Leyland and NFC are the only nationalised concerns in which staff costs per employee have increased significantly less than in manufacturing. In most of the undertakings manual earnings and/or staff costs per worker have risen faster than in manufacturing. This was true not only for BSC but also for gas, coal, electricity, telecommunications, postal services and the state buses. Their above average increases can be explained partly by the fact that before 1968 the weekly earnings of miners and electricity workers had fallen behind, and partly perhaps to productivity payments. However it is also notable that the concerns where the increases have been no greater than in manufacturing are those which have been subject to competition — BL, NFC and BA — or, as in the case of BR, have been under some financial pressure. The relative earnings of railwaymen increased after financial discipline had been relaxed but fell back when it was reasserted.[54]

Cost and price changes have naturally tended to go hand in hand. Prices fell by 30–35% in telecommunications, airways and gas, where there were large reductions in unit costs; but almost all of the concerns where costs rose made price increases. In some cases these were very large, viz. an increase of two-thirds in coal, 40% in postal services, a third for the buses and about a quarter at BL. Although BSC and NFC had more modest increases they amounted to 18%, while BR had a rise of 12%. Electricity was once again the exception to the rule because its charges were no higher in 1978 than they had been in 1968. However in electricity and most of the other undertakings there was a considerable contrast between the first and second half of the decade. Between 1973 and 1978 prices tended to increase more or fall less than they had during the years 1968–73, although NFC — with a bigger increase between 1968 and 1973 — was an exception.

Prices tended to increase less rapidly than unit costs, or to decline more sharply. As a result gross margins fell except in postal services and the NFC, where charges increased more than unit costs, and in telecomms and gas where prices fell less sharply than costs. During 1968 all of the nationalised undertakings except NFC and BR were covering their depreciation at replacement cost, and even British Rail earned sufficient to meet its operating costs. In 1978 the public enterprise sector was much less profitable and, after allowing for stock appreciation, there were gross losses at BR, the buses, BSC and the mines. Although British Leyland showed a small gross profit it had a net margin of −3%, at the NCB the figure was −8%, at National and Scottish −13%, at BSC −15%, and at BR −43%. The remaining undertakings made profits after depreciation but they were very small in relation to the value of the assets employed in electricity, the airways and NFC. Only telecommunications, postal services and gas appear to have been reasonably profitable and even BGC's net profit would have vanished if it had had to pay the market price for natural gas.[55] However it must be remembered that during the course of the decade there has been a considerable decline in the profitability of the private sector and that the financial position of most of the nationalised undertakings has improved since the mid-1970s.

ARE RESOURCES BEING MISALLOCATED?

As a general rule prices should be equivalent to marginal costs and output should be expanded or contracted until the marginal cost is just being covered. If this happens the value of the resources used in producing the final units of output will be just equal to the value which consumers place upon those units, as reflected by the price that they pay. That so many of the nationalised undertakings are operating at a loss is therefore a cause for concern because it would seem to indicate that resources are being misallocated. This conclusion may be queried on the ground that the only costs that are relevant are those that can be avoided and capital charges are therefore irrelevant because the capital expenditure to which they relate has already been made and cannot be recovered. However this argument wears thin if the net loss continues year after year, and even in the short run it does not excuse operating deficits. It should also be remembered that the use of capital assets often involves an opportunity cost because they have an alternative employment. Mining machinery, for instance, can be transferred from loss-making to profitable pits, and buses and railway rolling stock can be switched from one service to another. But BSC should not be expected to meet all of its capital charges because its plant and equipment have little or no alternative use and excess capacity exists.

It may be urged that it is not desirable that BR should cover its costs in full because much of its expenditure is fixed and its marginal costs are lower than its average costs. This argument has little substance because, among other reasons, the fixed element in BR's expenditure on infrastructure is only some £80 million.[56] However it is clear that the reverse situation, in which marginal costs exceed average costs, obtains in coal and gas. A substantial part of the NCB's tonnage is produced at a very high cost. During 1978–79 its loss-making collieries incurred a deficit of approximately £180 million but were cross-subsidised from the profits earned at other pits and from opencast output.[57] BGC has to pay about 12p per therm for natural gas from the northern part of the North Sea but is still buying gas from the southern fields for about 2½p. Instead of basing its prices on gas from the northern sector the Corporation charges its domestic customers an average cost price, and large amounts of gas are being supplied to other users at a low charge, although renewal contracts are being negotiated on a marginal cost basis.[58]

Extensive cross-subsidisation is also to be found at those public corporations that produce a range of goods and services. In the postal services, first class mail earns a net profit of around £50 million whereas second class mail incurs a loss of about £30 million. Moreover the same price is charged regardless of where letters are delivered although the cost is high in rural areas and low where mail is received in bulk.[59] In telecommunications, charges are unduly low for exchange connections, private lines and telex, but excessively high for trunk calls.[60] British Airways not only cross-subsidises its secondary services but also appears to engage in predatory pricing. Its standard fares, which are mainly paid by businessmen whose price elasticity is low, are often pitched far above costs. However discount fares are frequently set below cost in order to meet or discourage competition from the charter operators.[61] In buses prices are not related to costs, and cross-subsidisation appears to be widespread within BR's Inter-City sector.[62]

It is frequently maintained that public transport should not be expected to pay its way because of the hardship that will be inflicted if loss-making services are withdrawn and because of the social costs that will be inflicted if traffic is transferred from public to private transport. However subsidies for BR's unprofitable passenger services were provided without any detailed examination to discover which of them were worth retaining; and the decision to grant support was taken despite official surveys which showed that the withdrawal of little-used rail services caused no great hardship, and that the availability of rural bus services had little effect on mobility. It was never envisaged when subsidies were introduced that they would be increased and extended as they have. Indeed the rail subsidy arrangements in the 1968 Transport Act were specifically designed to limit the amount of financial support that BR would receive.[63] Nor were the politicians who agreed to provide more public money solely concerned with the welfare of the nation. Sir Richard Marsh recalls that, when he was Chairman of BR and the desirability of providing the railways with a greatly increased subsidy was being discussed, he 'played a slightly underhand political trick'. He showed Peyton, the Conservative Minister of Transport, 'a complete map of the existing British Rail network. We then removed that and put up a much smaller British Rail network on which we superimposed the political map. He suddenly realised that all the closed lines were in rural areas and, by sheer coincidence, happened to be Conservative seats. He said something to the effect, "Well I don't know why you did not show me that at the beginning, and why we wasted all that time this morning".'[64] It has now become almost unthinkable that any rail service should be withdrawn and, although the situation is more fluid in buses, most counties take it for granted that existing levels of service, wherever possible, should be maintained.[65]

A number of cost-benefit studies of rail passenger services have been made and from these it appears that at least fifty of BR's two hundred provincial stopping services do not provide a benefit which is sufficient to cover even their specific costs. Moreover, it seems highly improbable that there can be any cost–benefit case for maintaining many of the bus and rail services which now receive support as their loads are extremely light and they are wildly unprofitable. Survey evidence suggests that lift-giving increases as the provision of buses falls, and it is evident from the detailed investigations that are being carried out within NBC that it is often possible by re-routing and reshaping services to make them viable.[66] The provision of public transport at a loss is often supported on the ground that private road users do not pay sufficient in the form of fuel and other taxes to meet the cost of providing the road system. This is true only for buses themselves and for heavy lorries, but the divergence between costs and prices is much greater for rail freight. Moreover, it seems doubtful whether allowance for road congestion and other social costs would greatly modify the conclusion that misallocation is occurring because public transport fails to cover its costs. It must, for instance, be remembered that they include the costs of the congestion on BR's London commuter services.[67]

The desirability of contracting output where a loss is being made may be further disputed on the ground that it will only lead to higher unemployment. However, during the first half of the decade the labour market was, whatever official figures may seem to show, fairly tight. During 1973 both state and private concerns were having recruitment difficulties and as late as 1978 the PO's large city sorting offices were short of labour and NBC reported that, 'Staff shortages tended to persist or increase, particularly in the urban north-east and around London'.[68] Towards the end of 1979 BR declared that 'staff shortages bedevil significant areas of Kent and Essex'. Let us, however, assume that these are isolated exceptions and pose the question of whether it is desirable, at a time of general unemployment, to improve efficiency. Where workers are being employed unnecessarily, as a result of over-manning and inefficiency, no output will be lost if they become unemployed. Disguised unemployment may be regarded as preferable to open unemployment because of the demoralisation and humiliation to which the latter is supposed to give rise. However it seems doubtful whether those who are out of work any longer regard this as a cause for shame and it must surely be corrupting to have employment that is only nominal. Is it really more demoralising to be registered as unemployed or to be a fireman on a diesel train?

Where workers are genuinely helping to provide goods and services it does, at first sight, appear that society will be worse off if output is reduced or discontinued. If however the unprofitable activity was being cross-subsidised it will become possible to reduce prices where excessively high profits were having to be earned, and hence there will be some compensating increase in output and employment. Moreover the government should be able to make good any net reduction in output and employment by expansionary fiscal and monetary policies. If, as at present, it feels unable to do this because of inflation, the maintenance of employment in the nationalised industries will mean fewer jobs elsewhere. Nor, even in the case of coal, is there a convincing argument for continuing to produce at a loss on the ground that the unprofitable production is taking place in areas where unemployment is high.[69]

PART TWO — GOVERNMENT OWNERSHIP

The performance of the nationalised industries over the past decade has ranged from being good in parts — telecommunications and gas — to being almost wholly bad — BSC and postal services. Although the picture is not wholly black, most of the industries display serious inefficiency because they do not use the minimum quantities of labour and capital to produce the goods and services that they provide. Furthermore resources are being misallocated because of the widespread failure to pursue the optimum policies for pricing and production. Far too many of the nationalised industries produce at a loss, engage in average cost pricing or practice cross-subsidisation. In general the nationalised industries' performance has been third rate, though with some evidence here and there of first class standards. What is particularly disappointing is that the progress that was being made prior to 1968 has not in general been maintained, although a falling away was only to be expected in view of Britain's growing economic difficulties.

The public corporations' relatively favourable performance during the 1960s was in part due to the decision by the Government that they should behave less like social services and more like normal commercial undertakings. This was the message of the first White Paper on *The Financial and Economic Obligations of the Nationalised Industries*, published in 1961, and of the appointment of Dr Beeching with the remit of making the railways pay.[70] The White Paper was followed up by the establishment of financial targets. These had the weakness of being set without regard for the pricing and investment policies that the industries should adopt and might in some cases be met simply by raising prices. However, at that time price increases were more apparent because inflation was lower and after 1965 rises began to be vetted by the Prices and Incomes Board. The targets appear to have led not only to an improvement in profitability but also to the adoption of better methods for evaluating investment and to a general tightening up in efficiency; and Beeching certainly produced a marked improvement in BR's performance.

The second White Paper of 1967 on the nationalised industries' *Economic and Financial Objectives* was intended to strengthen and refine the system of financial targets and, though the object of making BR cover its costs was abandoned, the 1968 Transport Act was designed to put BR under greater financial discipline. However before long it was decided to provide BR with a virtually open-ended subsidy and the financial targets were waived. Despite a certain amount of equivocation the White Paper criticised cross-subsidisation and advocated marginal cost pricing, but this turned out to be no more than a pious hope. A related proposal was that the discounted cash flow method should be used to estimate the likely return from investment projects. Here departmental and Treasury promptings had some effect but it was disappointingly small because so much of the public corporations' investment was regarded as unavoidable. Nothing came of the proposal that departments should develop 'indicators of performance' to 'provide regular and systematic information about each industry's success in controlling its costs, increasing efficiency, and economising in the use of manpower and capital resources'.[71] Moreover the Heath Government abolished the Prices and Incomes Board which had devoted much of its time and energy to investigating and improving the nationalised industries' efficiency.

That the 1967 White Paper had so little effect is perhaps hardly surprising in view of the way in which it originated. It was the work of officials and did not represent a commitment by the Government. According to Dick Crossman, the Cabinet 'had exactly twenty minutes to consider it. Having rung Harold [Wilson] beforehand and prepared a number of amendments . . . I insisted on tabling them, much to the annoyance of my colleagues. As I got up from the table I said to Callaghan [who as Chancellor was formally responsible for the White Paper], "This is a very poor paper." "What does it matter?" he said. "It's only read by a few dons and experts." "Well I'm one don", I said, and he replied, "You're a don who knows nothing about the subject. Personally as Chancellor I couldn't care less. I take no responsibility and took no part in composing it." '[72]

Politicians of neither party are interested in devising better pricing structures or seeing that investment projects show a satisfactory return. If they belong to the Labour Party they are, like Dick

Crossman, instinctively opposed on the ground that this has nothing to do with Socialism but will, on the contrary, make the nationalised industries more commercial. If they are Conservatives they are wedded to the private enterprise model and believe that those who manage the public corporations should, in so far as possible, be left to get on with their jobs.

The system of financial targets was not adopted because the Government had suddenly become concerned that resources were being misallocated. The nationalised industries had for years been earning low rates of return on their assets and engaging in cross-subsidisation without Ministers displaying any interest. What happened was that the Treasury became worried during the late 1950s that public expenditure was getting out of control and starting to rise in relation to the national income.[73] Moreover British Rail's deficit was beginning to become a serious burden on the Exchequer. These were obviously matters which did concern the Government because of their implications for taxation. The principal aim of the 1961 White Paper was not to improve the allocation of resources but to ensure that the nationalised industries financed a greater proportion of their capital expenditure out of their profits.

By the early 1970s the public corporations' finances were no longer a cause for anxiety. There had been a considerable improvement in profitability and BR's losses had at least been stemmed. Although the public corporations were still borrowing fairly heavily from the Exchequer this was of no great moment because the public sector borrowing requirement was at a very low level as a result of the severe measures which had been taken after devaluation in 1967. What was worrying the Government was unemployment and rising prices. The Heath Government's initial policy for curbing inflation was that the nationalised industries should make wage awards which were slightly lower than the prevailing norm and in this way progressively reduce the size of the going rate. This strategy, known as X-1, led to confrontations in electricity and in the postal services, where industrial relations were permanently soured. Inflation continued to rise and in mid-1971 the Confederation of British Industry proposed that firms should not increase their prices by more than 5% during the next six months. The nationalised industries were expected to conform and to go on restraining their prices after the end of the period. As a result most of them made smaller increases than they would otherwise have done.

Hence it seemed unreasonable to expect the corporations to meet their financial targets and these were, in effect, suspended. At the beginning of 1973 statutory price control was established and, although this applied to industry as a whole, the nationalised industries were a special case because they were not permitted to raise their prices when trading at a loss and because of direct restraint by the Government. It was therefore decided to provide gas, electricity and the Post Office with compensation and this was effected by the Statutory Corporations (Financial Provisions) Act of 1974.

By then the other nationalised industries were being, or had already been, assisted financially by the Government in ways that were not envisaged at the time of the 1967 White Paper and the 1968 Transport Act. The limited support which BR had received under the 1968 Act was extended into a general subsidy for passenger services; and assistance for unprofitable rural bus services, which had been initiated by the 1968 Act, was broadened into general support for loss-making routes. In addition BR had a large part of its capital written off and the NCB and BSC were also helped in this way. However, what was of greater assistance to British Steel was that its debt had been converted, soon after nationalisation, into public dividend capital on which very little was ever paid to the Exchequer.

This is not the place for a detailed examination of how these policies came to be adopted and something has already been said about BR and the buses. There are however a number of general points that can be made. The White Paper, with its emphasis on the possible divergence of social and private costs and the need for a cost–benefit approach, helped to legitimise the provision of subsidies. So, of course, did the 1968 Act and the continual suggestion that public transport was a social service. It was difficult, once subsidies were being paid in order to maintain little-used rail services and loss-making rural bus services, to resist their extension to unprofitable urban bus routes and to rail services that were intensively used. Moreover once BR had been provided with large-scale financial support it could not long be denied to the buses. The growing concern with the environment also played a part, but what was probably even more important was that there had been a general reaction against Beeching type policies. The same was true in the case of pit closures which would have been necessary if the NCB had been denied a financial reconstruction in 1972. What was even more important was that the miners were now strongly opposed and their industrial power had been demonstrated by the national coal strike of 1972. Moreover the case for closures seemed much weaker now that unemployment was so much higher. As for the Government's failure to insist that BSC should pay greater dividends this was due to a combination of price restraint and to the inherent weakness of the device. It is impossible to insist that the necessary profit be earned during a year which has already passed by.

By the mid-1970s the nationalised industries' finances were in chaos. During 1974–75 they received £1,725 million of revenue support of which £1,065 million was compensation paid to gas, electricity and the PO, £545 million was handed over to the Railways Board and £115 million was paid to the NCB. In addition the nationalised industries borrowed £1,040 million from the Exchequer to finance their capital expenditure, bringing their total call on public funds to over £2,750 million. In 1975, as part of a general attempt to reduce the enormous public sector borrowing requirement, it was decided that the nationalised industries should increase their prices and reduce their deficits. NFC was told to put its house in order and BR had its passenger subsidy cut and was instructed to eliminate its freight deficit. Nevertheless few of the nationalised industries were under much financial pressure because they could now jack up their prices and attribute this to previous restraint or to inflationary pressures. The NCB, which had not previously possessed much latitude to raise its prices was now able to make a huge increase because of the rise in the cost of oil; and British Leyland and BSC, which could not increase their prices very far, were provided with funds by the Government. Moreover the amount of discipline that was imposed on BR and the nationalised buses should not be exaggerated because not only have they been able to raise their prices but they have continued to be provided with large-scale support. The Coal Board has also been insulated from market forces by the provision of subsidies and the discouragement of imports.

What in retrospect seems remarkable is not that the Government changed course in 1975 but that there was such a small alteration in direction. The Labour Government was no more willing than the Conservatives to exert any pressure on the nationalised industries to make them cut their costs and tighten up their efficiency. In order to do this they would have had to shed labour at a time when unemployment was high and the Government was trying to keep men at work. What was perhaps even more important was the anxiety of Labour Ministers not to alienate the trade unions. Not only were the unions now playing an increasingly powerful part within the Labour Party but their support was essential if the Social Contract was to be preserved and wage restraint was to have any hope of success. Moreover Mr Tony Benn, who played a crucial part first at the Department of Industry and then at Energy, placed enormous emphasis on the preservation of jobs and cooperation with the unions. As a result the Government failed to put pressure on the nationalised industries and the Boards could not, as the Steel Corporation found, rely on the support of Ministers if they tried to cut employment and raise productivity.

The policies which Governments have pursued towards the nationalised industries since 1970 seem almost to have been devised to depress their performance. They have created confusion about the nationalised industries' objectives. During the 1960s the nationalised industries were told to operate at minimum cost, earn reasonable profits and in general to behave commercially, at least in the sense of behaving as if they were operating under conditions of perfect competition, which is what a marginal cost approach to pricing and investment really means. This objective was, of course, hedged about with qualifications but the general message was clear and it became established that where 'wider social considerations' were to be taken into account the industries would, like British Rail, be provided with a specific subsidy in order to preserve their commercial remit. During the 1970s the nationalised industries have been expected to pursue a variety of policies which have often been contradictory and have seldom been of long duration. Although the message emanating from Government has in one sense been very confused in another way it has been all too clear: the nationalised industries are instruments of economic and social policy and are not commercial undertakings. The contrast between the 1960s and the 1970s is not, of course, absolute but it is, I believe, real.

Government policies and the aribitary intervention in which they have engaged have demoralised the nationalised industries. They have not only lowered the morale of their managements but they have also reduced their sense of responsibility. It has been all too easy for those in charge to excuse themselves on the ground that the

Government has been at fault. The way in which the Steel Corporation attributed its poor financial results to price restraint and ignored its own inefficiency is an obvious case in point. In his autobiography Sir Richard Marsh, who presided over British Rail's financial débâcle, blames the Government and never even considers the possibility that his own policies might have been mistaken.[74] Moreover because of the way in which it has behaved it has been difficult for the Government to hold the Boards accountable for their actions. Although the nationalised industries have been subject to many constraints they have been under remarkably little discipline. This has weakened the Boards' resolve to stand up to the unions and their members in order to secure improvements in efficiency which are being resisted. Moreover the unions' will to resist has been increased by the absence of tight financial limits and the belief that further Government assistance will be made available. This was well illustrated by the recent steel strike which would have ended sooner but for the union's belief that it did not have to agree to measures that would lead to greater efficiency because the Government would provide extra money.

It is important to recognise that the various factors that have been mentioned have not operated in isolation and that the causal process has not all been in one direction. For instance price restraint destroyed BR's feeble belief that, the social passenger services apart, it was to behave commercially and provided it with an alibi for failing to meet its financial objective. The Board then argued strongly that it required large-scale financial assistance because railways were inherently unprofitable and that this assistance, together with much larger funds for investment, should be provided on environmental grounds. When this was conceded and financial discipline was relaxed BR launched a recruitment drive and there was a large wage award. This led to a further increase in the subsidy. When it began to be questioned Sir Richard Marsh, who as Minister of Transport had been responsible for carrying the 1968 Act through its final stages, complained that BR had not been set any clear or lasting objective. Moreover he became angry and embittered when the Treasury began to cut back the excessive programme of capital expenditure that had been sanctioned.[75] Instead of trying to get the unions to agree to the modification of restrictive practices the Railways Board joined them in campaigning for the provision of massive state finance. British Leyland provides another example of cumula tive causation. One reason why the Ryder Team's proposals were so weak was the knowledge that the Minister was strongly opposed to anything that would anger the unions. However, the Government was scarcely able to dissent when Ryder recommended a policy of faith, hope and charity.

There has during the past year or two been evidence of a shift in Government policy towards the nationalised industries and also of a diminution in union power. Perhaps the first straw in the wind was the decision during 1977 that BSC could end steelmaking at a number of smaller works ahead of the dates that the Government had previously laid down. However too much should not be made of this as the Government had in fact been remarkably slow to recognise that action was necessary. What was far more significant was the decision to back Michael Edwardes, the new Chairman of BL, when he decided, for instance, to shut the Speke factory, although the unions were opposed and it was located in an area of high unemployment. The year 1978 also saw the publication of a new White Paper, the *Nationalised Industries*, which was intended by the Treasury to establish new and more effective financial guidelines for the public corporations.[76] Its centrepiece was the proposal that they should be expected to earn a return of 5%, as estimated using dcf, on their total capital expenditure. It was hoped that as a result prices would be based on costs and that stricter control would be exercised over investment. Since the Conservatives have been in power there has been a further and more radical break with the past. BGC has been told to raise its domestic prices in order that marginal costs may be covered, and BL and BSC have been encouraged to rationalise their activities and reduce their capacity. Moreover the Government withstood union demands that it should intervene in their dispute with BSC and finance a wage award which the Corporation was insisting should be covered by higher productivity.

It is, however, important not to exaggerate the advances that have taken place or to minimise the difficulties of securing a more efficient use of resources. BR and the buses are still being treated as sacred cows and the Government continues, in the holy name of energy policy, to support the expansion of coal production although on any rational view output should be reduced. The Coal Board is now being permitted to defer the payment of interest on its major schemes of capital expenditure, although it obviously has scope to improve its profitability by closing down loss-making collieries.

There have been false dawns before and there are formidable obstacles to reducing misallocation and cutting costs. Most of these have already been discussed but there are two general impediments which have so far been ignored. First, the fact that the nationalised undertakings are so large and are in public ownership converts what would otherwise be a collection of local difficulties and decisions into a national problem about which pressure groups and trade unions become concerned and politicians adopt policies. Corner shops have been quietly closing for years, but if retailing had been nationalised there would have been a great outcry some years ago when it became known that the Shops Board had a ten-year plan to close many of its uneconomic local outlets, and the process would probably have been slowed down. If the Coal Board did not exist and the railways had not been nationalised the problems of closing down loss-making pits and withdrawing unprofitable rail services would be less formidable. Moreover if the electricity industry had been less centralised different utilities would have chosen different types of reactors and some of them at least would have made the right choice. The great advantage of decentralised decision-taking is that bets are hedged, change is gradual and issues are not politicised. Second, public ownership raises expectations. Consumers expect 'fair' prices and the provision of unprofitable services, and workers come to believe they have a right to jobs and that wages should be paid regardless of whether they are earned. Both groups believe that the Government will, if necessary, be able to provide the public corporations with money and ask the seemingly unaswerable question of why, since they have been brought into public ownership, the nationalised industries should, like private undertakings, be expected to cover their costs and respond to market forces.

It would however be wrong to attribute the nationalised industries' failings simply to public ownership. Almost any collection of British industries would have shown up badly and, as BL's disastrous record under private ownership shows, bad management and poor labour relations are by no means confined to the public enterprise sector. Moreover the operation of industries that belong to the public enterprise sector poses particular problems because they tend to be natural monopolies and/or to be in decline. Many of the weaknesses which appear from British experience to be a consequence of public ownership are displayed by the same industries abroad under private ownership. The German and Belgian coal industries, which are in private hands, fail to cover their costs and are heavily subsidised. In America natural gas has been sold at an artificially low price and AT and T makes a loss on its local telephone service which it cross-subsidises out of the monopoly profits which are earned on trunk calls. Moreover, the establishment of Amtrack, to continue operating loss-making rail passenger services, suggests that in railways public ownership should be seen as the instrument of misallocation, not as its cause. It can therefore be questioned whether public ownership has in itself contributed to the poor performance of the British nationalised industries, although my own verdict would be that it has. But I do not believe that public enterprise always tends to perform worse than private industry. I suspect that nationalised undertakings function efficiently when economic conditions are generally favourable but particularly badly when the economy is in difficulties; and Italian experience seems to bear this out.

What, however, is perhaps an even more important issue than ownership is the question of monopoly status. In a number of industries there is obviously scope for greater competition and a prima facie case for moving in this direction.[77] Even where monopoly is inevitable it would be possible to move away from a unitary form of organisation and this may well be desirable.

References

In these references the Select Committee on Nationalised Industries is referred to as SCNI, the National Board for Prices and Incomes as NBPI, the Department of the Environment as DoE, the Department of Energy as D of E, the *Financial Times* as FT and the *Sunday Times* as ST. All Command Papers and publications of Committees, Commissions, Departments and Ministeries were published by Her Majesty's Stationery Office unless it is indicated to the contrary by the use of the word 'from', e.g. 'from D of E'. All publications by nationalised industries and other bodies were published by themselves unless otherwise stated.

Chapter 1 : Introduction

1 Chancellor of the Exchequer, *Nationalised Industries: A Review of Economic and Financial Objectives*, Cmnd 3437 (11.67).
2 Richard Pryke, *Public Enterprise in Practice* (MacGibbon and Kee, 1971).

Chapter 2 : British Gas

Principal statistical source for energy chapters: D of E etc. *Digest of United Kingdom Energy Statistics*.
1 Michael V. Posner, *Fuel Policy: A Study in Applied Economics* (Macmillan, 1973), p. 205.
2 Kenneth W. Dam, 'Oil and Gas Licensing in the North Sea', *Journal of Law and Economics* (1964), pp. 61, 62.
3 George Polanyi, *What Price North Sea Gas?* (Institute of Economic Affairs 1967); Kenneth W. Dam, 'The Pricing of North Sea Gas in Britain', *Journal of Law and Economics* (1970), p. 14.
4 M.V. Posner, *op. cit.* p. 207.
5 Ministry of Power, *Fuel Policy*, Cmnd 3438 (11.67), pp. 7, 8.
6 Ministry of Technology, *Report of the [Morton] Inquiry into the Safety of Natural Gas as a Fuel* (7.70), p. 37.
7 FT, 9.12.77.
8 FT, 7.10.77.
9 Price Commission, *British Gas Corporation — Gas Prices and Allied Charges* (7.79), pp. 23, 25, 29, 103, 115.

10 Department of Trade, *Overseas Trade Statistics of the UK.*
11 Price Commission, *op. cit.* pp. 23, 36, 40, 68, 103, 115.
12 NBPI Report 155, *Costs and Efficiency in the Gas Industry*, Cmnd 4458 (8.70), pp. 8, 11, 25.
13 Price Commission, *op. cit.* pp. 63, 65.
14 *Energy Projections 1979: A Paper by the Department of Energy* (from D of E 1979), p. 11.
15 Secretary of State for Energy, *Energy Policy: A Consultation Document*, Cmnd 7101 (2.78) p. 99; Gerald Manners, 'Alternative Strategies for the British Coal Industry', *The Geographical Journal* (1978), p. 227.
16 *Energy Projections 1979*, p. 6.
17 Peter R. Odell, 'The Potential for Natural Gas from the North Sea in Relation to Western Europe's Market for Gas by the mid-1980s', *Geoforum* (1977), p. 163.
18 FT, 24.2.78.
19 M. Prior and M. Teper, *The Supply of Gas from Coal and Alternative Resources* (IEA Coal Research Economic Assessment Service 11.79), p. 11.
20 Price Commission, *op. cit.* p. 38.

CHAPTER 3 : ELECTRICITY

Principal statistical sources: Electricity Council *Handbook of Electricity Supply Statistics*; CEGB *Statistical Yearbook.*

1 Richard Pryke, *Public Enterprise in Practice*, p. 299.
2 SCNI, *Ministerial Control* (Session 1967–68), Vol. 1, pp. 228–232.
3 FT, 14.6.74.
4 Minister of Power, *Report of the [Wilson] Committee of Enquiry into Delays in Commissioning CEGB Power Stations*, Cmnd 3960 (3.69), pp. 10, 14, 16, 21, 22.
5 Cmnd 3960, pp. 6, 7; National Economic Development Office (NEDO), *Large Industrial Sites* (1970), p. 12.
6 ST, 17.11.76, 9.7.78.
7 NEDO, Mechanical and Electrical Engineering Construction EDC, *What's Still Wrong on Site* (9.77).
8 Duncan Burn, *Nuclear Power and the Energy Crisis* (Macmillan, 1978), pp. 10, 121–3, 125, 153, 161; *The Political Economy of Nuclear Energy* (The Institute of Economic Affairs, 1967), pp. 28, 29, 62.
9 Burn, *Nuclear Power and the Energy Crisis* pp. 97, 100, 104, 105, 128, 129, 134.
10 Ehlert Knudsen, *Non-Availability of Thermal Power Stations* (International Union of Producers and Distributors of Electrical Energy Vienna Congress 5.76), p. 11; US Department of Energy, Economic Regulatory Administration, Division of Power Supply and Reliability, *Interim Report on the Performance of 400 Megawatt and Larger Coal-Fired Generating Units* (4.78), p. 27; CEGB, 1977–78, p. 9; 1978–79, p. 9.
11 Price Commission, *Area Electricity Boards — Electricity Prices and Certain Allied Charges* (7.79), p. 15.

12 F.H.S. Brown, *The Duty and Development of Modern Power Station Plant* (The Institution of Mechanical Engineers, 12.12.62), p. 10.

13 United States Department of Energy, Energy Information Administration, *Steam-Electric Plant Construction Cost and Annual Production Expenses 1977* (US Government Printing Office 12.78), p. xxxv; CEGB, 1978–79, p. 10.

14 Energy Commission, *Coal and Nuclear Power Station Costs* Paper 6 (from D of E), p. 4; *Choice of Thermal Reactor Systems: Report of the Nuclear Power Advisory Board*, Cmnd 5731 (8.74), p. 26.

15 Price Commission, *op. cit.* p. 21.

16 *Ibid.* p. 23.

17 Business Statistics Office, *Business Monitor Monthly Statistics Durable Goods Shops* SDM 3 (12.79).

18 *Which?* (4.75), p. 105; (1.77), p. 52; (2.77), pp. 62, 64, 65.

19 CEGB, *Corporate Plan 1978*, pp. 16, 17; R. Turvey, ed., *Public Enterprise* (Penguin Modern Economic Readings, 1968), p. 183.

20 Ronald S. Edwards and R.D.V. Roberts, *Status, Productivity and Pay* (Macmillan, 1971), pp. 109, 110, 137, 141, 150, 172, 173, 274, 295–9.

21 NBPI Report 79, *Electricity Supply Industry National Guidelines Covering Productivity Payments*, Cmnd 3726 (7.68), pp. 2, 4.

22 SCNI, *Reports and Accounts of the Energy Industries* (Session 1977–78), pp. 106, 107; Edwards and Roberts, *op. cit.* p. 274.

23 Edison Electric Institute, *Statistical Year Book* (1978), pp. 31, 49.

24 United States Department of Energy, Energy Information Administration *op. cit.*; Electricité de France, Direction de la Production et du Transport Thermique, *Rapport d'Activité 1977*.

25 United States Department of Energy, *op. cit.*, and *Statistics of Privately Owned Electric Utilities in the United States 1977* (US Government Printing Office, 1.79).

26 Price Commission, *op. cit.* pp. 49, 56.

27 *Ibid.* pp. 33, 34.

28 *Energy Projections 1979*, p. 7.

29 Colin Sweet, ed., *The Fast Breeder Reactor* (Macmillan, 1980).

30 Energy Commission, Paper 6, Fig. 1.

31 US Department of Energy, Economic Regulatory Administration, *op. cit.* p. 27.

32 Electricity Council, *Medium Term Development Plan 1979–86* (7.79), p. 21.

33 FT 4.4.80.

Chapter 4 : The Coal Mines

1 Cmnd 3438, p. 36.

2 Economist Intelligence Unit, *Britain's Energy Supplies* (9.68), Vol. 2, pp. 1–3; *Coal Industry Examination: Interim Report June 1974* (from D of E), p. 11.

3 SCNI, *National Coal Board* (Session 1968–69), Vol. 2, p. 479.

4 G.L. Reid, Kevin Allen and D.J. Harris *The Nationalized Fuel Industries*, (Heinemann, 1973) pp. 35–6, 40–3.

5 Chris Harlow, *Innovation and Productivity under Nationalisation* (George Allen and Unwin, 1977), p. 211.
6 *Coal Industry Examination: Final Report 1974* (from D of E), p. 12.
7 Harlow, *op. cit.* p. 210; R. Rawlinson, 'Producing Coal', *Colliery Guardian Annual Review* (8.76), p. 370.
8 NCB, 1965–66, p. 9.
9 *Colliery Guardian*, p. 361.
10 NCB, *Press Release* (7.7.76), p. 7.
11 R.G. Searle-Barnes, *Pay and Productivity Bargaining: A Study of the Effect of National Wage Agreements in the Nottinghamshire Coalfield* (Manchester University Press, 1969), pp. 12, 13, 26–9, Chapter 3.
12 *Ibid.* pp. 73–95.
13 *Ibid.* pp. 128–52, 166.
14 John Hughes and Roy Moore, *A Special Case? Social Justice and the Miners* (Penguin Books, 1972), p. 29.
15 Eurostat, *Coal Monthly Bulletin*, No. 5-1980.
16 *Coal Industry Examination: Interim Report*, pp. 10–12.
17 *Coal for the Future: Progress with 'Plan for Coal' and Prospects to the Year 2000* (from D of E), pp. 9, 11, 22.
18 *Interim Report*, p. 10; ST, 28.11.76.
19 *Coal for the Future*, p. 11; NCB, 1978–79, p. 16.
20 *Coal for the Future*, p. 11.
21 *Coal for the Future*, pp. 16, 17, 19.
22 *Energy Projections*, p. 7.
23 See below p. 207.
24 See above p. 19.
25 *Energy Projections*, Annex 1.
26 Cmnd 7101, pp. 74, 75, 87.
27 *Energy Projections*, p. 9; Cmnd 7101, p. 95.
28 *Coal Industry Tripartite Group Sub-Committee on the South Wales Coalfield* (from D of E 30.3.79), para 73.

CHAPTER 5 : BRITISH RAIL

Principal statistical source for transport chapters: Department of Transport, etc. *Transport Statistics Great Britain.*

1 Ministry of Transport, *Report on the Effects of Closing Three Rail Passenger Services* (from Ministry — now Department — of Transport, 7.67), pp. 1, 3, 4.
2 Ministry of Transport, *Railway Policy*, Cmnd 3439 (11.67), p. 5.
3 *Road Way* (10.79), p. 13.
4 *Railway Gazette International* (1.77), pp. 14, 15.
5 BRB, *A Comparative Study of European Rail Performance* (12.79), pp. 16, 19, 27.
6 I.S. Jones, *The Demand for Inter-City Rail Travel in the UK: Some Evidence* (from Department of Transport).
7 FT, 28.11.68.

8   Transport and Road Research Laboratory Report SR2, *Comparative Assessment of New Forms of Inter-City Transport* (from Laboratory 7.71), p. 4.

9   A. Paterson, 'Track and Signalling for the Railway of the Future', *Railway Students Bulletin*, Christmas Term 1968, p. 11.

10 Richard Pryke and John Dodgson, *The Rail Problem* (Martin Robertson, 1975), p. 8.

11 BRB, *Transport Policy: An Opportunity for Change* (7.76), p. 60.

12 SCNI, *Minutes of Evidence* (7.3.78), Q 266.

13 SCNI, *The Role of British Rail in Public Transport* (Session 1976–77), Vol. 2, Q 363.

14 *Railway Magazine* (3.71), p. 130; BR, *Press Release* 3/71.

15 Here and in following paragraphs I have drawn on Pryke and Dodgson *op. cit.* Chapter 8.

16 SCNI, 7.3.78, Q 252.

17 SCNI, 1976–77, Vol. 2, p. 379.

18 Pryke and Dodgson *op. cit.* pp. 108, 109, 117; Price Commission, *British Railways Board-Increase in Passenger Fares* (2.78), p. 19.

19 NBPI, Report 8, *Pay and Conditions of Service of British Railways Staff*, Cmnd 2873 (1.66), p. 21.

20 SCNI, 1976–77, Vol. 2, pp. 36, Vol. 3, pp. 510–15.

21 Stewart Joy, *The Train That Ran Away* (Ian Allen, 1973), pp. 92, 93.

22 Sir Henry Johnson, 'Railways', *Institute of Transport Journal* (7.69), p. 188.

23 Pryke and Dodgson, *op. cit.* Chapter 1.

24 Peter Walker, *The Ascent of Britain* (Sidgwick and Jackson, 1977), p. 53.

25 Committee of Public Accounts, *Eighth Report* (Session 1976–77), pp. xxvii, xxviii.

26 C.A. Rose, Presidential Address Railway Study Association (17.10.77).

27 Hansard Written Answers (23.1.78).

28 BR Southern Region, *Southern Facts and Figures* (3.79).

29 BRB, 1978, p. 15; Hansard Written Answers (13.7.78).

30 Hansard Written Answers (17.3.80), etc.

31 I.S. Jones, *op. cit.*

32 J.S. Dodgson, 'Cost-Benefit Analysis, Government Policy and the British Railway Network', *Transportation* (1977), pp. 153–61.

33 Finance National Taxation Division, Department of Transport, *Vehicle Excise Duty on Heavy Goods Vehicles* (from Department 8.79).

34 DoE, *Transport Policy: A Consultation Document* (1976), Vol. 2, p. 114; *Transport Statistics* 1965–1975, Table 1.

35 DoE, *op. cit.* Vol. 1, p. 59.

Chapter 6 : National and Scottish Buses

1   NBPI Report 50, *Productivity Agreements in the Bus Industry*, Cmnd 3498 (12.67), pp. 4, 52, 58; Report 99, *Pay of Maintenance Workers Employed by Bus Companies*, Cmnd 3868 (12.68), p. 9.

2   DoE, *Transport Policy: A Consultation Document*, Vol. 2, p. 36.

3 Peter R. White, *Planning for Public Transport* (Hutchinson, 1976), pp. 128, 134.
4 Cheshire County Council Transportation Unit, *Policy Options and Implications for Revenue Support: A Report for Consultation* (1977), p. 61.
5 SCNI, *Innovations in Rural Bus Services* (Session 1977–78), pp. xxix, xxx.
6 Graham Rees and Richard Wragg, *A Study of the Passenger Transport Needs of Rural Wales* (Welsh Council, 1975), pp. 22, 23.
7 NBC Marketing and Operational Research Report 23, *Discount Fares* (2.79), para 2.2.3.
8 Ministry of Transport, etc., *Public Transport and Traffic*, Cmnd 3481 (12.67), p. 19.
9 Cmnd 3481, pp. 18, 22.
10 *Study of Rural Transport in Devon [West Suffolk]: Report by the Steering Group* (from DoE), pp. 9, 24; Suffolk Study, pp. 14, 19.
11 DoE, *Transport Policy* pp. 1, 12, 28, 37, 38, 89.
12 Peat, Marwick, Mitchell and Co, *An Initial Report on Minimum Levels of Service for Rural Public Transport Prepared for the National Bus Company* (4.77) pp. 7, 17.
13 *Ibid.* pp. 27, 28.
14 DoE, *op. cit.* p. 12.
15 *A Policy for Transport?* (Nuffield Foundation, 1977), pp. 37, 39.
16 Cheshire County Council, *op. cit.* pp. 58, 96, 97, Network A, Table 2, Network G, Tables 2 and 3.
17 *Decision of the [East Midland] Traffic Commissioners* (9.5.77).
18 Advisory Council on Energy Conservation Paper 2, *Passenger Transport: Short and Medium Term Considerations* (D of E, Energy Paper No 10, 1976, HMSO), p. 5, etc.
19 *Study of Rural Transport in Devon*, p. 9.
20 *Public Transport in Malvern Hills* (Hereford and Worcester County Council), p. 12.
21 *Study of Rural Transport in West Suffolk*, p. 14.

CHAPTER 7 : THE NATIONAL FREIGHT CORPORATION

1 NBPI Report 162, *Costs, Charges and Productivity of the National Freight Corporation*, Cmnd 4569 (1.71), pp. 32–5.
2 S.L. Edwards and B.T. Bayliss, *Operating Costs in Road Freight Transport* (from DoE), p. 4.
3 BR, *The Reshaping of British Railways* (HMSO, 1963), p. 147.
4 Bernard Warner and Stewart Joy, 'The Economics of Rail Container Operation in Britain', *Rail International* (4.71), pp. 345–56.
5 H.C. Sanderson, 'The Future of Railway Freight Services', *Proceedings of the British Railways (Western Region) London Lecture and Debating Society* (1967), p. 12.
6 Stewart Joy, *The Train That Ran Away*, pp. 135, 136, 140.
7 P.A. Land, 'Freight Integration', *The Chartered Institute of Transport Journal* (3.72), pp. 369–71.

8   Brian T. Bayliss, *The Road Haulage Industry Since 1968* (DoE 1973), pp. 22, 25, 26; Price Commission, *The Road Haulage Industry* (10.78), pp. 96, 97.
9   Bayliss, *op. cit.*, p. 25.
10 NBPI Report 48, *Charges, Costs and Wages in the Road Haulage Industry*, Cmnd 3482 (11.67), pp. 20, 23.
11 *Road Haulage Operators' Licensing: Report of the Independent [Foster] Committee of Inquiry* (11.78), p. 36.

CHAPTER 8 : BRITISH AIRWAYS

Principal statistical sources: Civil Aviation Authority (CAA) *Monthly* and *Annual Statistics;* International Air Transport Association *World Air Transport Statistics;* International Civil Aviation Organisation *Digest of Statistics.*
1   *British Air Transport in the Seventies: Report of the [Edwards] Committee of Inquiry into Civil Air Transport* Cmnd 4018 (5.69), pp. 94–7.
2   CAA, *Decision on Applications to Vary the UK DAT* (21.3.79), para 46.
3   CAA, *European Air Fares* (11.77), Appendix 6.
4   BA, *Civil Air Transport in Europe* (1.77), Appendix 4.
5   CAA, *Decision*, paras 69, 74.
6   William M. Taussig, *British Airways — An Analysis of Efficiency and Cost Levels* (US Department of Transportation, 5.77), pp. 8–10.
7   SCNI, *Minutes of Evidence* (24.1.78), Q8–10.
8   J.H.T. Green, *Department of Trade: United Kingdom Air Traffic Forecasting* (1978), p. 6; Business Statistics Office, *Business Monitor Quarterly Statistics: Overseas Travel and Tourism*, MQ6, Fourth Quarter, 1978.
9   J.E.D. Williams, 'Holidays by Air', *Institute of Transport Journal* (5.68), pp. 372–5.
10 Michael H. Cooper and Alan Maynard, 'The Effect of Regulated Competition on Scheduled Air Fares', *Journal of Transport Economics and Policy* (5.72), pp. 171, 172.
11 CAA, *European Air Fares*, Appendix 5.
12 *Ibid.* p. 27.
13 J.H.T. Green, *op. cit.* pp. 10–12.
14 CAA, *op. cit.* p. 13.
15 CAA, *Decision on the Reconsideration of the Authority's Decision of 26 October 1977 . . .* (20.4.79), para 61.

CHAPTER 9 : POSTAL SERVICES

1   NBPI Report 58, *Post Office Charges*, Cmnd 3574 (3.68), pp. 9, 18; Report 121, *Post Office Charges: Inland Parcel Post and Remittance Services*, Cmnd 4115 (7.69), p. 3.
2   Cmnd 4115, p. 3.
3   Post Office Users' National Council (POUNC), *Report on Proposals for Increased Postal Tariffs* (10.70), p. 23.
4   Cmnd 3574, pp. 82, 83.

5   SCNI, *The Post Office* (Session 1966–67), Vol. 1, p. 40.
6   Cmnd 3574, p. 18.
7   SCNI, Vol. 2, p. 596.
8   *Appendix to the Report of the [Carter] Post Office Review Committee*, Cmnd 6954 (11.77), p. 178.
9   POUNC Report No. 12, p. 12.
10 POUNC Report No. 17, p. 27.
11 Cmnd 6954, pp. 109, 138–41.
12 *Report of the [Carter] Post Office Review Committee*, Cmnd 6850 (7.77), p. 29.
13 Cmnd 6954, p. 257.
14 POUNC, *Report on Proposals for Increased Postal Tariffs*, pp. 7, 22.
15 Monopolies and Mergers Commission, *The Inner London Letter Post* (3.80), pp. 54, 119, etc.
16 Cmnd 6954, pp. 257, 258.
17 D. Wesil, *A Survey of the New Inland Letter Service* (HMSO 4.69) para 103.
18 *Annual Report of the [US] Postmaster General*, 1972–73 and 1978; *Report of the [US] Commission on Postal Service* (4.77), Vol. 1, pp. 15, 16.
19 Cmnd 6850, p. 20; *Annual Report of the Postmaster General*, 1977 p. 17.
20 Monopolies and Mergers Commission, *op. cit.* pp. 49, 57.
21 *Report of a Committee Appointed by the Post Office and Union of Post Office Workers* . . . (1971), pp. 13, 14.
22 Cmnd 6954, pp. 474, 475; Cmnd 3574, pp. 15, 16.
23 Cmnd 6954, pp. 111, 255.
24 Cmnd 6954, p. 259.
25 POUNC Report No 17, pp. 18, 39.
26 SCNI, Vol. 2, p. 440.
27 POUNC Report, January 1972, p. 22.
28 Cmnd 6954, pp. 115, 142–5; SCNI, *The Post Office's Letter Post Services* (Session 1975–76), p. xxvi.
29 Monopolies and Mergers Commission, *op. cit.* pp. 65, 66.
30 Michael E. Corby, *The Postal Business 1969–1979* (Kogan Page, 1979), p. 200.
31 Cmnd 6954, pp. 319, 320, 321, 326, 327, 338.
32 Monopolies and Mergers Commission, *op. cit.* p. 30.
33 Cmnd 6954, p. 110; Cmnd 3574, p. 18.
34 Monopolies and Mergers Commission, *op. cit.* pp. 31, 32.
35 See SCNI 1975–76, p. 139 and Cmnd 6954, p. 134.
36 Monopolies and Mergers Commission, *op. cit.* pp. 52, 84, 88.

Chapter 10 : Telecommunications

Principal statistical source: P O *Telecommunication Statistics* (the PO).

1   Francis Cripps and Wynne Godley, *The Planning of Telecommunications in the United Kingdom* (Department of Applied Economics, Cambridge 1978), p. 45.
2   Chris Harlow, *Innovation and Productivity under Nationalisation*, pp. 110–12.

3   Prescott C. Mabon, *Mission Communications: The Story of Bell Laboratories* (Bell Telephone Laboratories, 1975), pp. 69, 70, 74, 75.
4   Harlow, *op. cit.* pp. 117, 118.
5   John Brooks, *Telephone: The First Hundred Years* (Harper Row, 1976), pp. 278, 279.
6   Mabon, *op. cit.* pp. 80, 81; Cripps and Godley, pp. 44, 45; *Bell Laboratories Record* (3.77), pp. 59–63.
7   Mabon, *op. cit.* pp. 77, 78, 82, 83; AT and T *Annual Report* 1975, p. 9.
8   Cripps and Godley, *op. cit.* pp. 34, 45.
9   Harlow, *op. cit.* p. 126.
10 *Ibid.* p. 129.
11 *Post Office Orders for Telecommunication Switching Equipment: Report [by M.V. Posner] to the Secretary to State for Industry May 1977* (from Department of Industry), Table 5, para 6.
12 Cmnd 6954, p. 431.
13 Cmnd 6850, p. 99, etc.
14 Post Office Engineering Union, *The Modernisation of Telecommunications*, p. 67.
15 Posner Report, para 15, Appendix 2.
16 AT and T, *The World's Telephones* 1978, Table 2; Cmnd 6850, p. 100.
17 P. Luhan, 'The Breakthrough of Digital Switching in the World Market' *Telecommunications* (4.80), pp. 34, 35.
18 *Idem*; POEU *op. cit.* p. 20.
19 Posner Report, Appendix 1.
20 Cmnd 3574, p. 19.
21 FT, 22.11.77.
22 POEU *op. cit.* p. 24.
23 Cmnd 6850, p. 21.
24 AT and T, *1978 Statistical Report* pp. 2, 9, etc.
25 FT, 16.11.77.
26 National Economic Development Office, *A Study of UK Nationalised Industries: Appendix Volume* (1976), pp. 99, 100.
27 AT and T *Annual Report* 1976, p. 21.

CHAPTER 11 : BRITISH STEEL

Principal statistical sources: BSC, *Annual Statistics for the Corporation*; Iron and Steel Statistics Bureau, etc., *Iron and Steel Industry Annual Statistics;* OECD, *The Iron and Steel Industry*; Eurostat, *Iron and Steel Year Book* and *Quarterly Iron and Steel Statistical Bulletin*.
1   SCNI, *British Steel Corporation* (Session 1972–73), pp. 312, 313.
2   Federal Trade Commission Bureau of Economics, *Staff Report on the United States Steel Industry and its International Rivals* (11.77), p. 489.
3   See A. Cockerill, *The Steel Industry: International Comparisons of Industrial Structure and Performance* (Cambridge University Press, 1974), p. 25.
4   *Iron and Steel*, Special Anchor Issue 1972, pp. 69, 70; R.S. Pitt, 'Steelmaking in North-east England — the Next Ten Years', *Iron and Steel* (2.72), pp. 98, 99.

5   SCNI, *The British Steel Corporation* (Session 1977–78), Vol. 1, p. xlvii, Vol. 3, p. 287.
6   Iron and Steel Board, *Annual Report*, 1966, p. 43.
7   *The Steel Industry: The Stage 1 Report of the [Benson] Development Co-ordinating Committee of the British Iron and Steel Federation* (7.66), pp. 23, 24, 29.
8   Richard Pryke and John Dodgson, *The Rail Problem*, p. 56.
9   SCNI, 1977–78, Vol. 2, p. 18.
10 *Ibid.* pp. 125, 127, 128, 416, 430, 434, Q 739–41.
11 *Steelmanager* (6.77), pp. 12–15.
12 *Steel Review: The British Iron and Steel Federation Quarterly* (7.67), p. 3.
13 Campbell Adamson, 'Steel Shortages — Problems and Prospects', *British Steel*, Autumn 1973, p. 3.
14 US Department of Labor, Bureau of Labor Statistics, Office of Productivity and Technology, *International Comparisons of Productivity and Labor Costs in the Steel Industry; United States, Japan, France, Germany, United Kingdom; 1964 and 1972–78* (5.80, unpublished).
15 *The Steel Industry: The Stage 1 Report*, p. 87.
16 National Economic Development Office, Iron and Steel Sector Working Party, *A Hard Look at Steel: international Comparisons of Steel Works Efficiency*, Parts 1–3.
17 *Steel News*, 5.2.76.
18 *Steel News*, 26.7.79.
19 SCNI, 1977–78, Vol. 2, p. 18.
20 FT, 12.12.79; BSC, *News Release* 17.1.80, etc.
21 *Colliery Guardian* (9.75), p. 389; FT, 3.12.79, etc.

CHAPTER 12 : BRITISH LEYLAND

Principal statistical source: Society of Motor Manufacturers and Traders, *The Motor Industry of Great Britain*.

1   C.F. Pratten, *Economies of Scale in Manufacturing Industry* (Cambridge University Press, 1971), pp. 141–2.
2   Graham Turner, *The Leyland Papers* (Eyre and Spottiswood, 1971), p. 183; Expenditure Committee, *Public Money in the Private Sector* (Session 1971–72), Vol. 2, p. 222.
3   Expenditure Committee, *The Motor Vehicle Industry Minutes of Evidence* (Session 1974–75), Vol. 1, pp. 228, 231; *Autocar Supplement* (10.8.67), pp. 3, 81; Monopolies Commission, *The British Motor Corporation and the Pressed Steel Company* (1966), p. 9.
4   Graham Turner, *The Car Makers* (Eyre and Spottiswood, 1963), p. 182.
5   *Leyland Papers*, pp. 123, 124; ST, 6.11.66, 10.1.71.
6   ST, 10.1.71.
7   *Leyland Papers*, pp. 180, 181. See also Expenditure Committee, *Minutes*, Vol. 1, Q 412.
8   *Leyland Papers*, pp. 189, 190.
9   *Motoring Which?* (10.74), pp. 124, 125.
10 *The Motor Vehicle Industry*, p. 22, etc.

11 *British Leyland: The Next Decade* (1975), pp. 34, 35 (henceforth described as Ryder); ST, 10.1.71, 16.1.72; Expenditure Committee, *Minutes*, Vol. 1 Q 323.
12 Ryder, p. 12.
13 Ryder, pp. 6, 7.
14 Ryder, pp. 6, 29, 32.
15 D.T. Jones and S.J. Prais, 'Plant Size and Productivity in the Motor Industry: Some International Comparisons', *Oxford Bulletin of Economics and Statistics* (1978), p. 142; Central Policy Review Staff, *The Future of the British Car Industry* (HMSO, 1975), p. 80 (henceforth described as CPRS).
16 Ryder, pp. 29, 32.
17 *Motor Vehicle Industry*, p. 36.
18 CPRS, pp. 85–7.
19 CPRS, pp. 83, 119, 120.
20 FT, 30.3.78; CPRS, pp. 97, 117.
21 CPRS, p. 87.
22 Ryder, p. 61.
23 Expenditure Committee, *Minutes*, Vol. 2, Q 1919, 1921.
24 CPRS, pp. 35–50, 108; Ryder, p. 65.
25 CPRS, p. 108.
26 *The Motor Vehicle Industry*, p. 91.
27 Ryder, p. 42.
28 FT, 16.2.78, 14.12.77.
29 ST, 24.9.78.
30 *Motoring Which?* (1.79), pp. 19–21.
31 CPRS, pp, x, 70, 120.
32 BMH, *Annual Report*, 1966–67, p. 20.
33 Krish Bhaskar, *The Future of the UK Motor Industry* (Kogan Page, 1979), Table 7.1; *British Leyland Facts and Figures*, p. 52.
34 Ryder, pp. 37–42.
35 NEB, *Press Release* (3.4.78), p. 8.
36 Expenditure Committee, *Minutes of Evidence* (16.3.77), Q 110, 123.
37 ST, 8.1.78.
38 NEB, *Press Release* (30.3.79), p. 18.
39 FT, 4.4.79.

Chapter 13 : Public Enterprise – A Survey and Evaluation.

All references are to previous pages unless it is clear to the contrary.
1 193–7, 215–17, 219–22, 231–3.
2 119, 120, 122–4, 126.
3 129–39.
4 37–8, 48, 207.

5   121–2.
6   151.
7   100.
8   POEU, *The Modernisation of Telecommunications*, pp. 36, 40, 41.
9   80, 91.
10 100–1.
11 151–2.
12 167, 174.
13 13–15.
14 45–6, 51, 53, 78, 81.
15 51–3.
16 81.
17 97, 154–7, 183–4, 201–3, 211–12.
18 157–9.
19 201–2.
20 101–2.
21 82, 84, 102, 201–2, 221–2, 233.
22 152–3.
23 154, 157.
24 201–2, 206–7.
25 82, 84–5, 88.
26 101, 103–6.
27 53, 58.
28 225–7.
29 55–6.
30 215, 221–2.
31 153.
32 104.
33 157–9.
34 57, 85, 203.
35 85, 88.
36 80, 187–9, 191, 228.
37 83, 85.
38 215–17.
39 189–90.
40 86–7, 233.
41 16–17, 34, 175.
42 133–5.
43 34–6.
44 17, 34–7, 176–8.
45 25–8.
46 165–71.
47 132.
48 227–9.
49 44.
50 61–6.
51 126.
52 National Economic Development Office, *A Study of UK Nationalised*

Industries: Their Role in the Economy and Control in the Future (1976), p. 30.
53 188–9.
54 76, 87–8.
55 18.
56 92–3.
57 59–60.
58 14–16.
59 150, 160.
60 180.
61 131, 139–42.
62 108.
63 75, 77, 109, 114.
64 Richard Marsh, *Off the Rails* (Weidenfeld and Nicholson, 1978), p. 167.
65 111.
66 93, 94, 113–14.
67 94–5.
68 NBC, 1978, p. 21.
69 67–9.
70 Chancellor of the Exchequer, *The Financial and Economic Obligations of the Nationalised Industries*, Cmnd 1337 (4.61).
71 Cmnd 3437, p. 12.
72 Richard Crossman, *The Diaries of a Cabinet Minister* (Hamish Hamilton and Jonathan Cape, 1976), Vol. 2, p. 524.
73 H. Glennerster, *Social Service Budgets and Social Policy* (George Allen and Unwin, 1975), pp. 119, 120.
74 Marsh, *op. cit.*
75 Marsh, *op. cit.* pp. 192–7 and in *Daily Express*, 27.11.75.
76 Chancellor of the Exchequer, *The Nationalised Industries* (3.78), Cmnd 7131.

Index

F₂